THE RUSSIAN HEART: DAYS OF CRISIS & HOPE

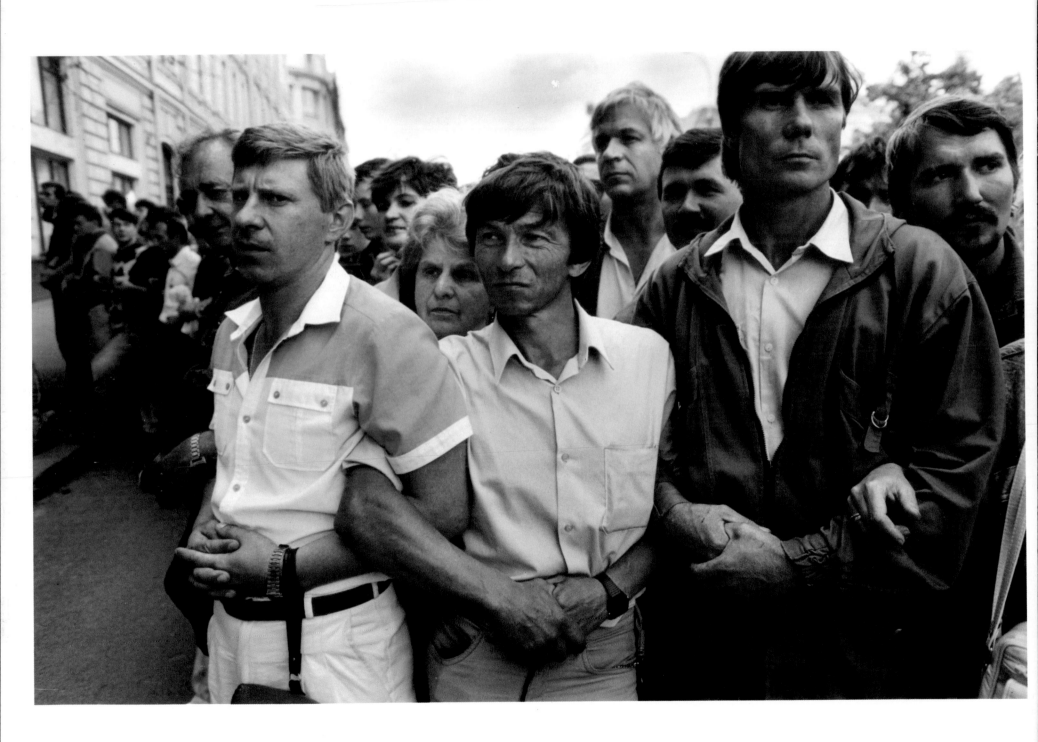

Coup D'Etat, Moscow
Soviet citizens surround the Communist Party Building on August 22, the day after the failed coup d'état.

THE RUSSIAN HEART: DAYS OF CRISIS & HOPE

PHOTOGRAPHS AND JOURNAL BY DAVID C. TURNLEY

INTRODUCTION BY WILLIAM KELLER

Φ

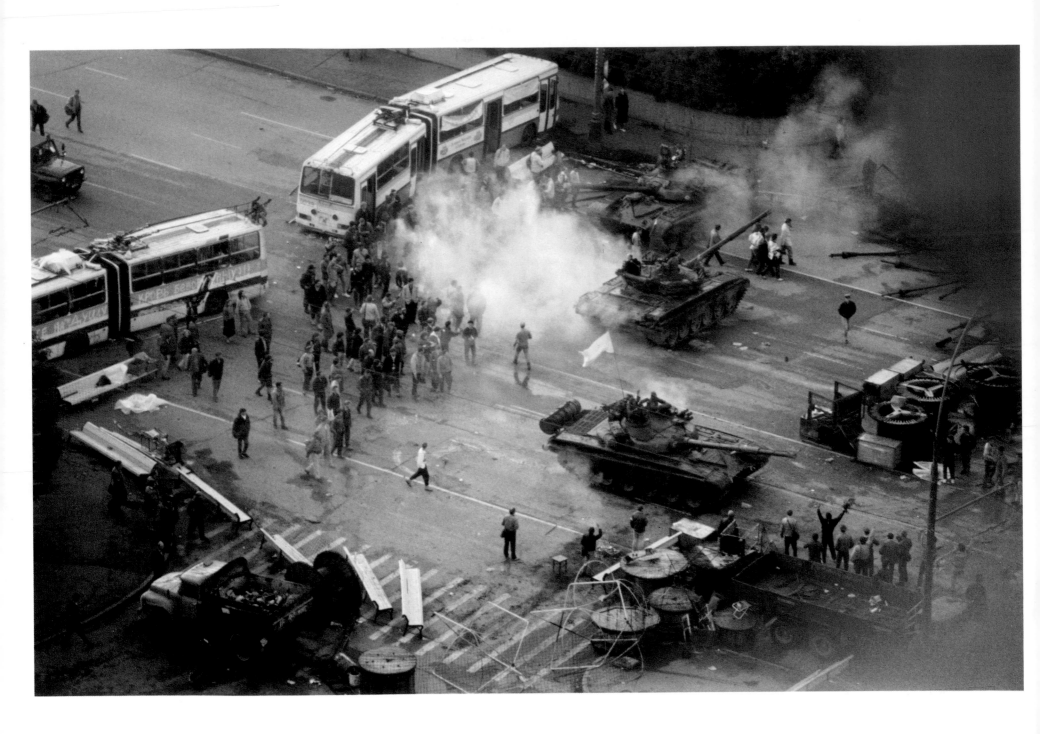

Coup D'Etat, Moscow
Soviet tanks and buses barricade the
streets of Moscow.

INTRODUCTION

BILL KELLER

The Russians have a wonderful idiom, *glaza razbegaiyutsya*, which means literally "the eyes run in all directions." Russian friends have used it to describe the confusion they felt when they entered an American supermarket for the first time and stood paralyzed by the choices entailed in buying something as simple as a box of salt. It must be the way photographers feel when they first encounter the empire that used to be the Soviet Union.

Even during the gray decades of fear and inertia, the Soviet Union offered up a dizzying profusion of landscapes, faces, cultures, moods, and eras. For all the grim enforced silences of life under the old regime, the Soviet Union even then could amaze a newcomer with its unabashed public theater. President Reagan, the noted linguist, used to claim that there is no word in Russian for freedom. He was wrong, there are several. But there is no word for privacy, as Westerners understand it. Thanks in part to native openness and in part to a desperate shortage of private places, Russia's intimate moments— flirtations, celebrations, grief—often happen in public, within reach of the attentive lens. Depending on where his curiosity (or in the suspicious old days, his official handlers) led him, a photographer could portray the Soviet Union as almost whatever kind of country he chose—as gentle as a birch forest, as brutal as a blast furnace, as cultured as the confectionery architecture along Leningrad's canals, as modern as a rocket, as primitive as an old woman stooped like a serf over a muddy potato field, as uninhibited as a wild laugh in the streets, as cold as a funeral. The Russians were just like us, or they were not really like us at all. The great visual truism was: Soviet Union, Land of Contrasts.

Just because this is a cliché does not make it untrue. As the great émigré philosopher Nikolai Berdyaev wrote more than half a century ago, "Russia and the Russian people can be characterized only by contradictions." But a volume that is merely a collection of contradictions as much as says that nothing matters. A photographer without a focus could compile an album of arresting images adding up to nothing in particular. A photographer who wants to take home something more is forced to choose.

If anything the photographer's (and the writer's) predicament has worsened in the Gorbachev years, as his opportunity has multiplied. The freedom to travel has opened up so many new directions in which the eyes can run. Places where foreigners were forbidden, such as prison camps and army bases, or where they were strongly discouraged from going, such as the squalid rural settlements that populate the vast spaces between the cities, are now accessible. And to the dazzling variety of people and places has been added the new dimension of tumultuous change. At least before things stood still. Now events tumble past like trees uprooted by a hurricane. An empire dissolves, an ideology dies, an enemy ceases to frighten us, politicians arise from the streets. We don't even know what to call this place from month to month; at the time of this writing, habit still calls it the USSR, though it is really, as one wit suggested, the UFFR—the Union of Fewer and Fewer Republics. In the midst of this maelstrom we try to figure out what is constant and what has changed, which moments are profound turning points and which are false leads, what really matters. With each twist of the kaleidoscope, yesterday's headlines and images are suddenly today's clichés—the empty shop, the angry mob, the toppled statue of Lenin. Not long ago a journalist in the Soviet Union could delight his audience simply by reporting what was there. Now nothing less will do than to foretell the future. These are dicey times for anyone who wants to put something, pictures or text, between hard covers and hope it will outlast the month.

David Turnley has found his focus in the human heart, and his prevailing mood in the hope and yearning that reside there. It is a loving choice, and a wise one. He has not prettified life in the diminishing empire, or recoiled from the misery that seems to be Russia's greatest natural resource. This collection includes scenes from not just one prison camp, but two, not a single funeral, but three, and even the scenes of workaday life are often virtually indistinguishable from the prisons. Except for the regulation matching dresses on the grim and aimless inmates, the Mozhaysk Women's Prison could be the yard of almost any Soviet housing project. No, this is not a lighthearted tour. Yet Turnley has produced a collection that is optimistic at heart.

The hope is sometimes out in the open, in the joy of the sailor and his girlfriend dancing on the Arbat, in the relish of the Muscovites waltzing on the Manezh Square after vanguishing the tanks of the August coup. Hope is explicit in the enduring images of families and faiths, and implicit in the momentary flickers of humanity in a dehumanizing world. Turnley finds a tender hug in a prison, the incongruous oompah of a brass quartet in a mud-spattered funeral procession, the pride underlying the grief as the three martyrs of the August putsch are escorted to the graveyard.

Looking at these pictures, I thought of Andrei Sinyavsky, a writer of essays and short stories who was imprisoned and then exiled after a celebrated 1966 trial. I met Sinyavsky, now a professor of Russian literature at the Sorbonne, when he returned to Moscow in early 1989 for the funeral of his co-defendant, Yuli Daniel. The conversation turned to his six years in a prison camp, and to my amazement Sinyavsky's face lit up with heartfelt nostalgia.

"I really loved the camp," he said, without irony. "In the concentration camp, I found myself in a fantastical reality. Since I'm an author of fantastical tales and strange things, I found myself in a reality that suited me as a writer. Of course the tale is frightening, but it is an interesting one." Somehow in that confined world of unrepentant criminals and born-again Christians and illiterates and intellectuals, Sinyavsky said he came to know Russia, whose spirit was free even if its body was enslaved. This is the Russian heart, which not only survives the rigors of the concentration camp, but makes of it a university and later thinks back fondly on its alma mater.

By whatever name, the former Soviet domain is still inescapably a land of contradictions, and Turnley has seen them, too. The not-ready-for-prime-time sunbathers at Round Lake, arms akimbo and surgical scars on display, and the stylish, bikini-clad sun worshippers on the River Neva in Leningrad could be a before-and-after advertisement for the go-go Gorbachev years. The young navy officers crossing themselves in the cathedral before sailing off to defend what was supposed to be the world's greatest atheist state remind us that here is a country looking for something dependable to believe in. I particularly like the serendipitous picture of the stolid babushka in L'Vov, sweeping the sidewalk with her twig broom beneath a torrid movie marquee. (The film it advertises is called *Bezumstvo*— "Madness" or "Frenzy.") What secret madness lurks in the peasant soul?

But the constant in this collection is the resilience of the Russian spirit, its ability to endure and even, occasionally and in the face of all reason, to rejoice under conditions of overpowering duress. I don't know whether this is intuition or calculation on the photographer's part, but it is not accident. You put down this book thinking, "Maybe, just maybe, they can make it."

I can well imagine having to defend this collection in arguments with Soviet and Western friends. Many of the onlookers who observed this time of troubles, and perhaps a majority of the Russians who are sentenced to live through what comes next, would quarrel with Turnley's decision to strike a relatively uplifting note. Russia, they would say, must be shown enveloped in gloom. I have heard the view from Russian aesthetes, for example, that only black-and-white photography is appropriate for capturing the brooding monochrome of Russia. Russia, its leaden skies, its weathered faces and weary landscapes, can only be rendered in grays. To which I can only say: Trust me, this is the way Russia looks. Turnley's photographs reflect the real colors of Russia, not some Hollywood colorized version of reality.

Others might object that it was naive or misleading to conclude this volume with the victory over the inept, reactionary coup of August, 1991. Sure, those days may have been a heady interlude for the men and women who faced down tanks, but after all most Soviets sat on the sidelines during the coup. Within days the delirium on the faces of those who did participate had sagged into uncertainty, and within weeks talk had turned again to the *next* coup, this time sure to be bloodier and perhaps successful. Hope in this period of upheaval has been ephemeral and, so far, unrewarded. The non-Russian republics sampled by Turnley's lens have since hurtled off into independence and who knows what civil calamities. Not long after Gorbachev's victory jaunt through downtown Moscow, he seemed to have marched on into the shadows of history. The Russians and the other peoples of the Soviet empire have gone from being frightened of today to being frightened of tomorrow. How can anyone find a straw of optimism in a place that is simultaneously running out of food and fuel and faith?

Counsel for the pessimists would have a strong case if Turnley had set out to make a journalistic narrative of a period. But this collection, which covers only 70 days and for the most part keeps its distance from the headlines, does not pretend to add up to a comprehensive portrait of the Soviet Union, or a chronicle of its liberation and collapse. Much of that was, in any case, invisible. The country did not overthrow communism in August. It grew out of communism over the course of a generation. It raised up a middle class, it developed a taste for free speech, it wearied of its forged history, it learned that politicians can be held accountable. It peeked at the West and liked what it saw. Like the collapse of the Berlin Wall, which only preceded a long and murky period of reconstruction, the August coup was not really the beginning or end of anything. For a photographer, I think, the August coup was most of all a window. It was one of those grand moments when people and institutions are tested; gaze into the eyes of people at such moments, and it seems you can see deeper. This will not tell you how the story comes out, but it tells you something of the human resources that brought these people through so much wretchedness and that remain at their command in the chapters ahead.

To be hopeful about the Soviet Union requires a prodigious effort of memory and faith. The importance of memory was neatly put by Roald Sagdeyev, a genial space scientist, member of the Soviet parliament, and incurable optimist. One day during the first tumultuous meeting of the new parliament in early 1989, I ran into Sagdeyev munching on a sandwich in the huge top-floor cafeteria of the Kremlin Palace of Congresses. "A madhouse, isn't it," I asked. He nodded happily and replied: "As the Bible says, in the beginning was chaos. But better such chaos than the kind of order we had before."

As for faith, you can find it in these pictures. I, for one, think Turnley's focus is true. After the system has dissolved, after the ideology has died the death of all false dreams, after the leaders have come and gone, after the euphoria has passed, the resilience of the free Russian heart is what remains.

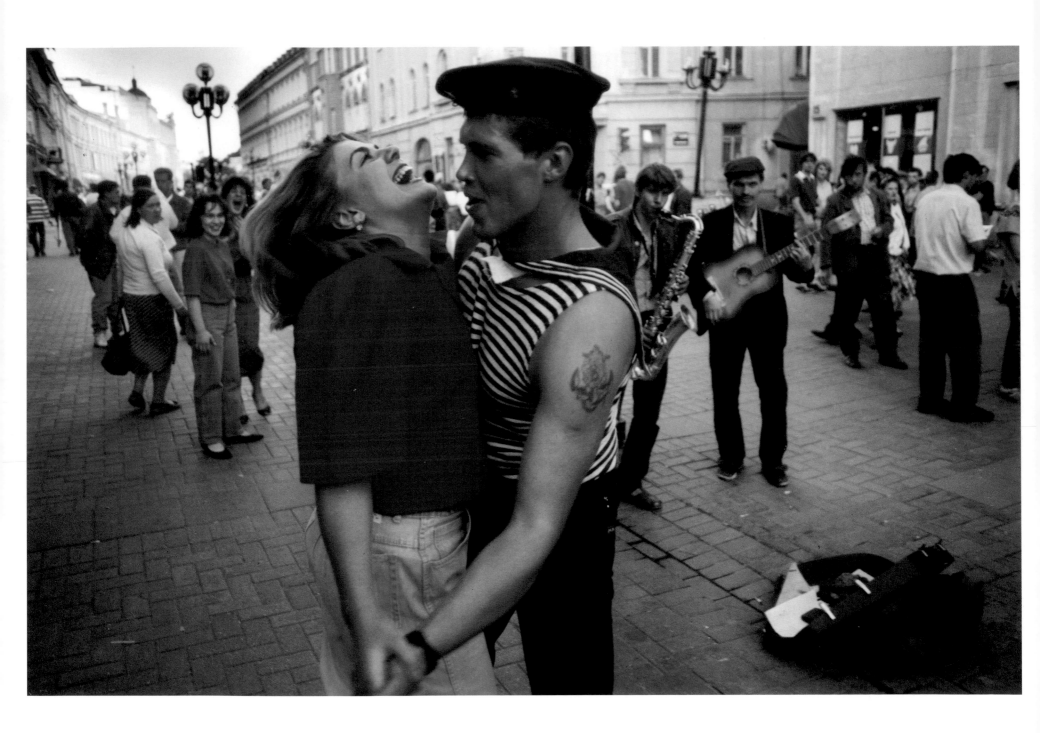

Moscow
On a national holiday honoring the navy, a sailor enjoys a dance with a friend on Moscow's Arbat Street, famous for its street vendors, artists and musicians.

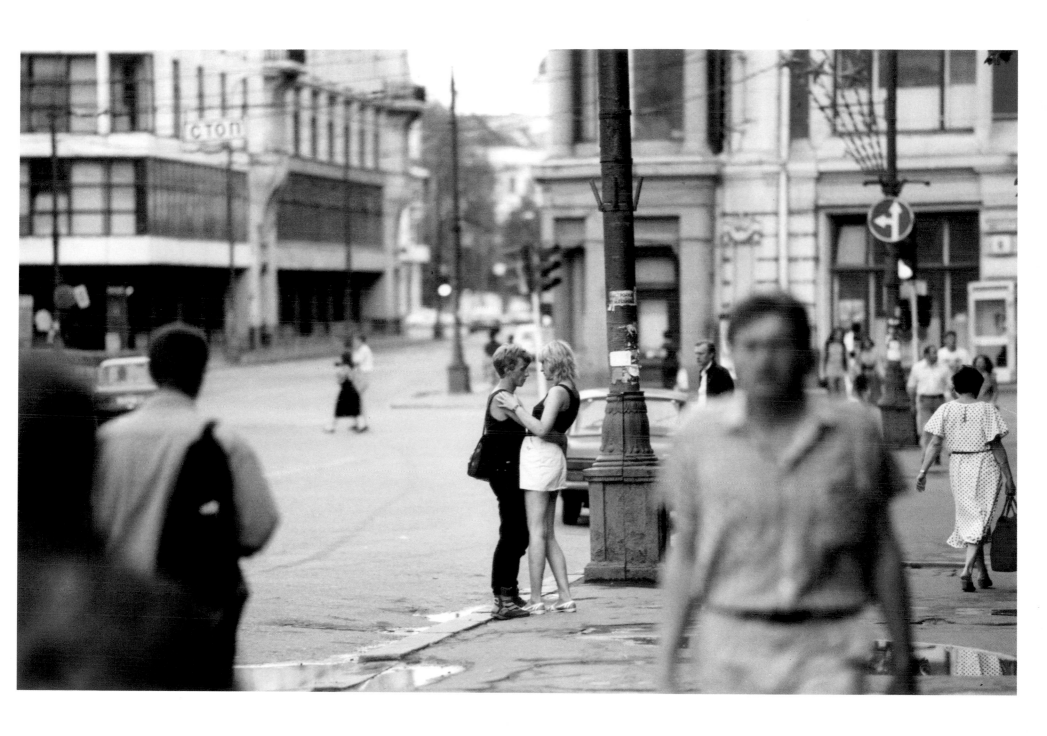

A young couple embrace near the Bolshoi Theatre in the center of Moscow.

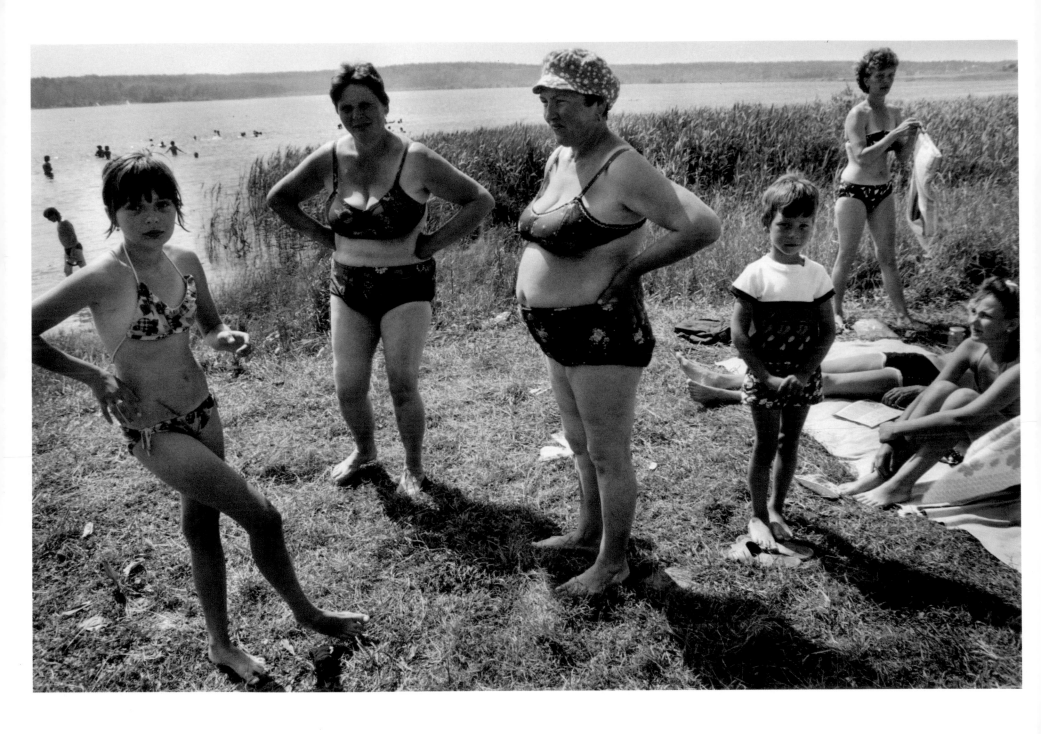

Russians swim and sunbathe on
Round Lake, 40 kilometers outside
Moscow.

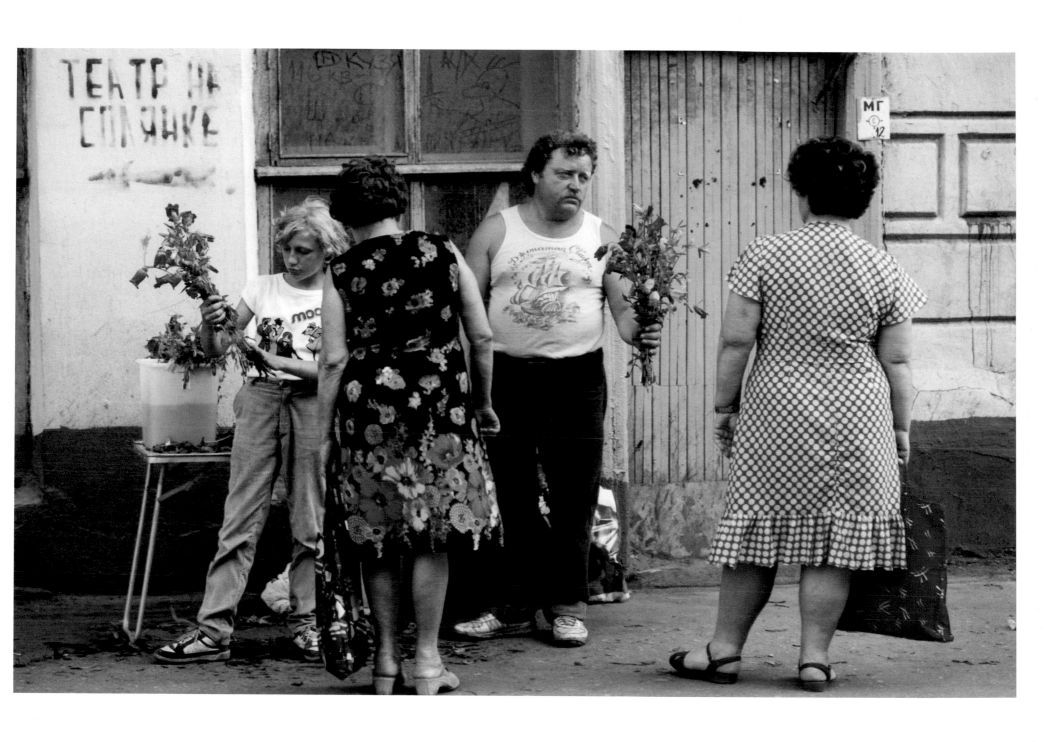

Not far from Red Square, vendors tempt women returning from work with bouquets of flowers. In a country where the average salary is very low, flowers are still an important part of life.

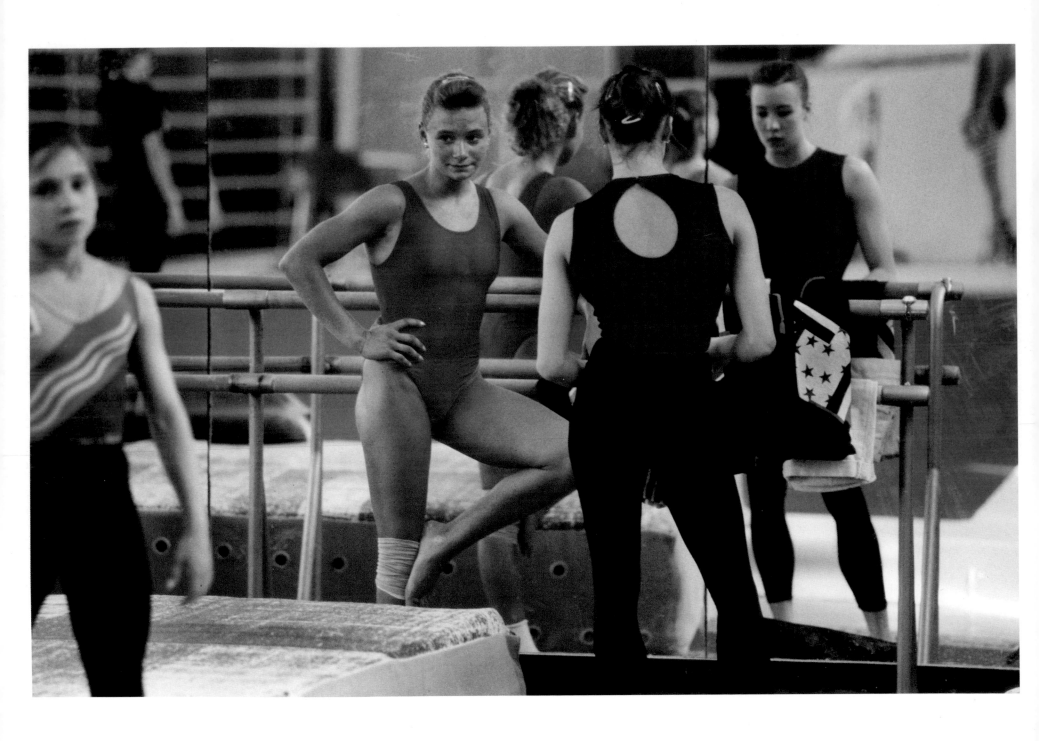

Olympic gold medalist, Svetlana
Boguinskaya, trains at the Round
Lake Olympic training center outside Moscow. Athletes train from
6:30 A.M. until 7:00 P.M. all year.
Foreign travel is one of the primary
motivations for this hard work.

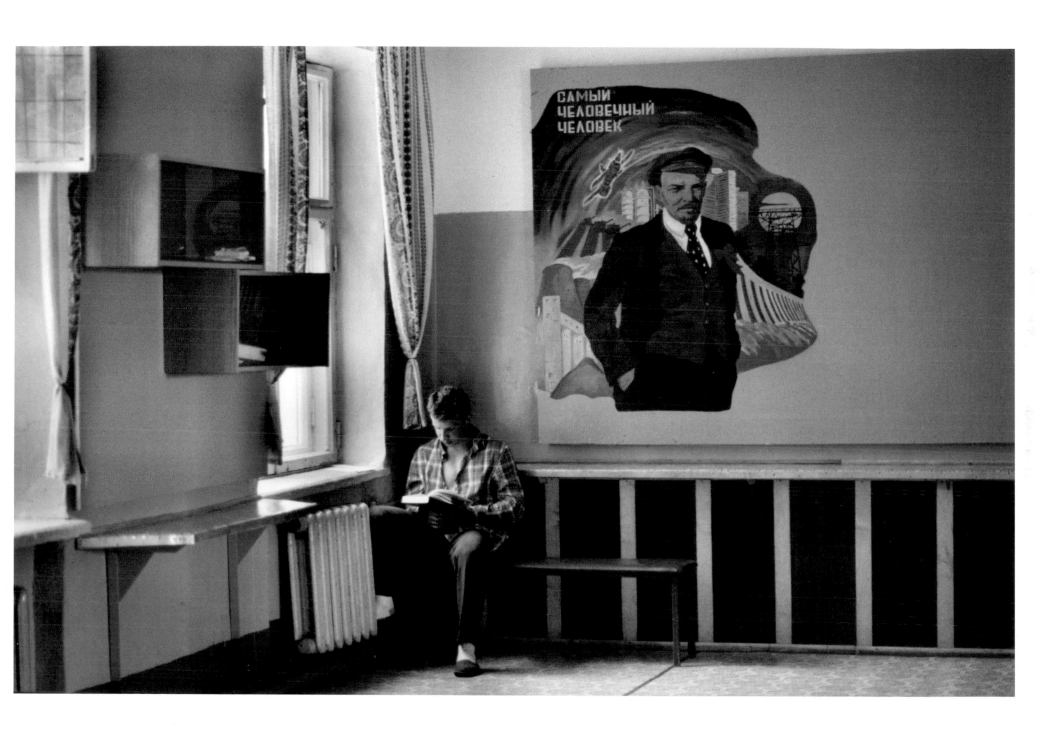

A young prisoner reads in the library of the Mozhaysk Boys' Prison, which holds boys aged 14-20. The warden says the economic crisis in the Soviet Union has caused an alarming increase in robbery.

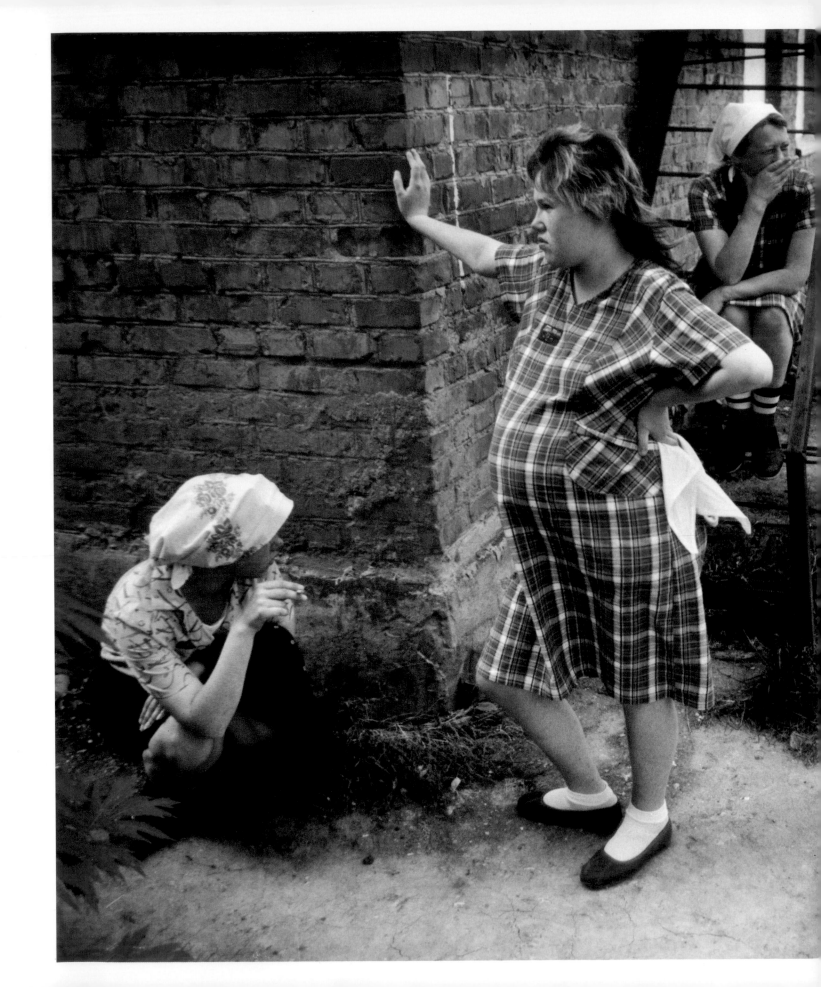

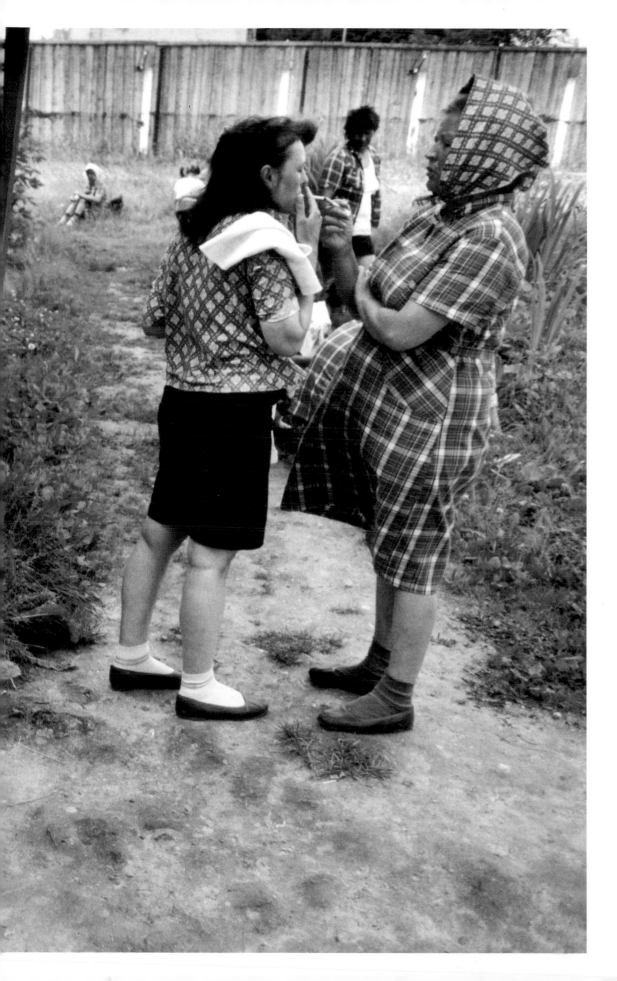

The Mozhaysk Women's Prison, 100
kilometers outside Moscow, was
built during World War I. Prisoners
await their shift in the textile factory
making Soviet policemen's
uniforms.

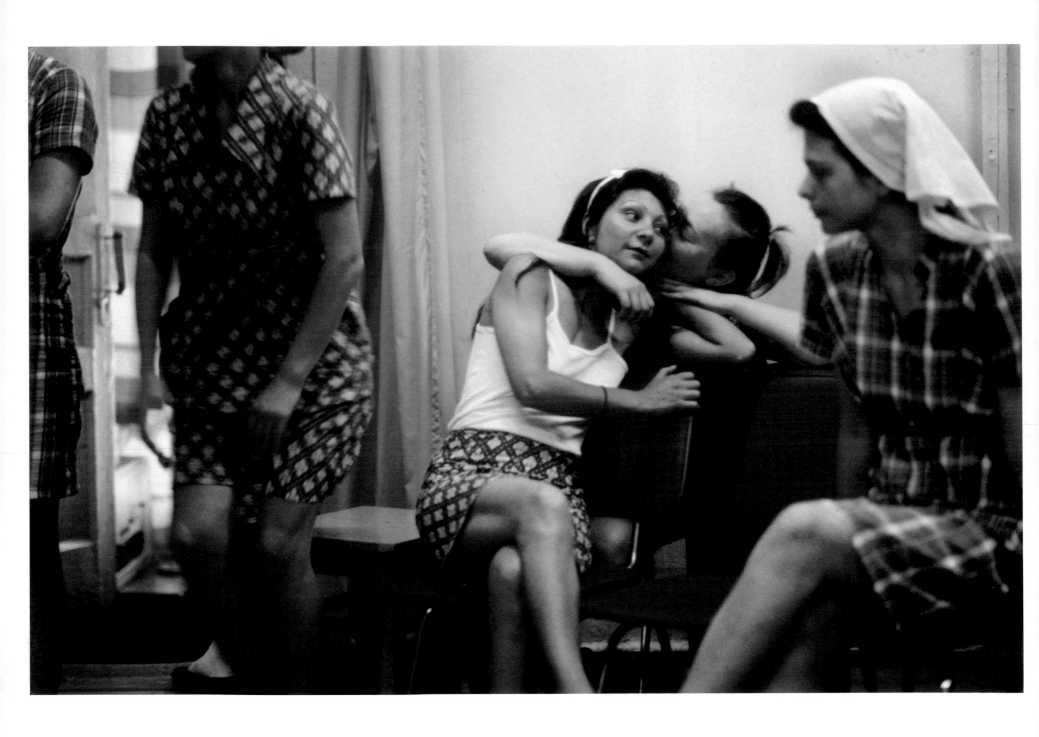

Women prisoners prepare for a play
rehearsal.

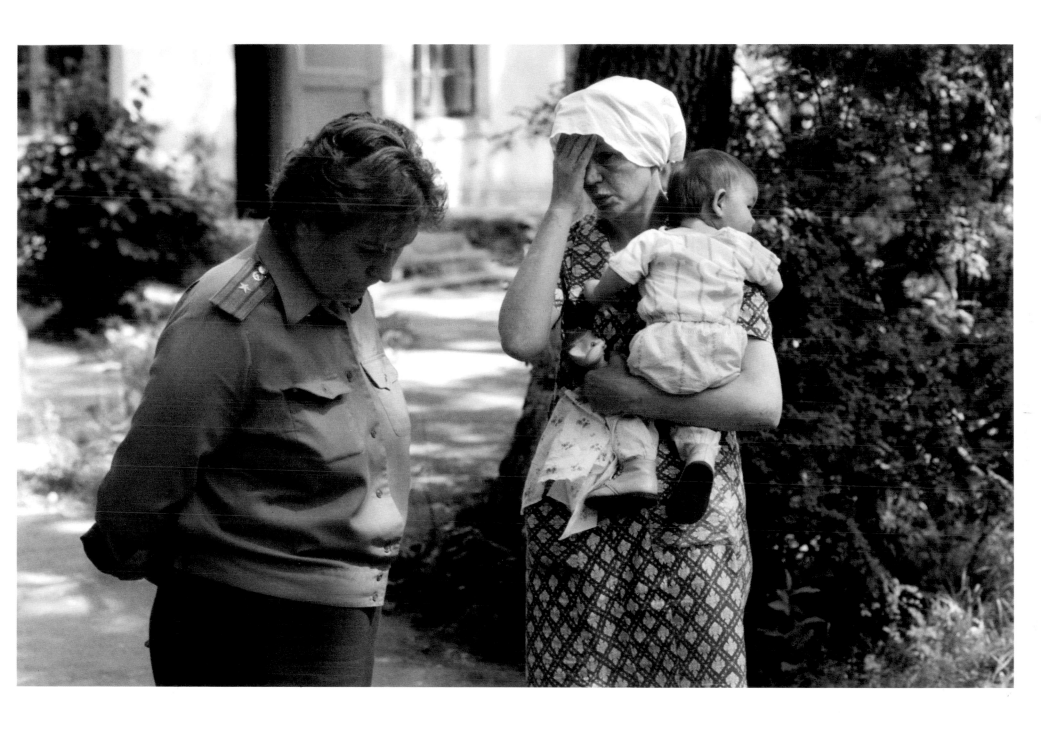

Tatiana Ivanova holds her baby while talking to the prison warden. Prisoners with babies under three years old are able to visit their children for two hours a day.

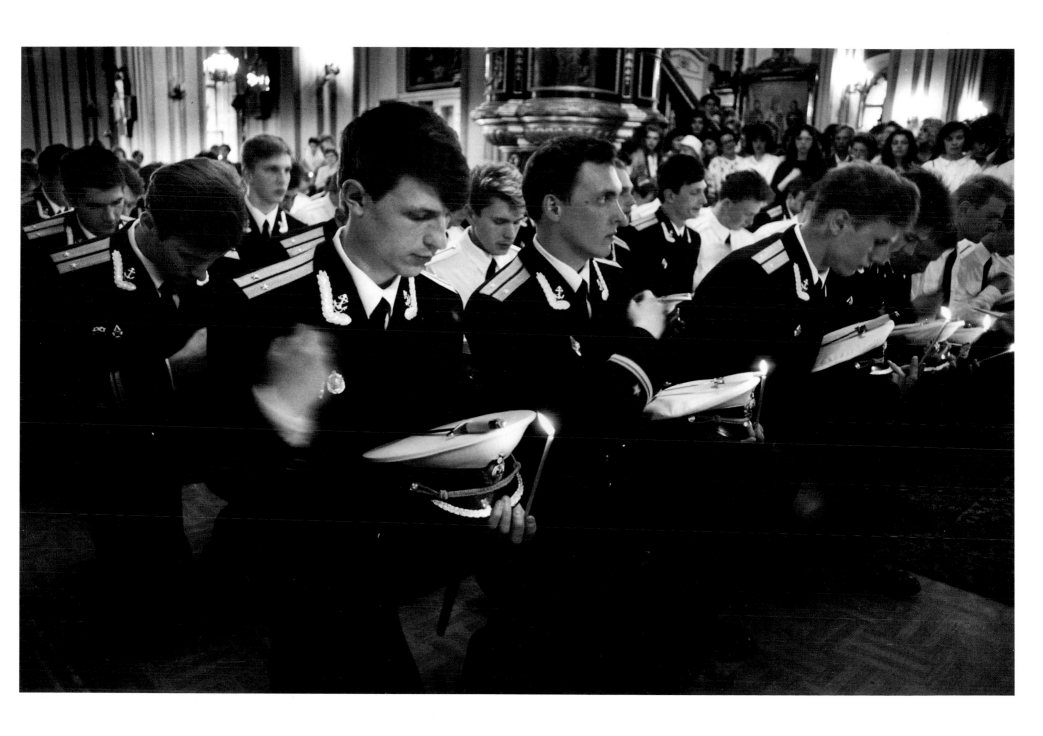

Leningrad
For the first time since the Russian Revolution in 1917, a Naval Cadet class celebrates its graduation at the St. Isaac Russian Orthodox Church in Leningrad. Asking for divine guidance for trips to sea was a tradition celebrated by the Soviet Navy before the Bolshevik Revolution, and is being revived.

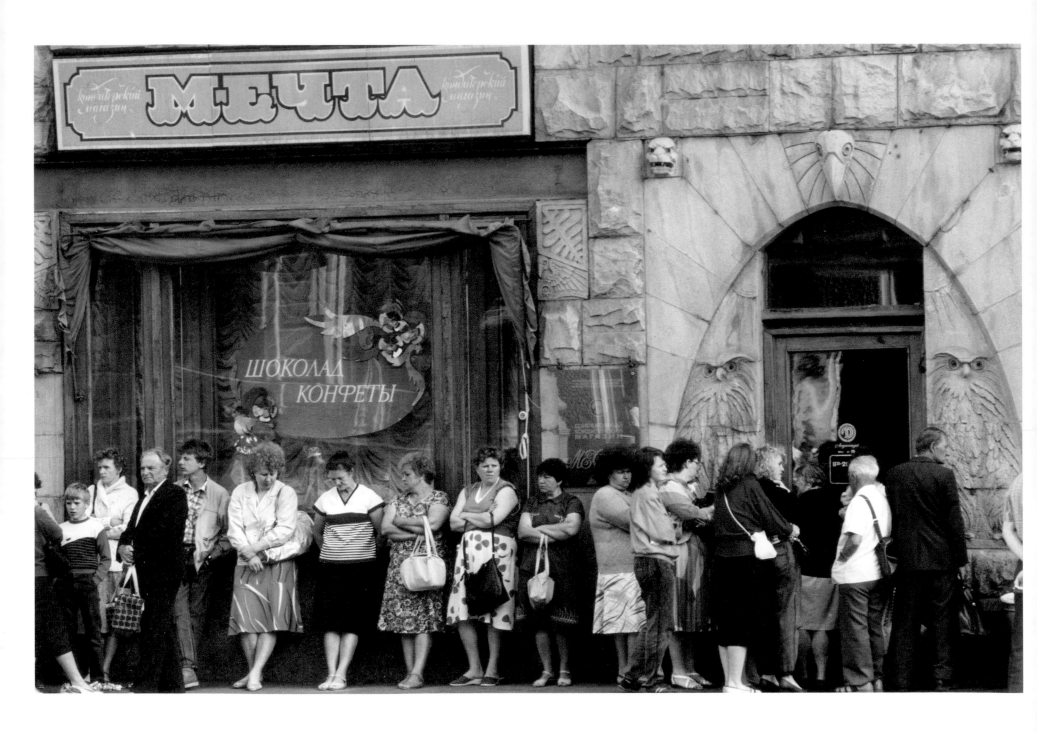

Shoppers stand in a queue waiting for a grocery store to open. Food is scarce in state-managed stores and very expensive in private markets.

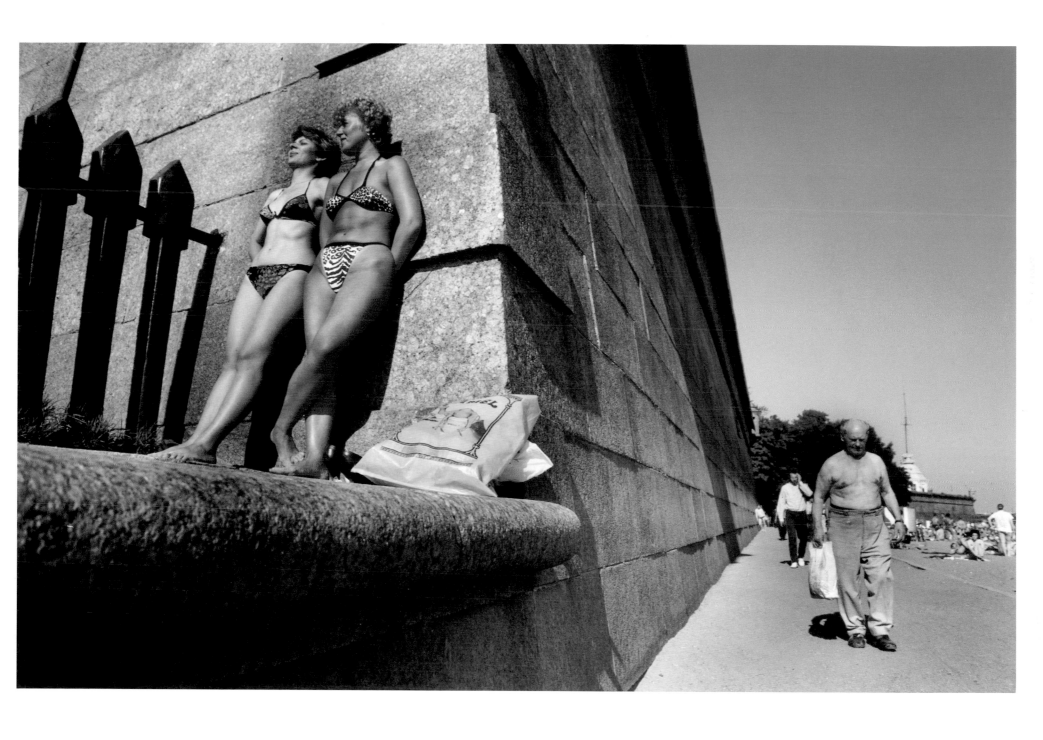

Women sunbathe on an island along
the River Neva, in the heart of
Leningrad.

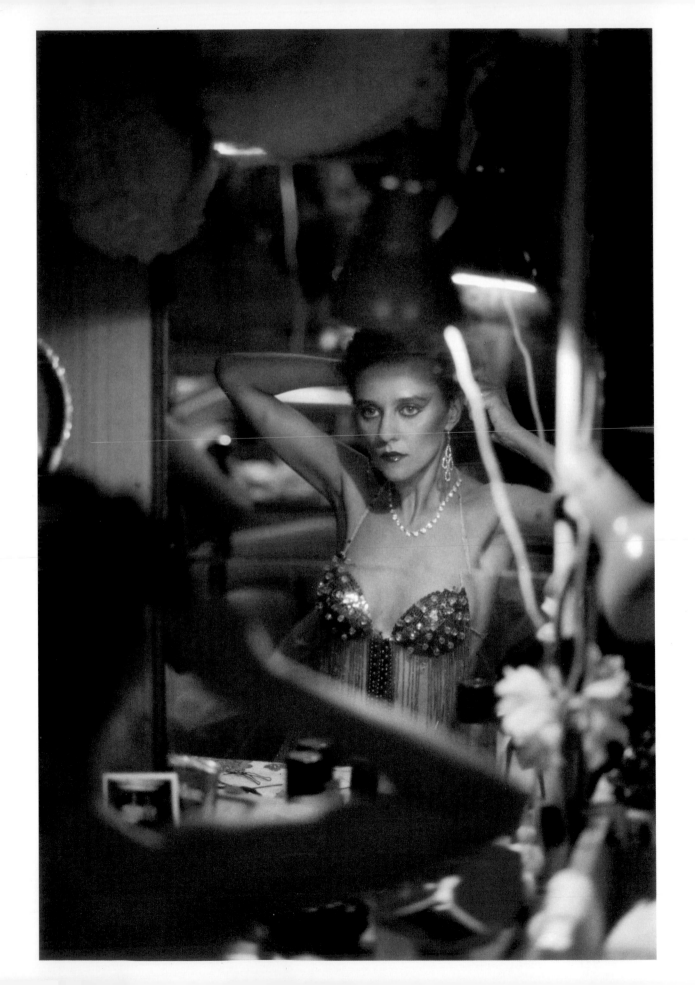

Backstage during a cabaret at the
Troika Restaurant in Leningrad.

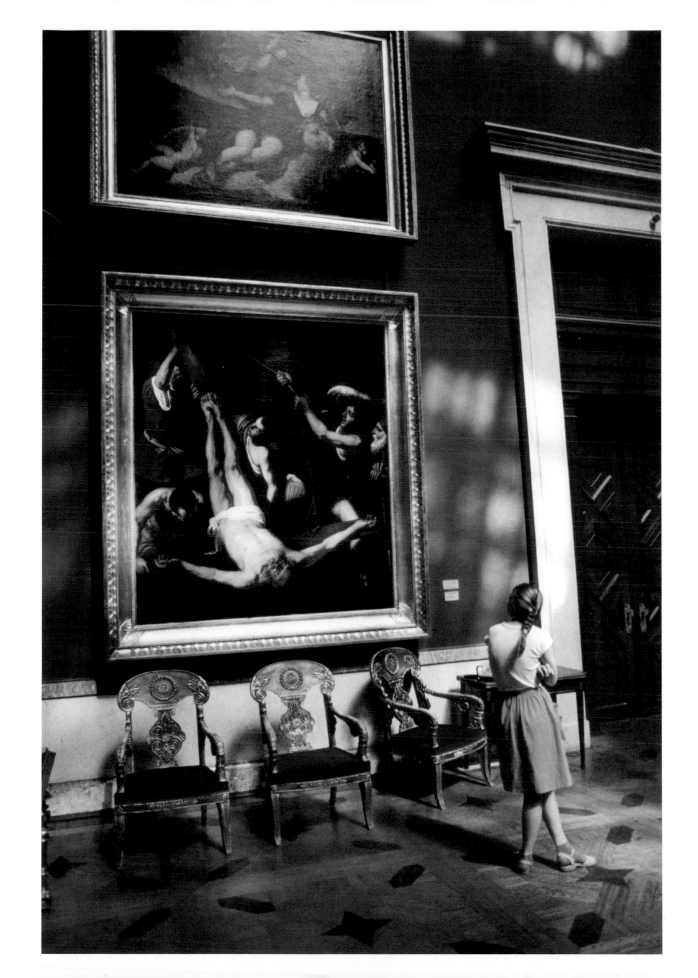

Inside Leningrad's Hermitage
Museum.

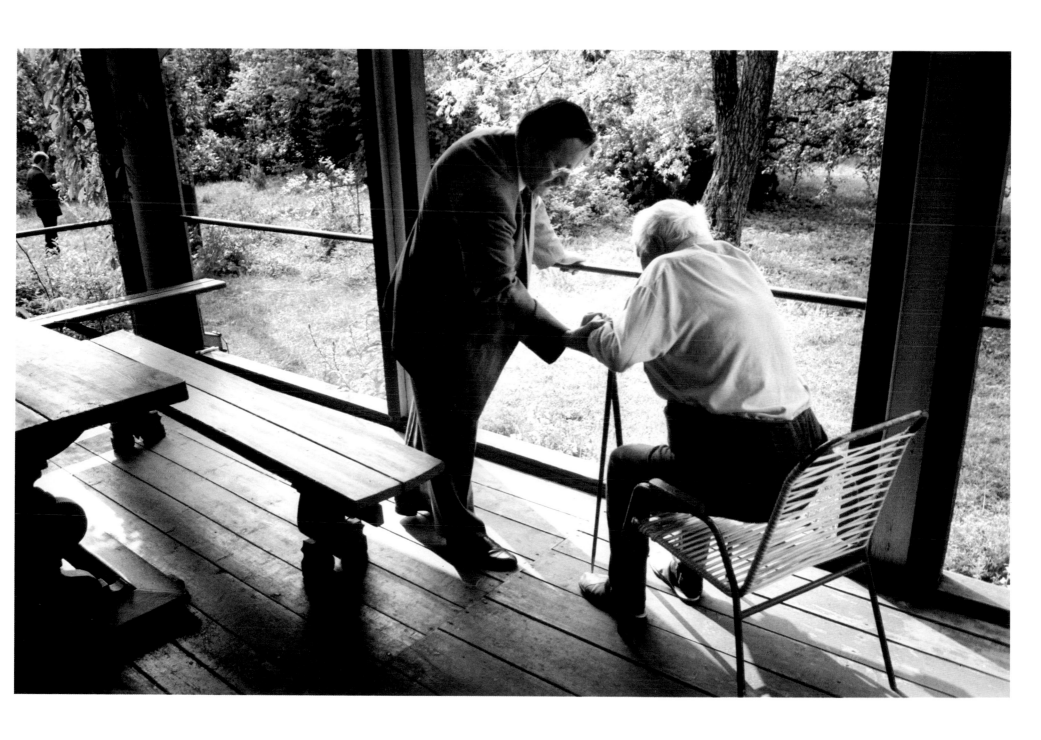

Kaunas, Lithuania
At the family dacha, Lithuanian President Vytautas Landsbergis helps up his 98-year-old father. Once an officer in the Czar's White Russian Army, his father is still one of the president's most valued advisors.

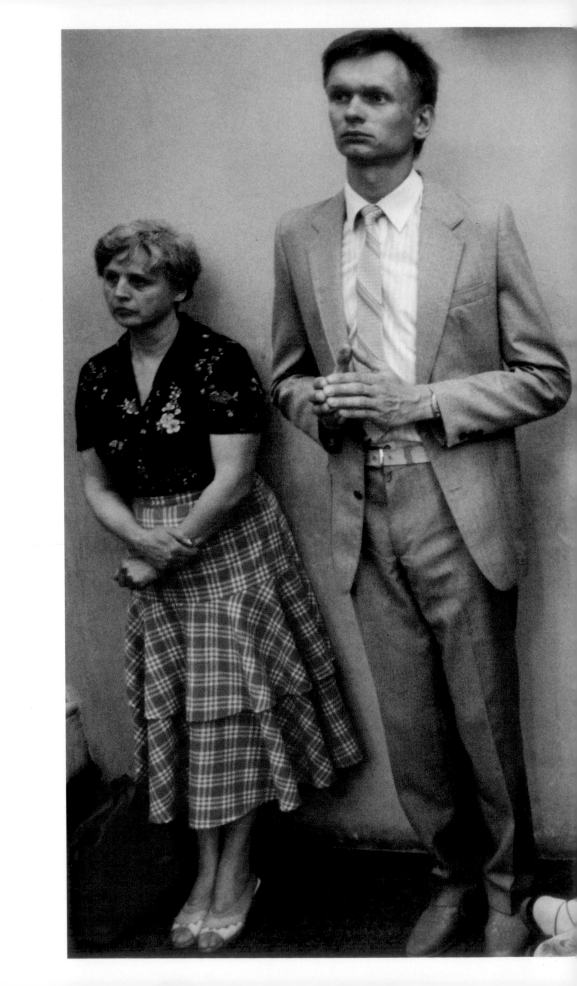

Vilnius, Lithuania
Confession during a Sunday service
at the Vilnius Roman Catholic
Cathedral.

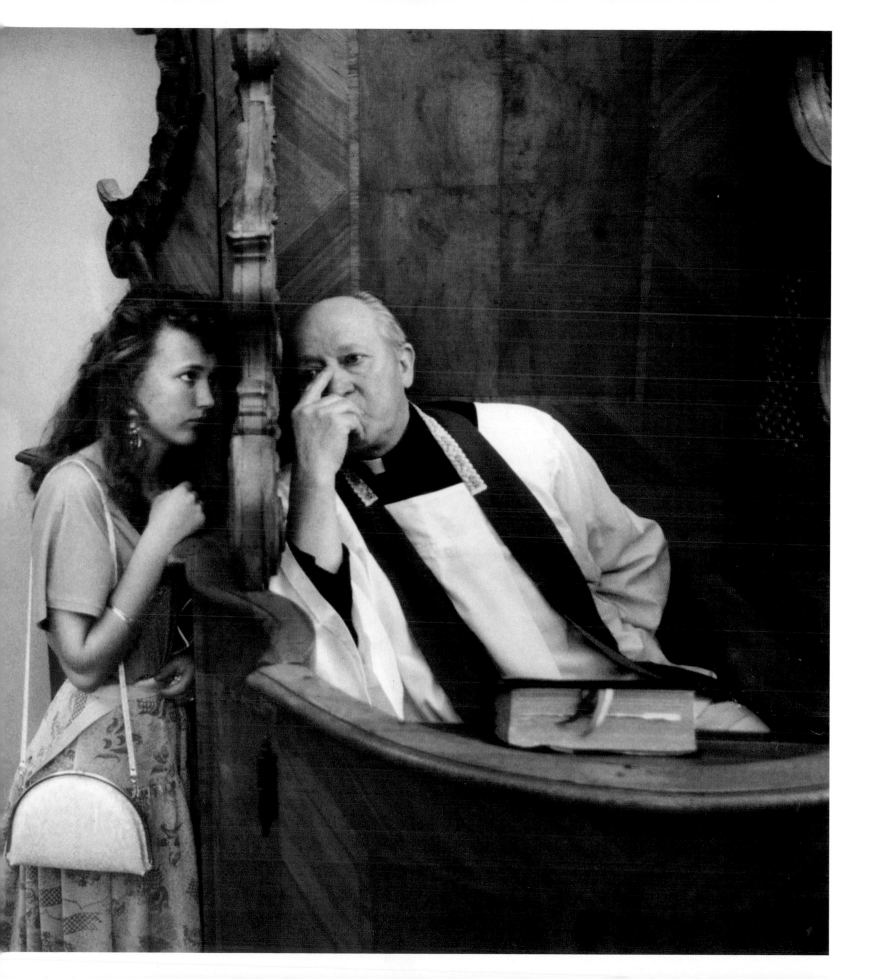

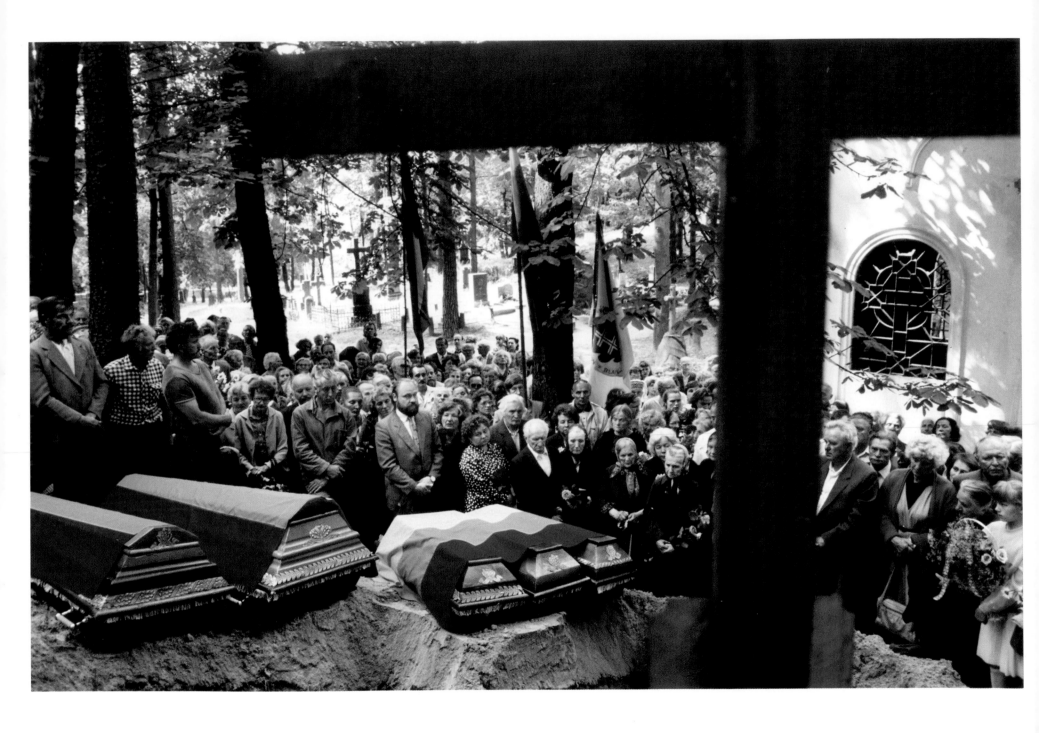

Lithuanians commemorate the deaths of members of a family who had been killed by Stalin in the 1940s, and whose bodies had been brought back from Siberia.

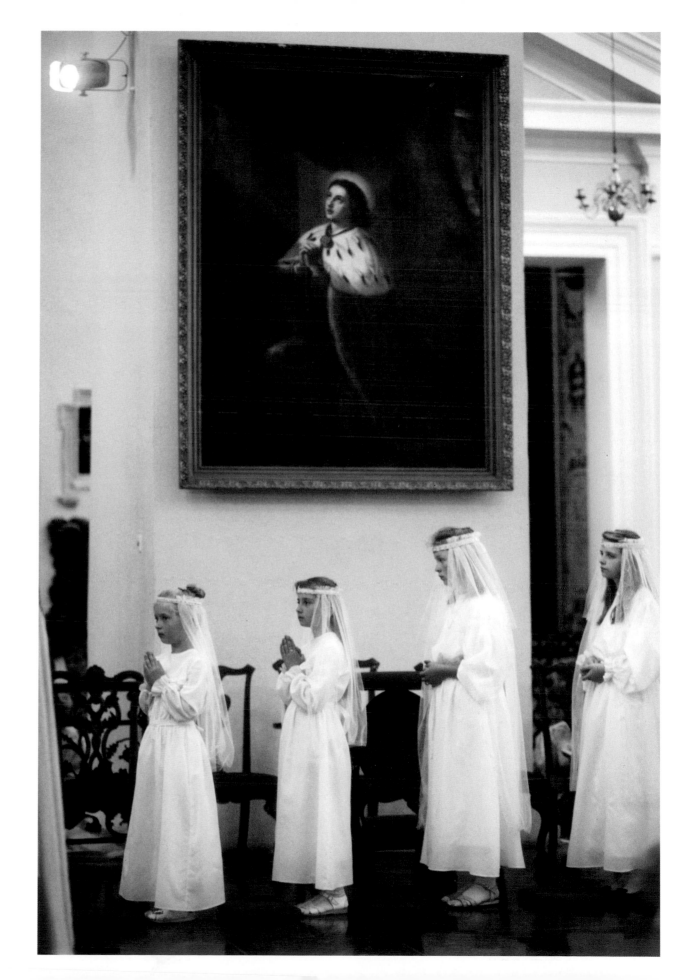

Altar girls of the Vilnius Cathedral.

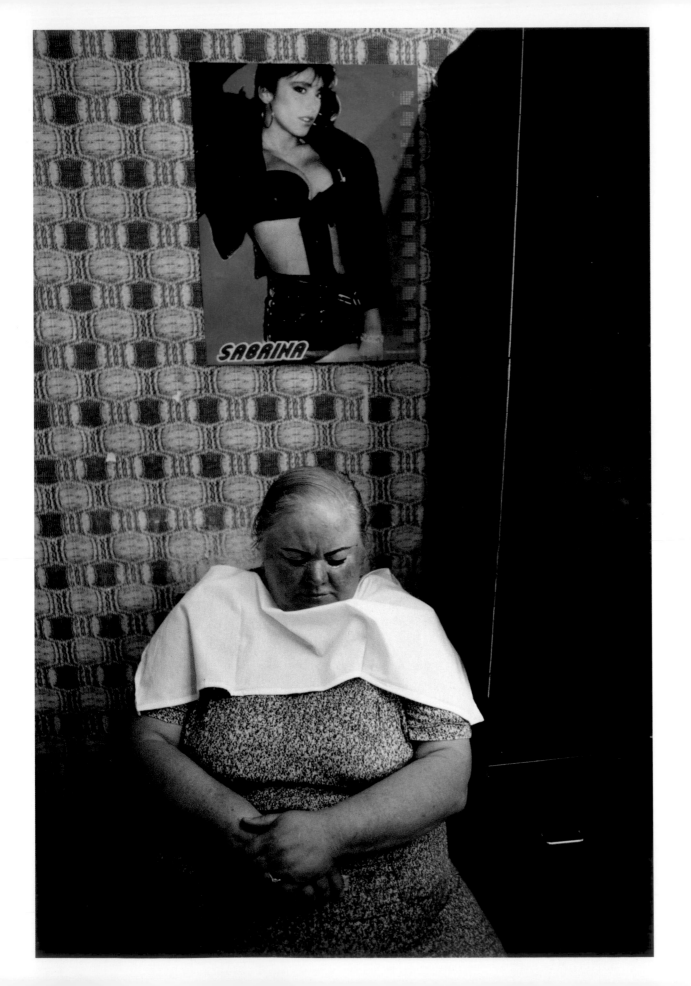

In a Vilnius beauty parlor, a woman has her eyebrows bleached in front of a poster of Sabrina, an Italian rock music star.

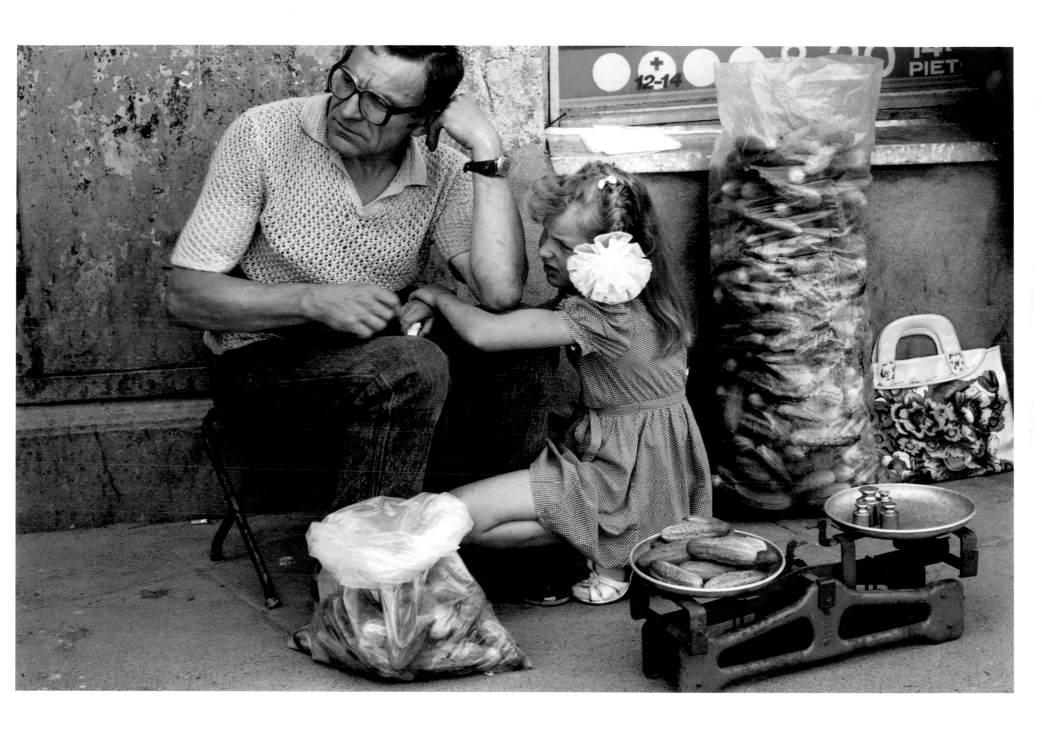

A farmer and his daughter sell cucumbers in Vilnius.

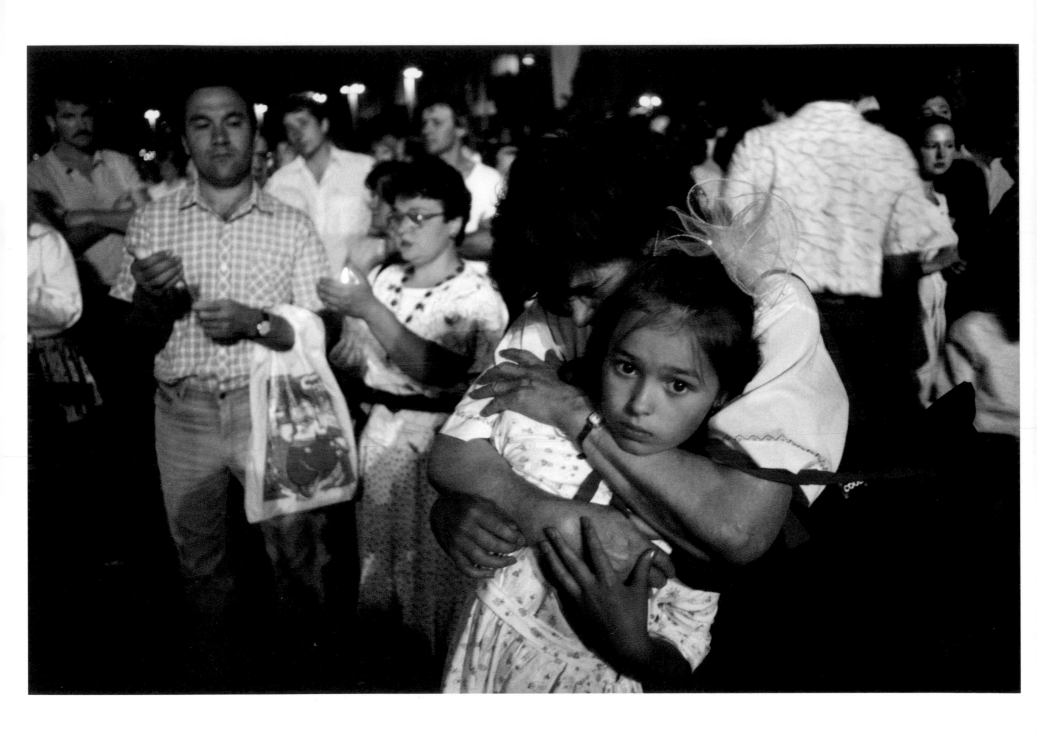

Kiev, Ukraine
Ukrainians celebrate the first anniversary of declared independence with folk dancing, music, and the lighting of candles.

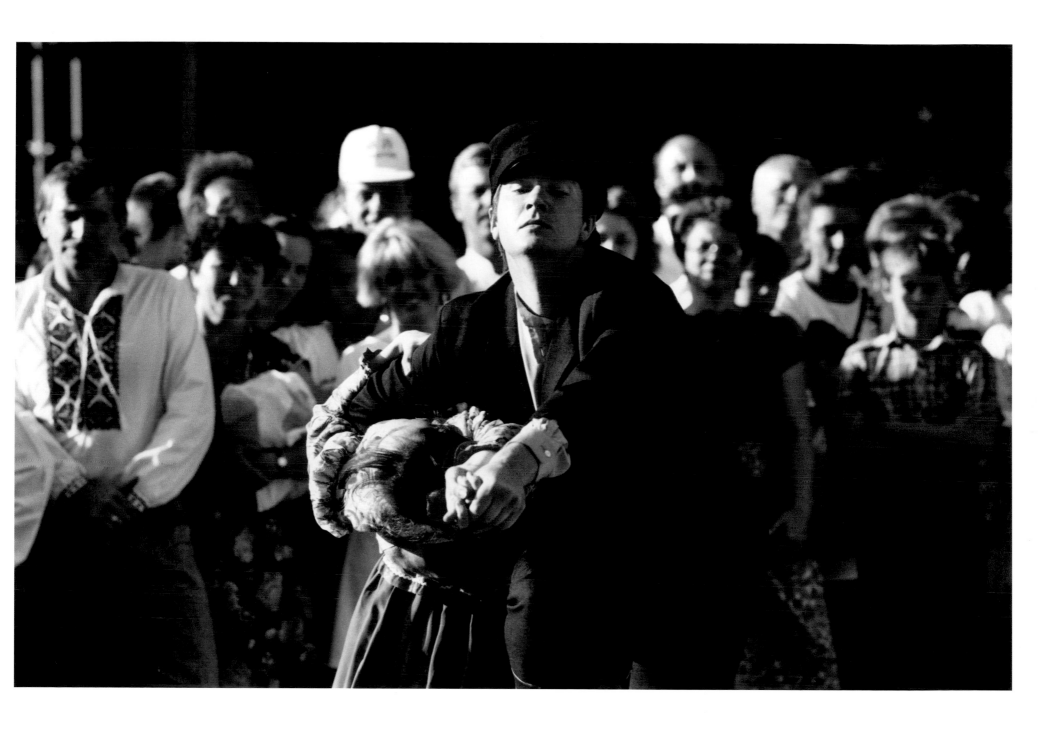

Gidzivka, Ukraine

In a collective farming village dating back to the ninth century, families and friends celebrate the wedding of Roman and Luba. Traditionally, before the bride and groom can marry, they must each bow in front of their parents and grandparents and kiss loaves of homemade bread to symbolize the transition from their old family to a new one. The couple also visited the gravesite of Luba's father to pay their respects. Dancing, a feast, and much vodka were all part of the three-day ceremony.

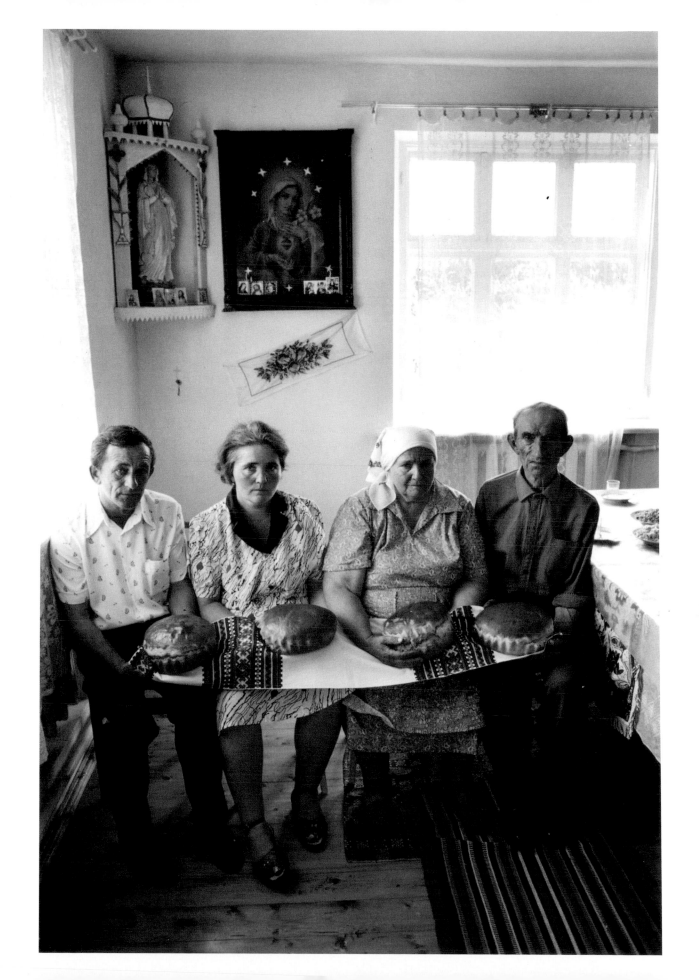

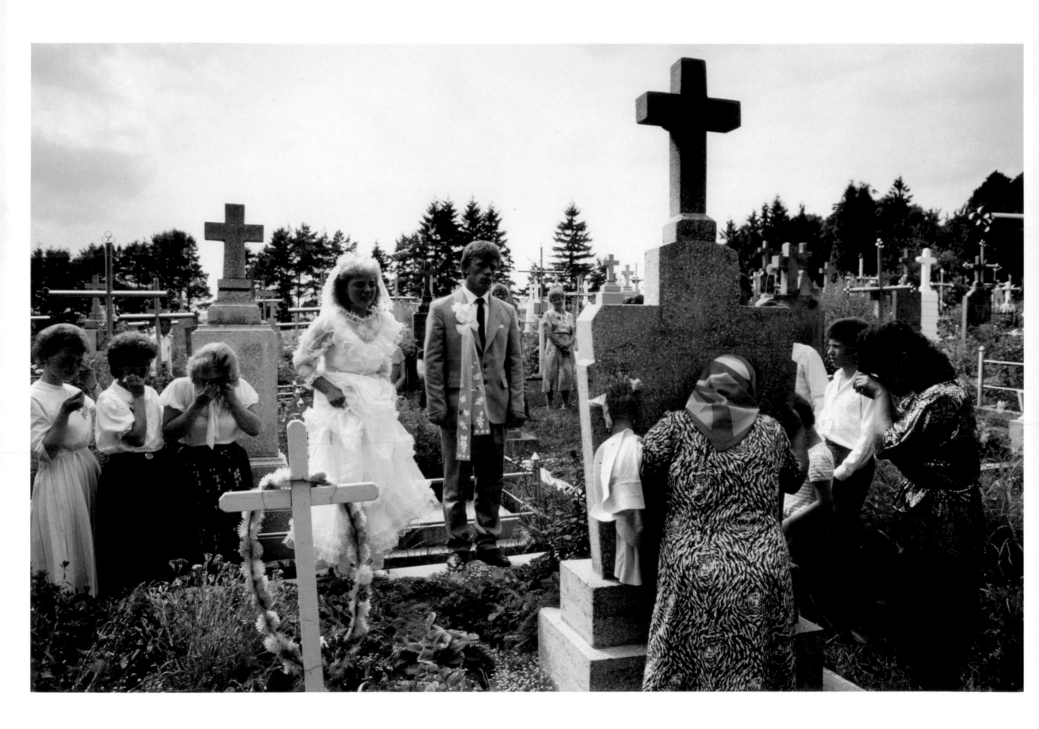

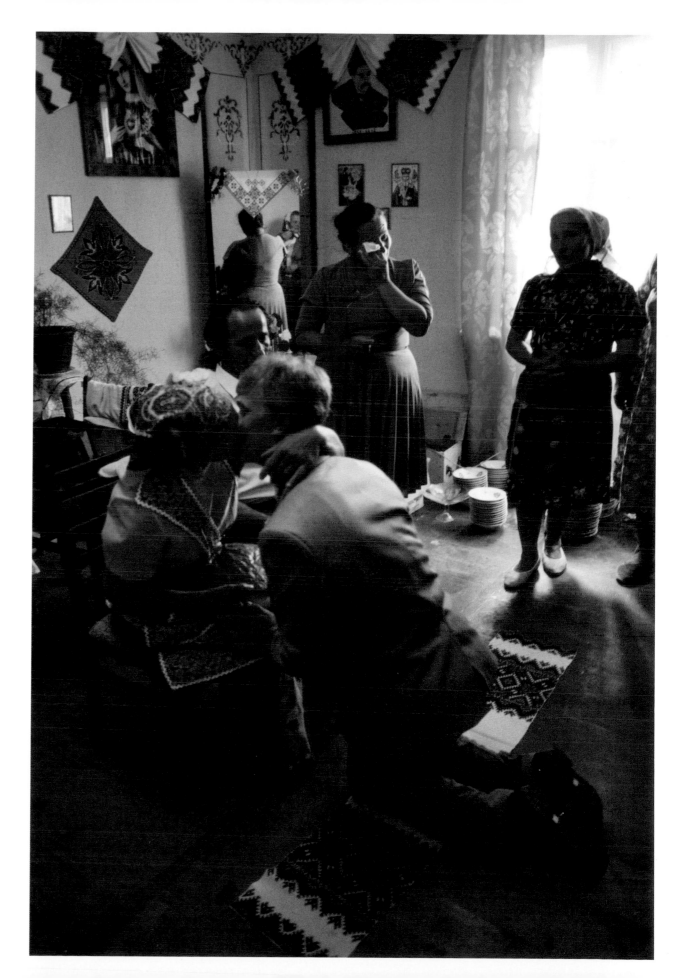

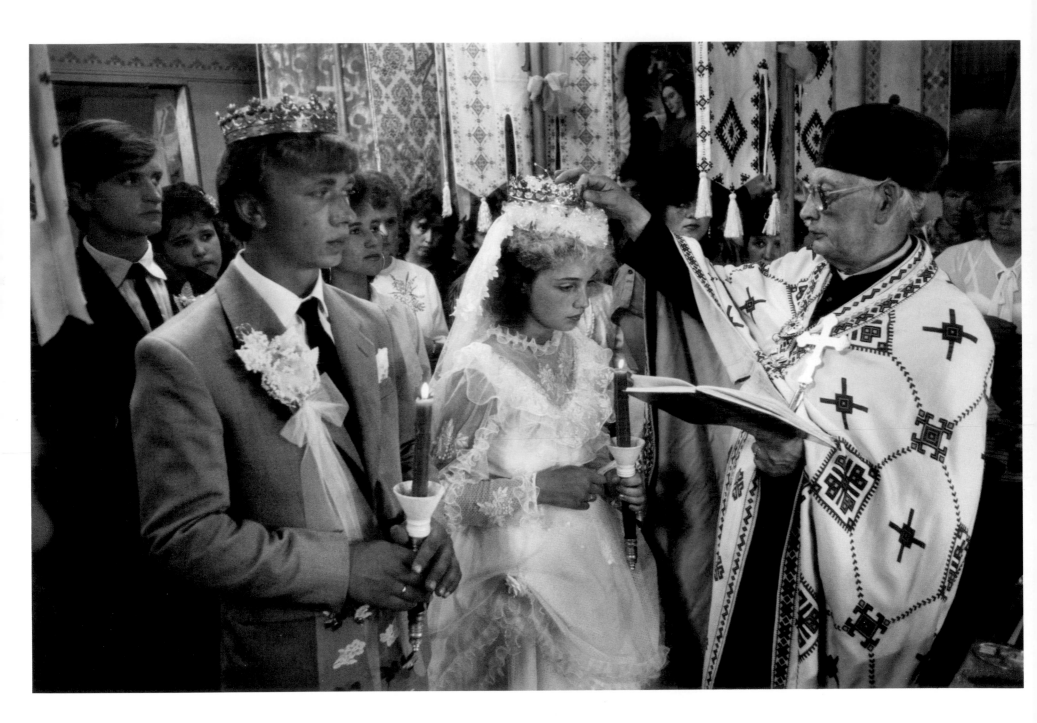

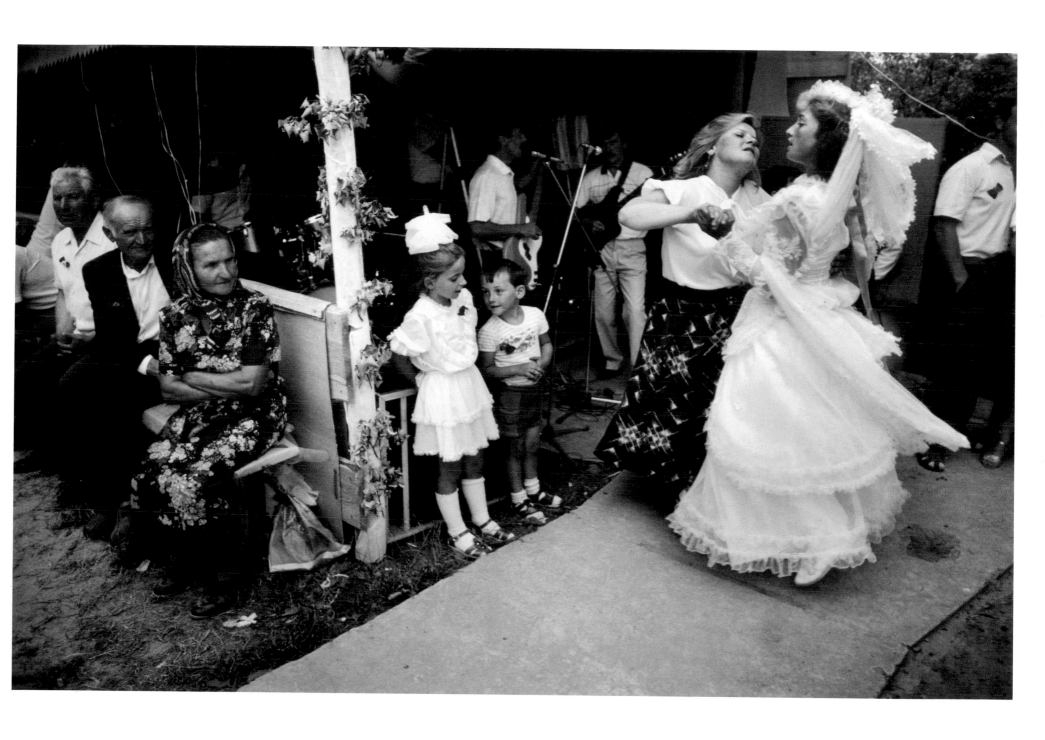

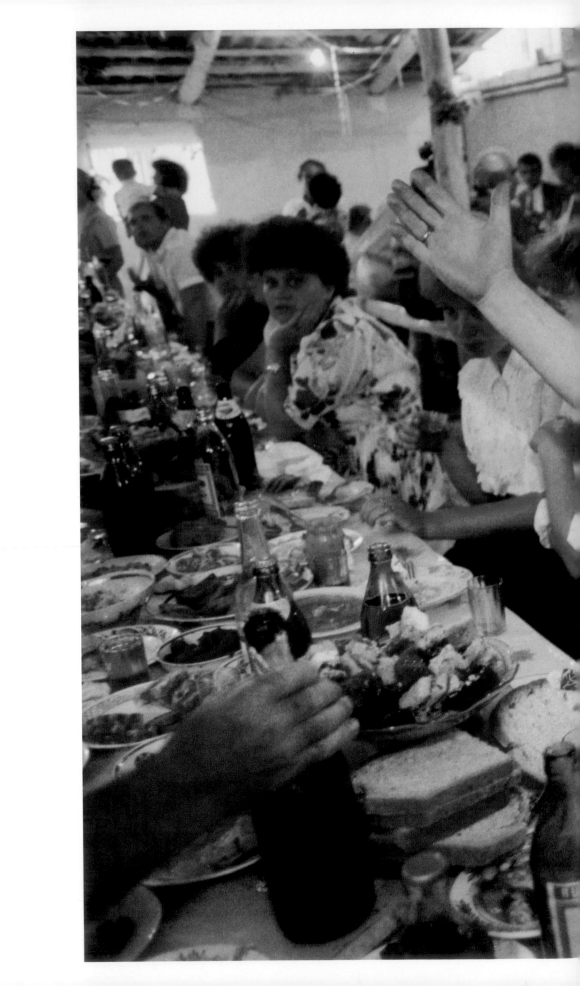

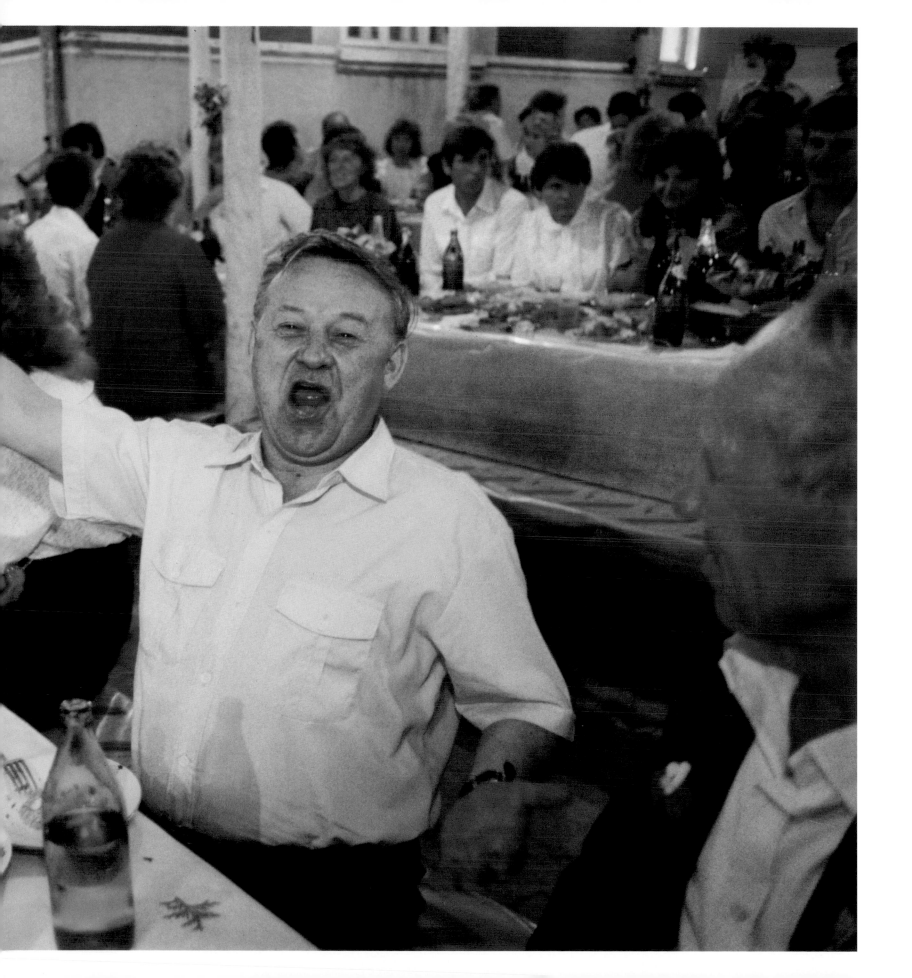

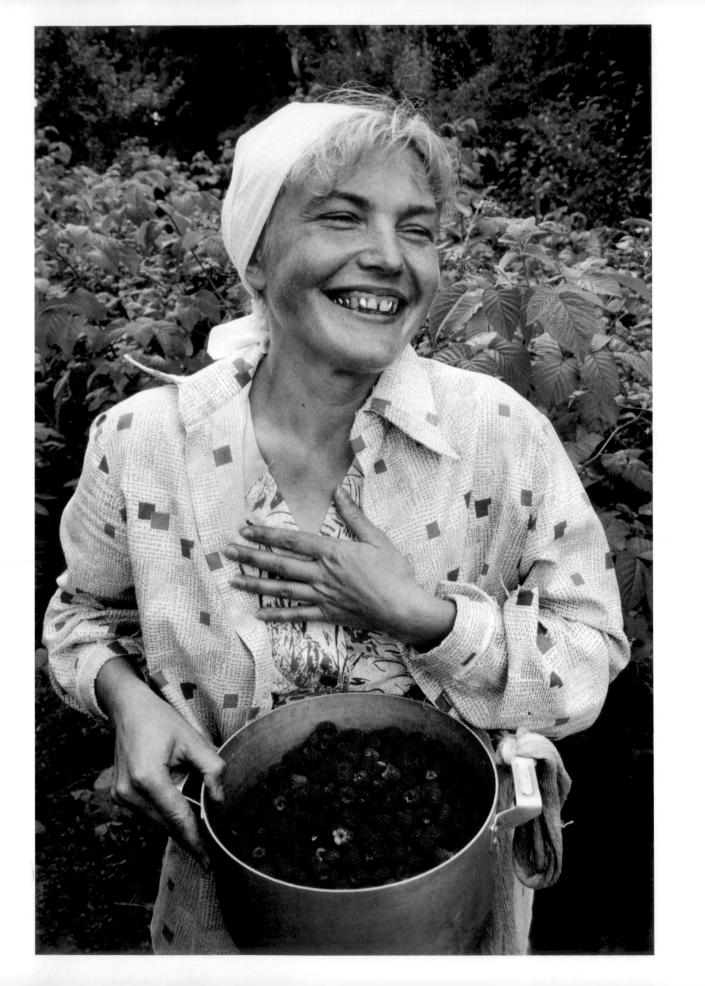

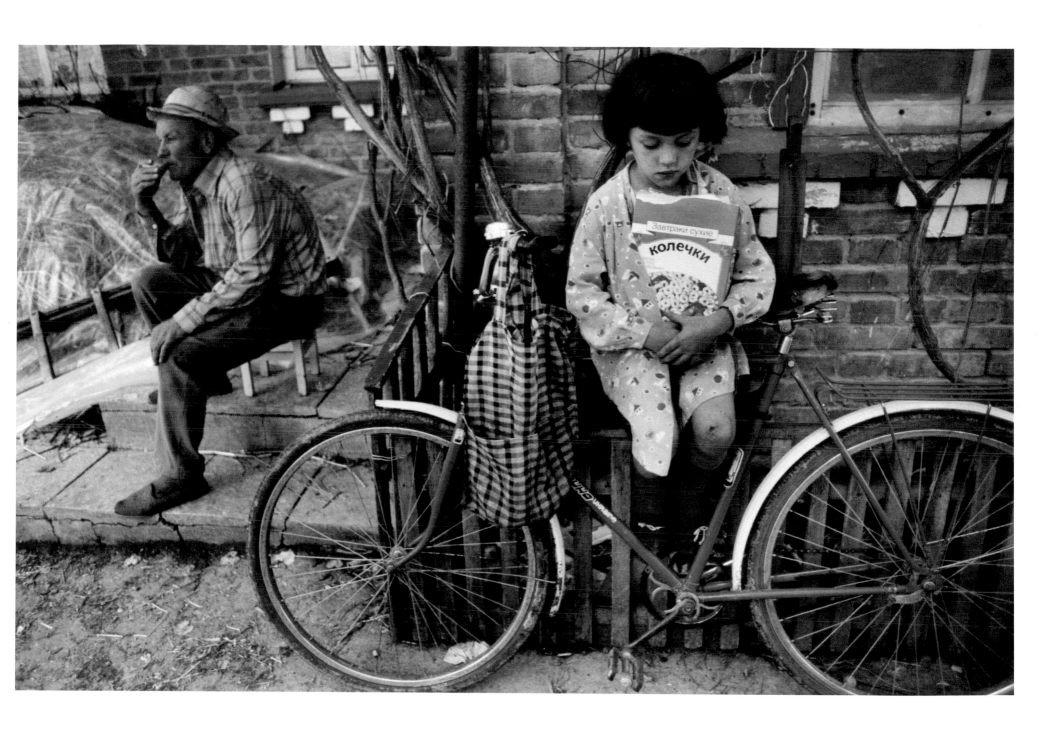

On his private farm, Sebastian
Fedorenko and his granddaughter
take a break from their farm chores,

while his daughter-in-law, Lela,
picks raspberries.

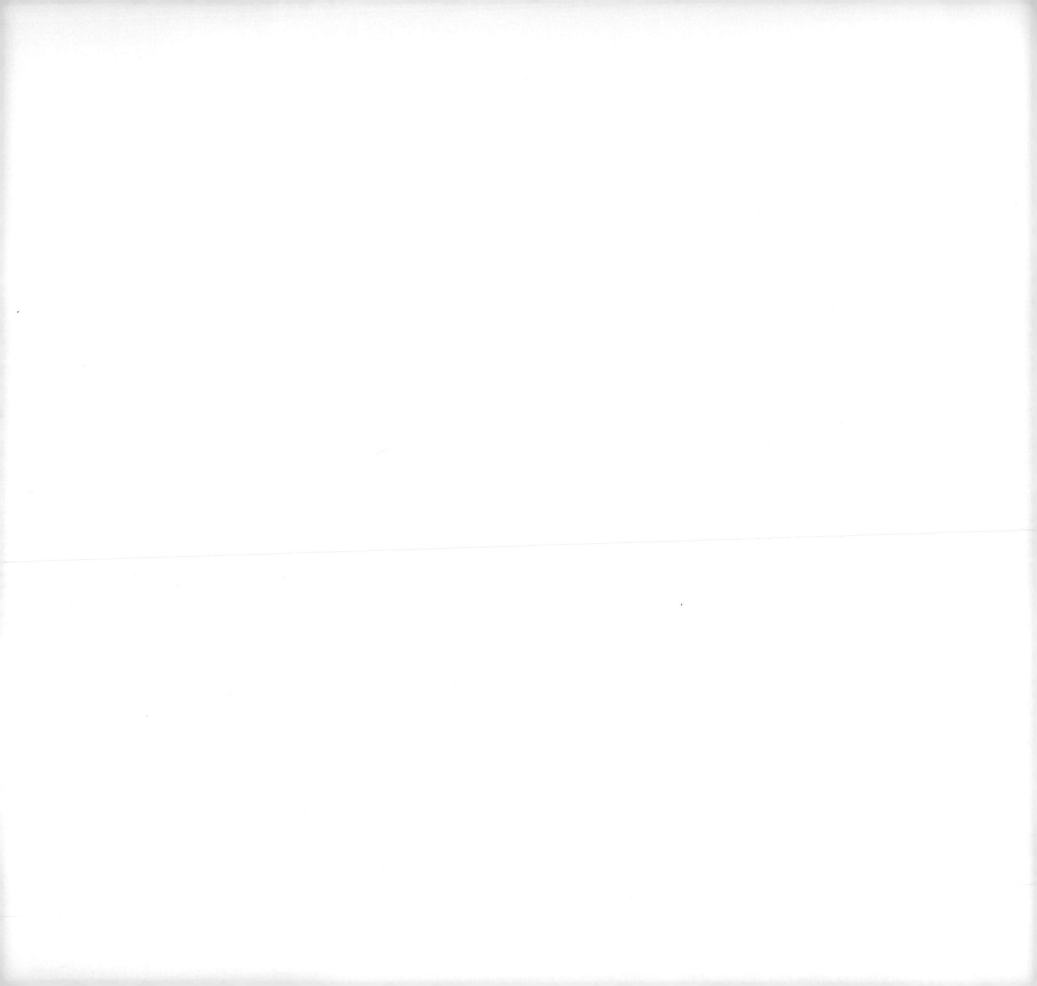

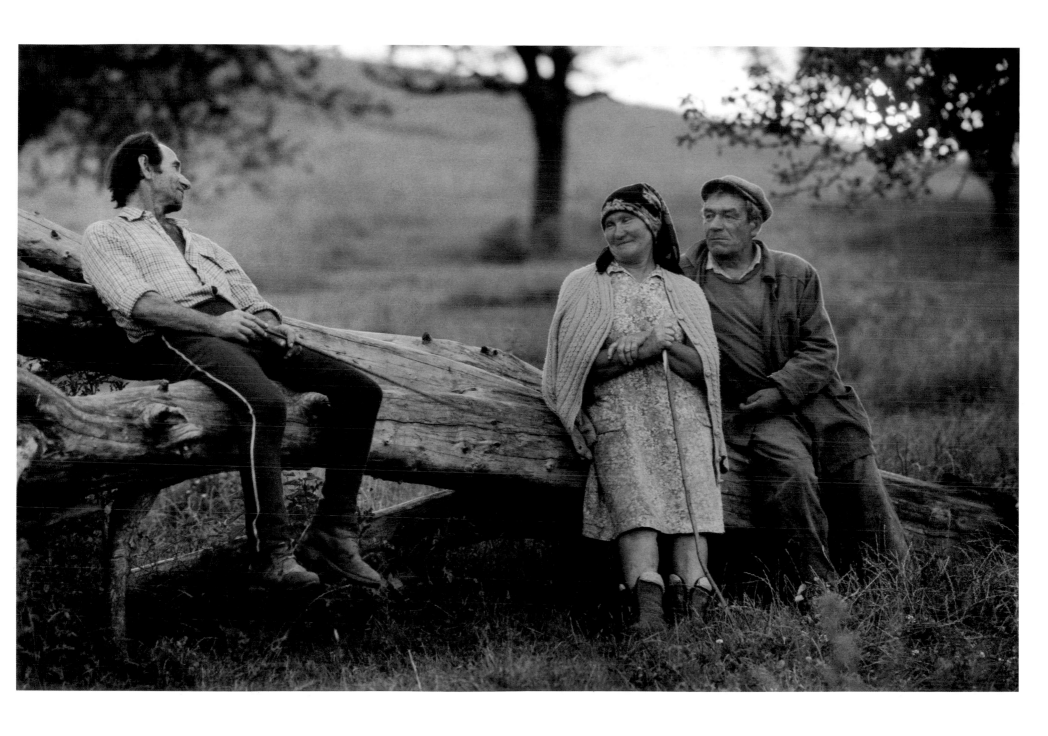

Farmer Yaroslav Popovich and his neighbors chat in the late afternoon as they graze their cows on a collective farm in the village of Gidzivka, where 450 families work. Farmers earn about 250 rubles a month (less than ten dollars), working 12 hours a day.

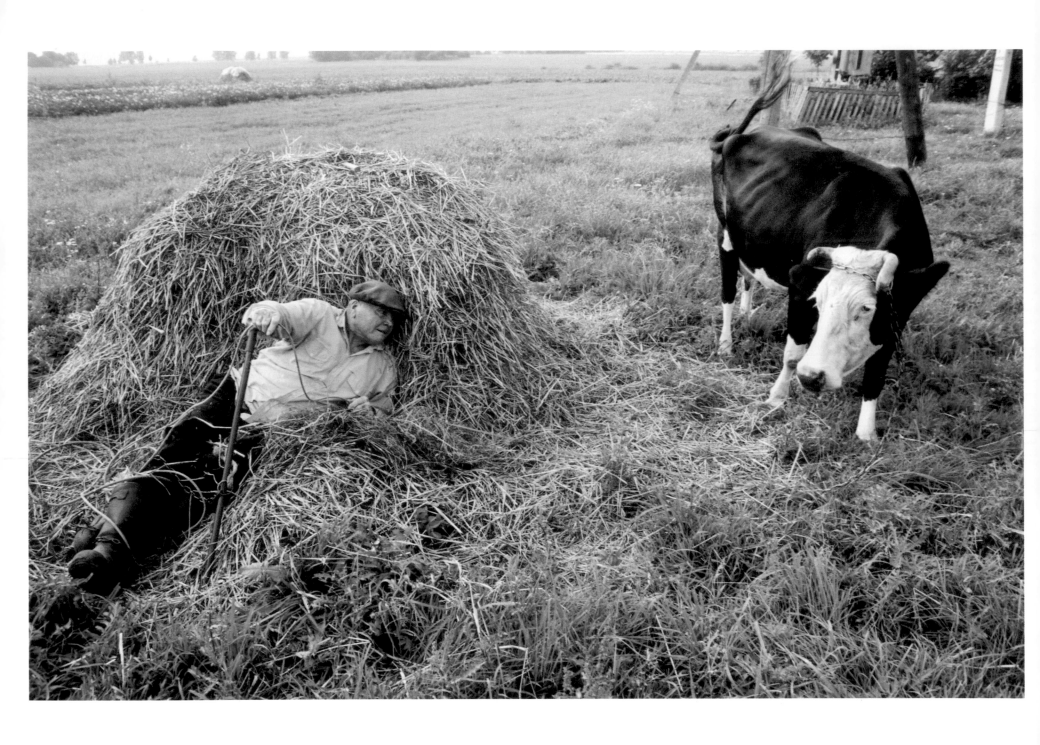

Outside L'Vov, Ukraine
An 80-year-old retired farmer grazes
his cow on his farm.

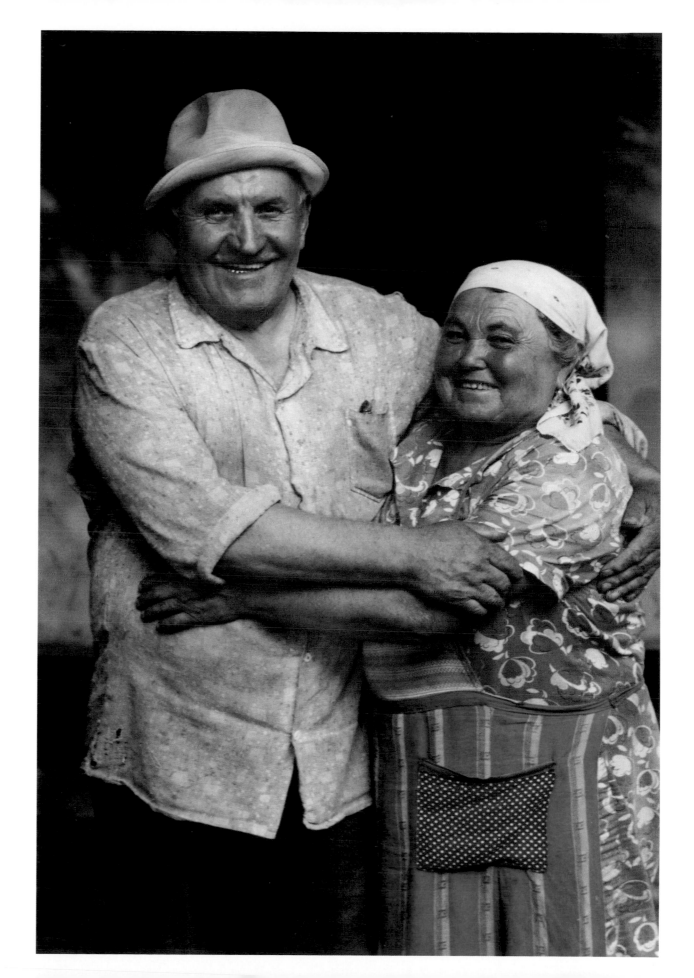

Carpenter and farmer Panas Shanal
with his wife Anna.

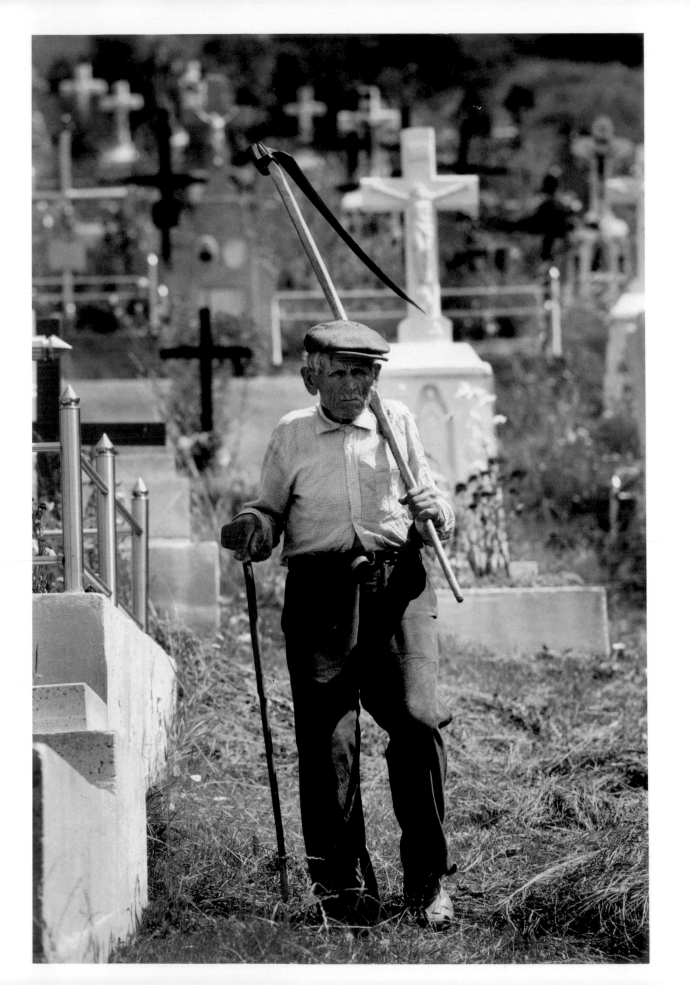

An elderly man returns from cutting grass in the hillside cemetery in Gidzivka, a ninth-century collective farming village.

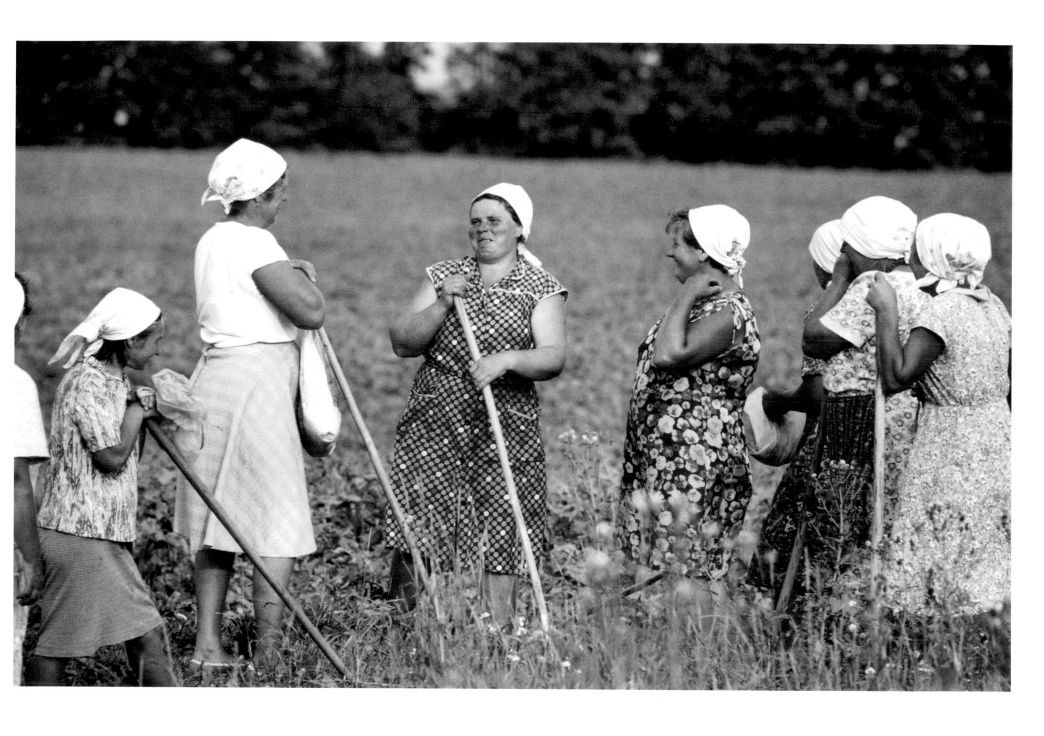

Ukrainian collective farmers take a
break from hoeing a field of tomato
plants.

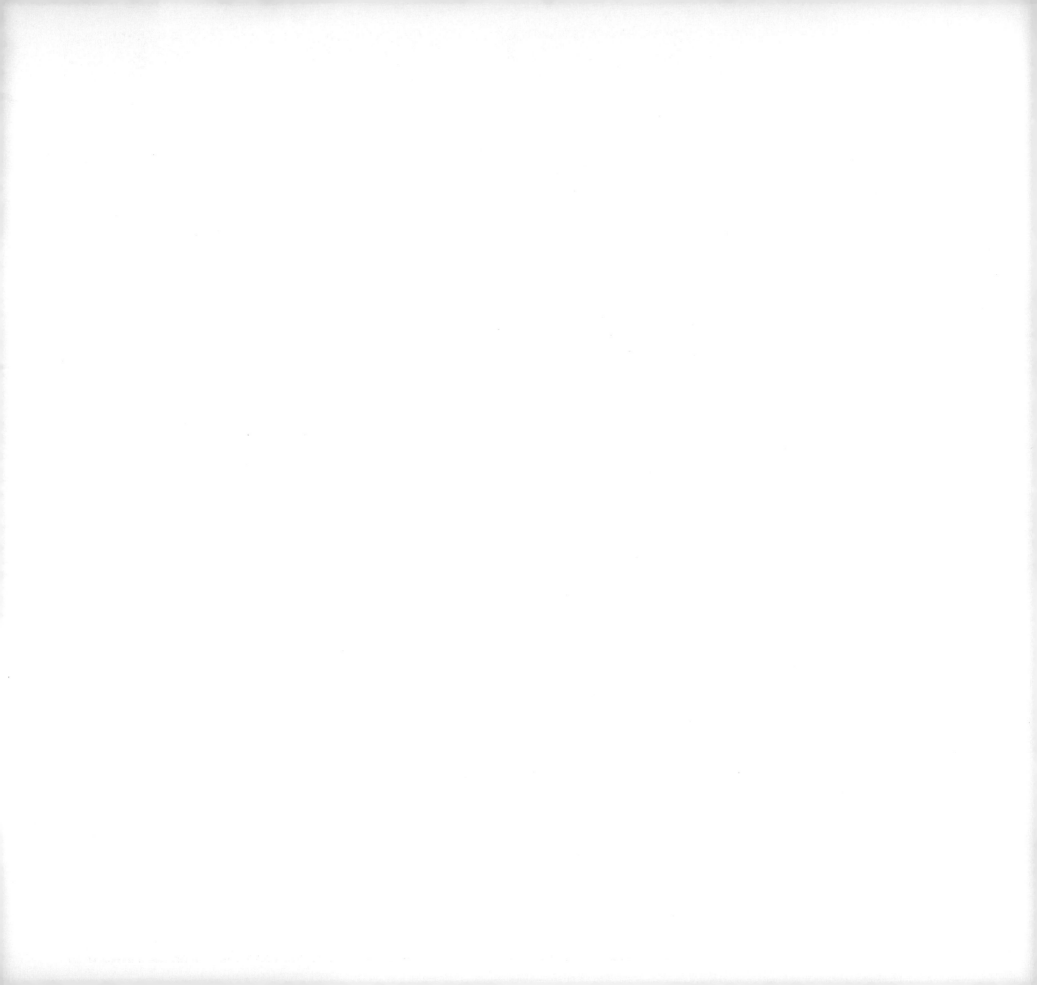

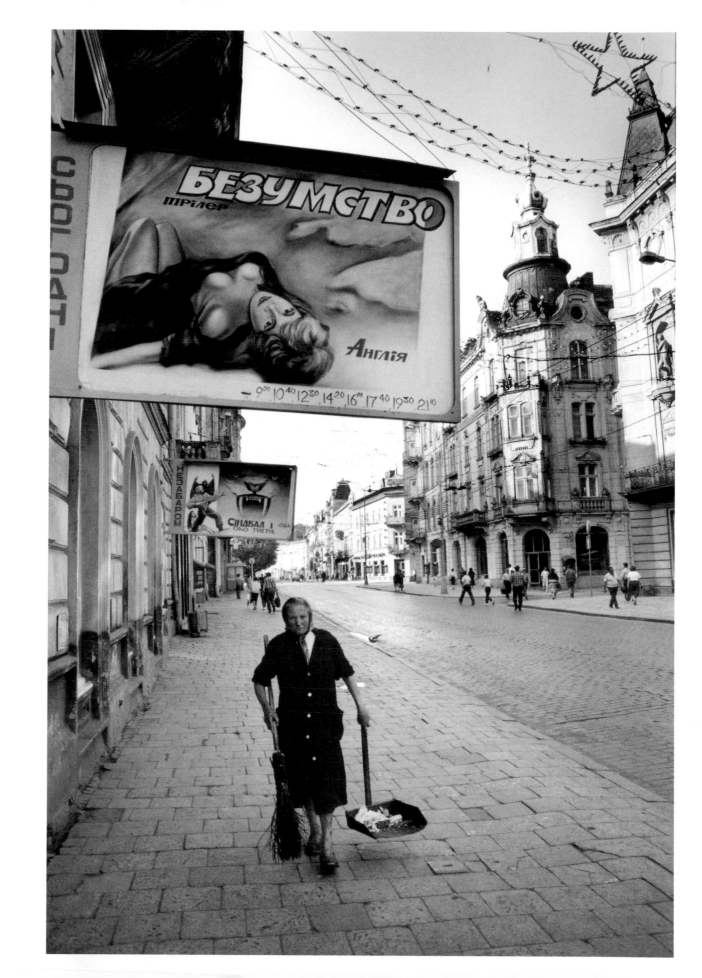

L'Vov, Ukraine
A woman cleans the streets of
L'Vov, under a hand-painted cinema
marquee.

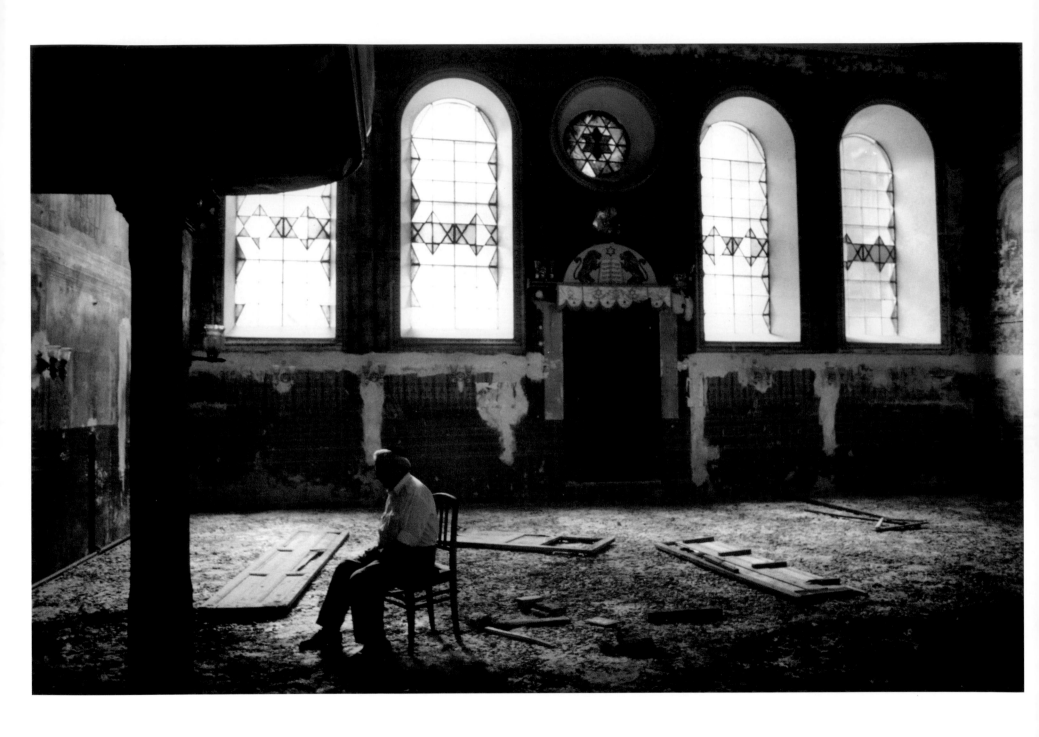

The Torah is read in the last functioning synagogue in L'Vov, a city that once had a population of 50 thousand Jews and 80 synagogues. This synagogue, which has only recently been reopened after 70 years of repression, was used by the Germans as a horse stable during the Second World War.

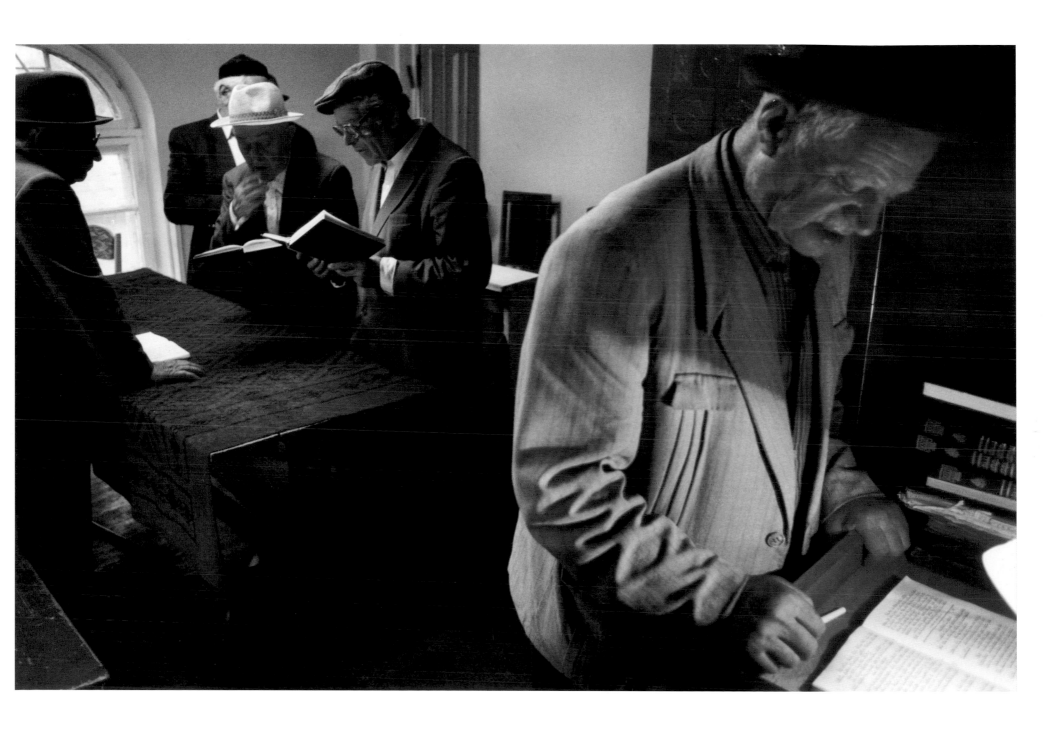

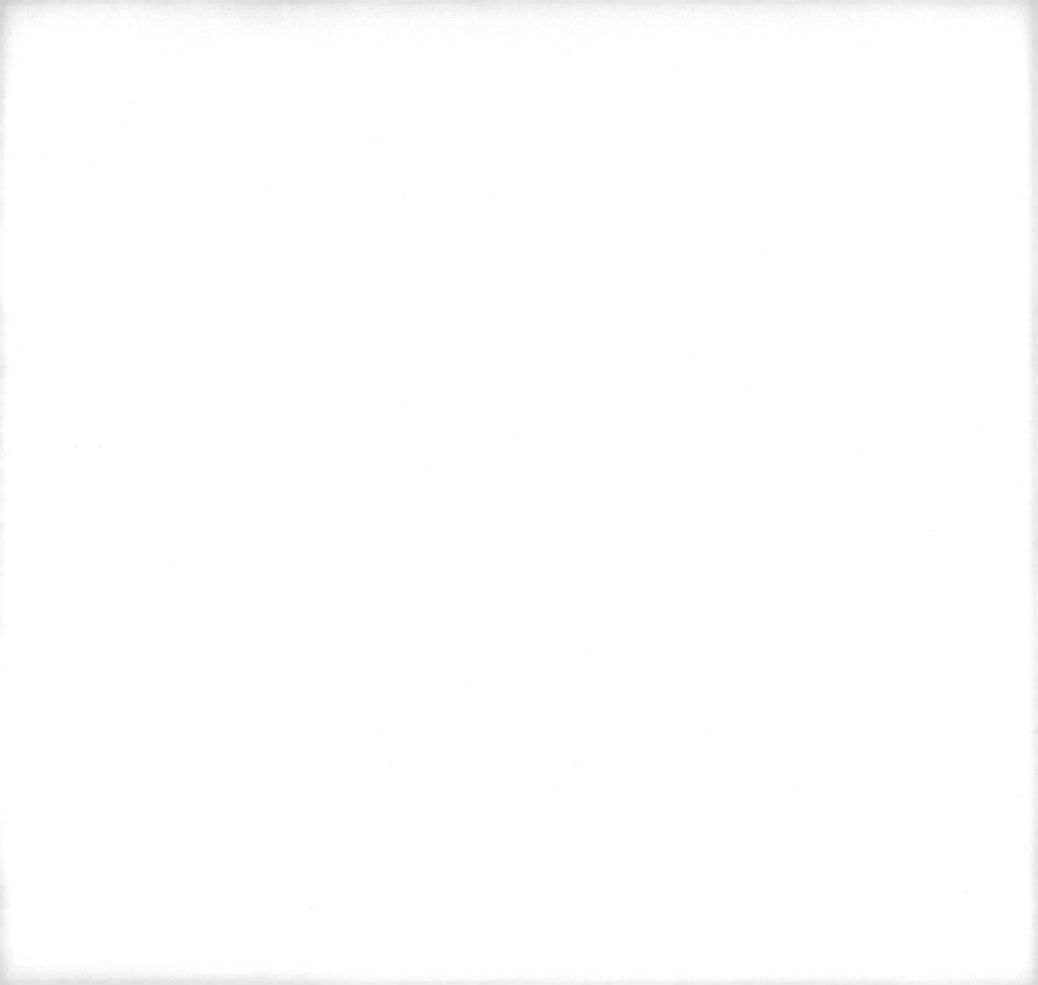

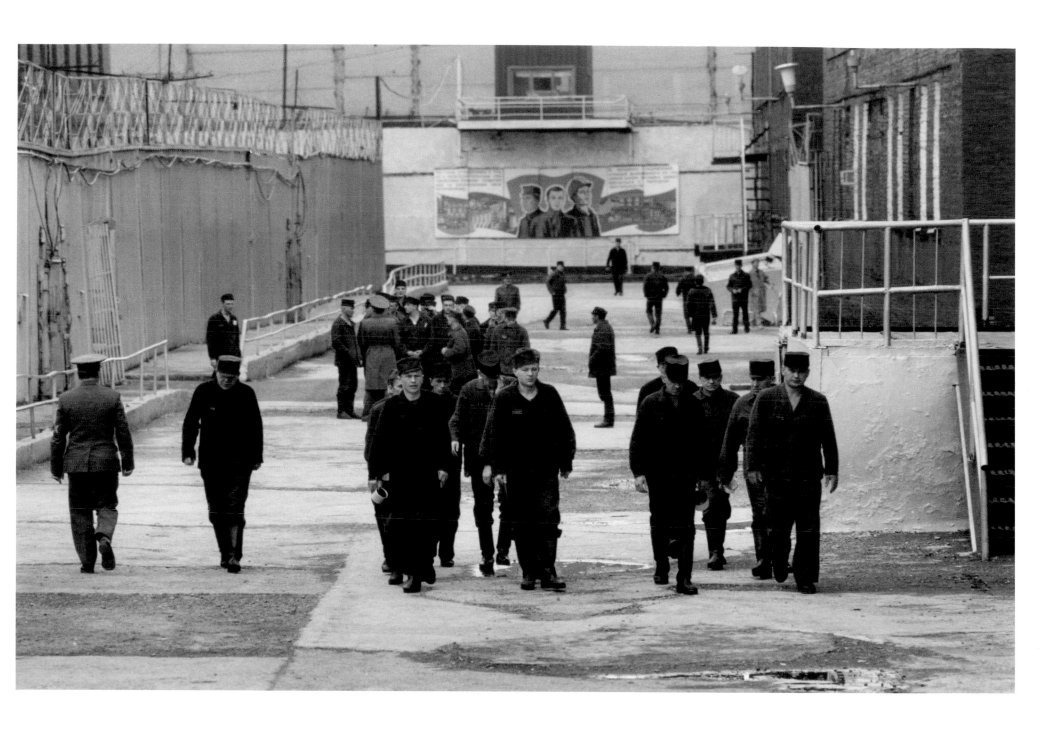

Norilsk, Northern Siberia

In "severe regime" Prison #288/15, temperatures fall to 50 degrees below centigrade during the winter. The prison, which was once used as a gulag for political prisoners, is reputed to be one of the most repressive prisons in the country. Built 30 years ago, the prison holds 1,400 inmates.

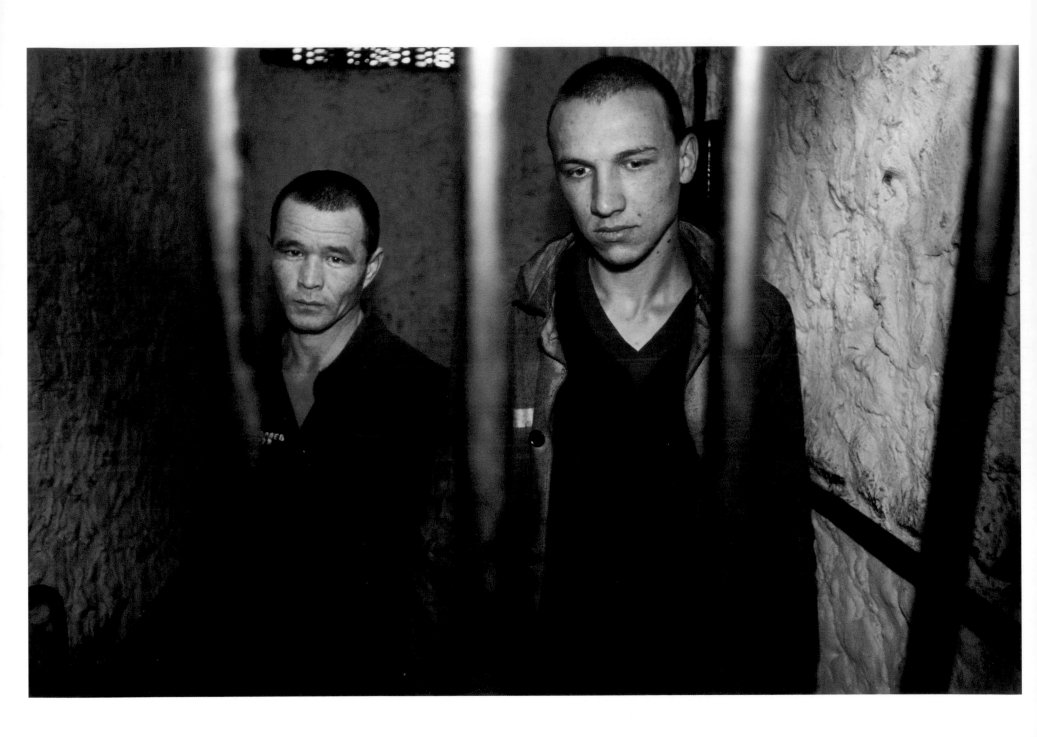

Officials say that prisoners can only be held in solitary confinement for 15 days, but prisoners contend that they are often held for up to six months. The cells have very little light, no beds, and a hole in the corner which serves as a toilet.

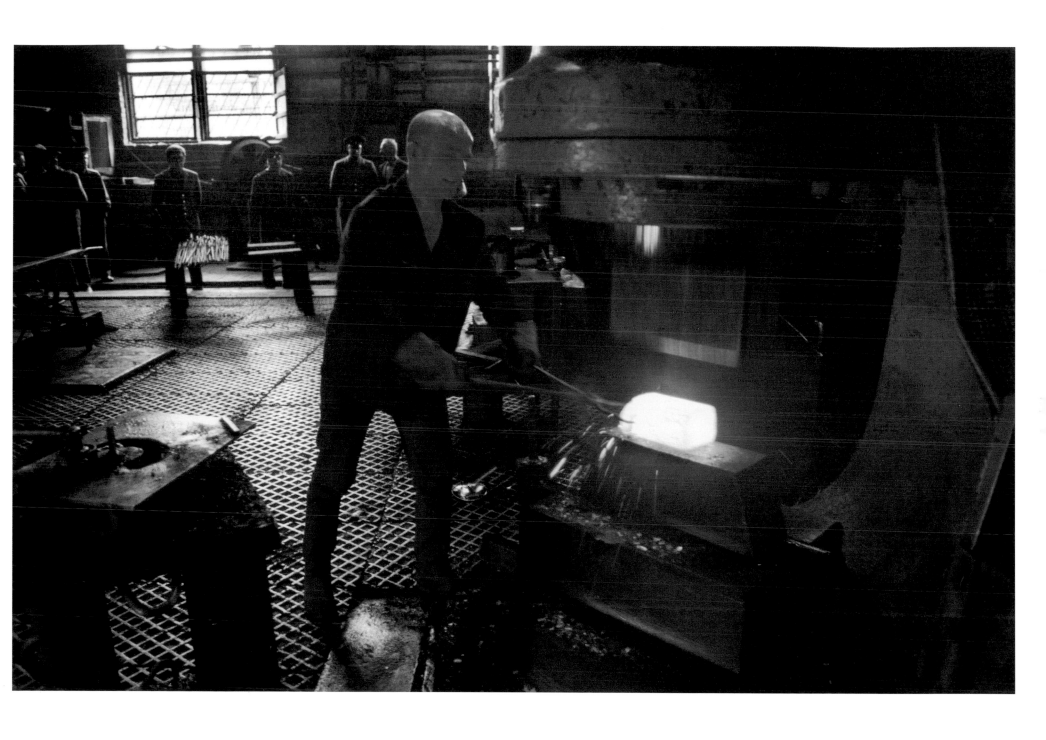

Prisoners work in a foundry making
metal containers to be used to ship
refined nickel to foreign countries.

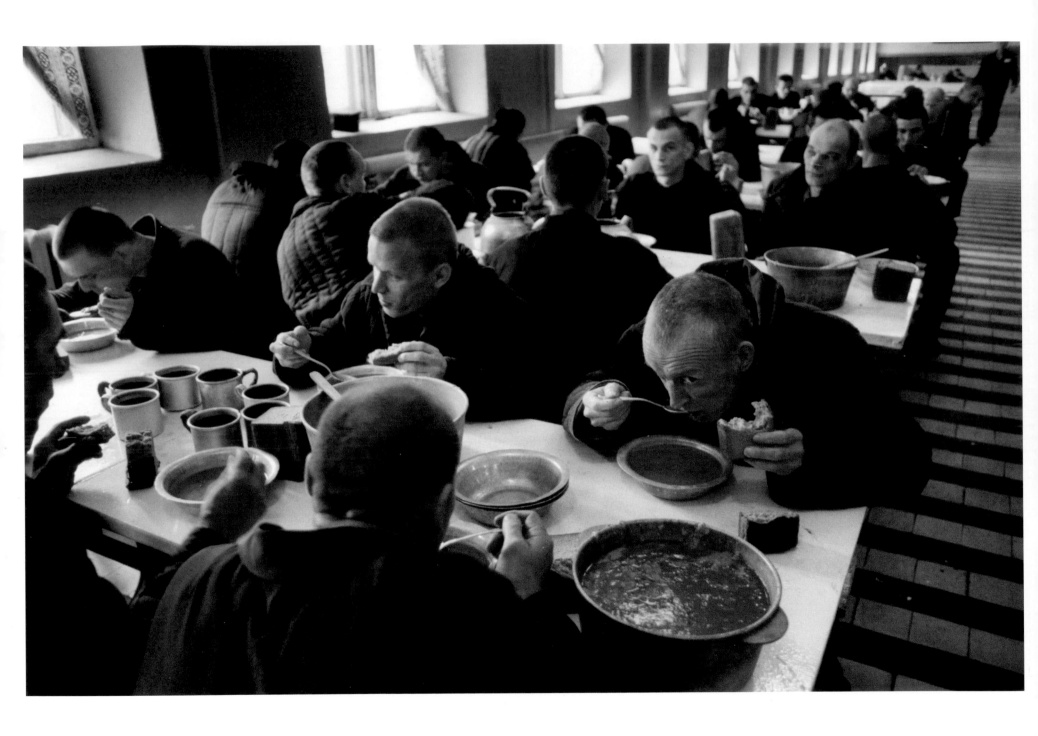

Prisoners are given 15 minutes to eat
their lunch, which consists of bread,
soup, and black tea.

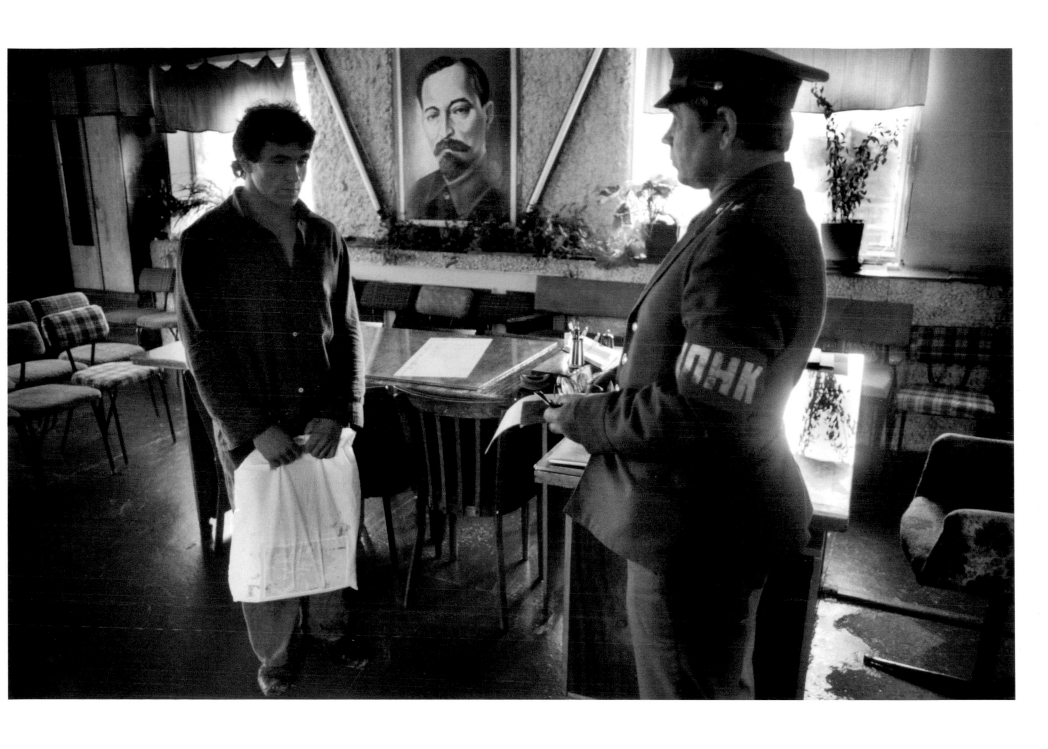

A prisoner from the Far East awaits
his release.

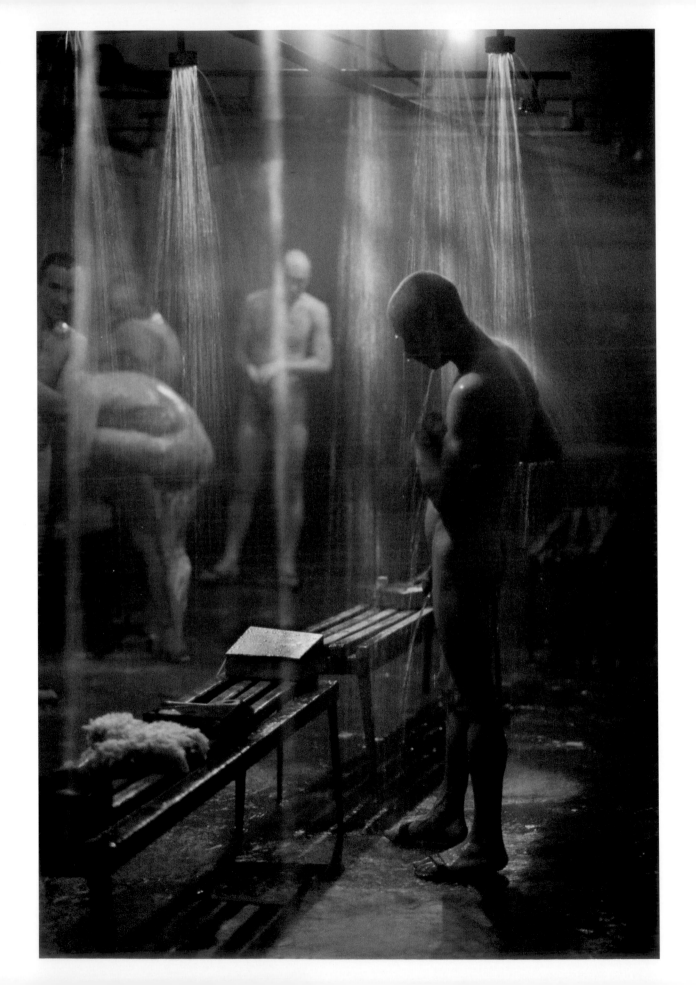

Prisoners are allowed a five-minute shower at the end of their shift in the prison's foundry.

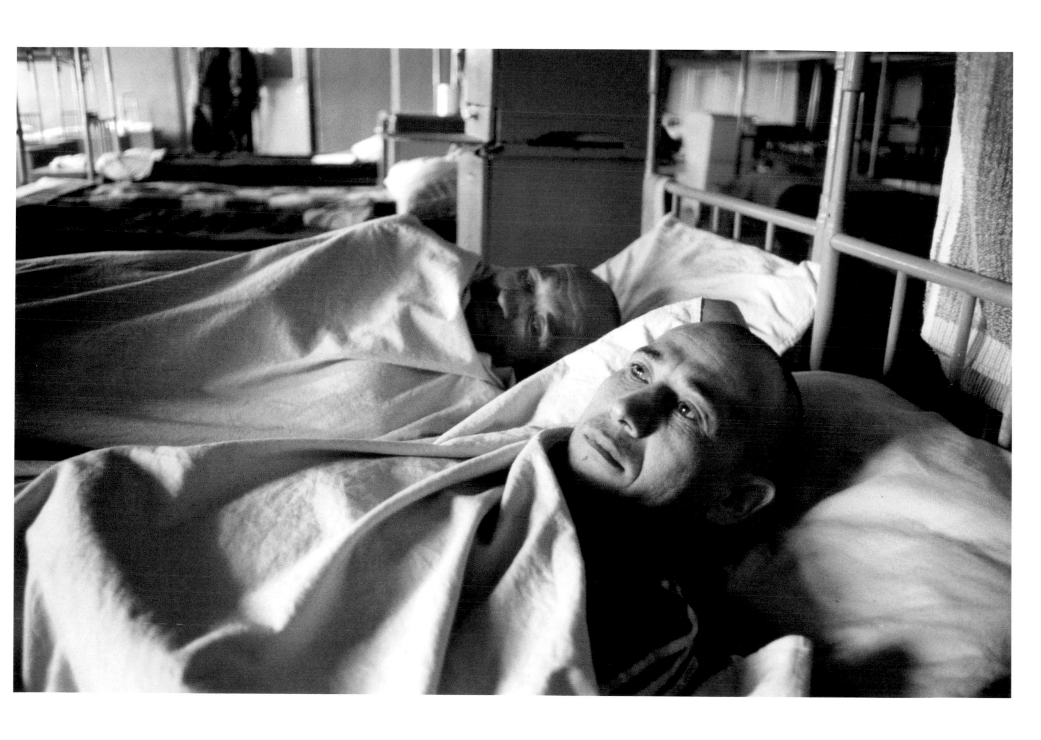

Prisoners sleep in barracks 60 men
to a unit.

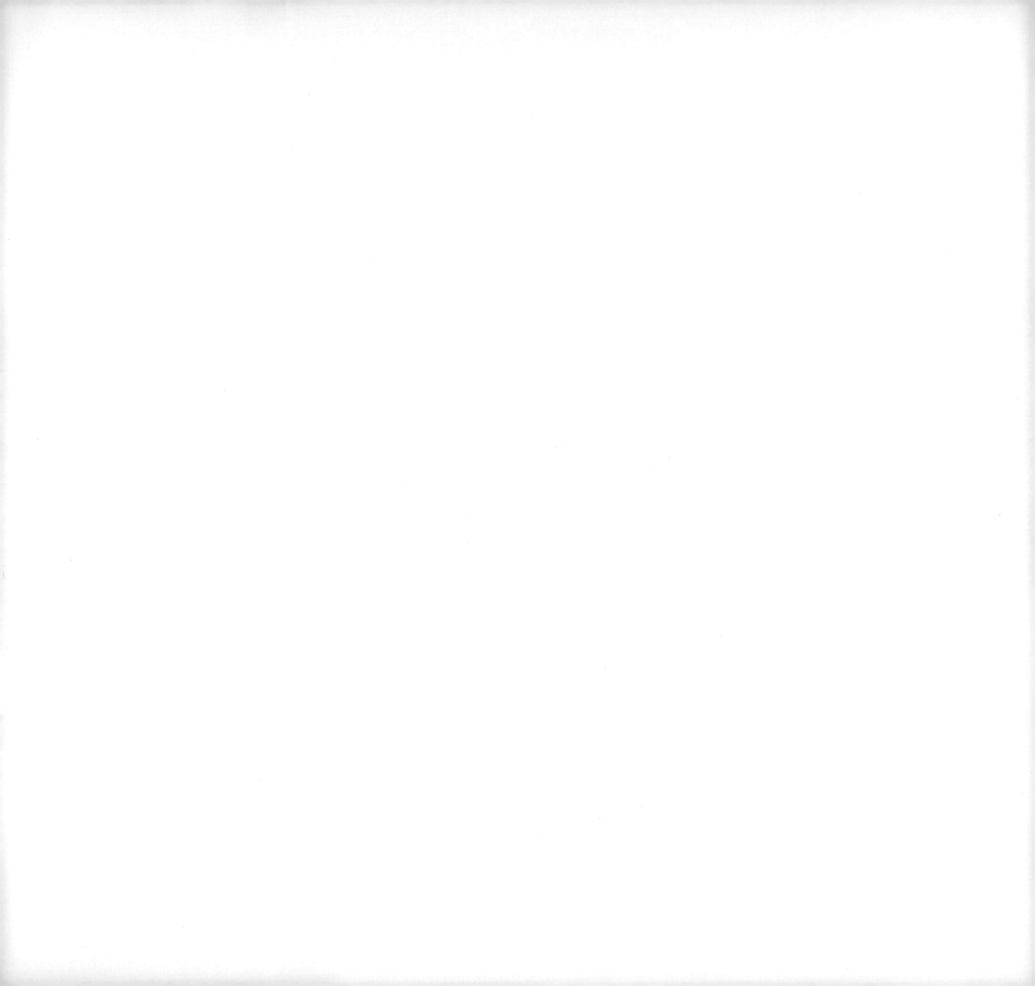

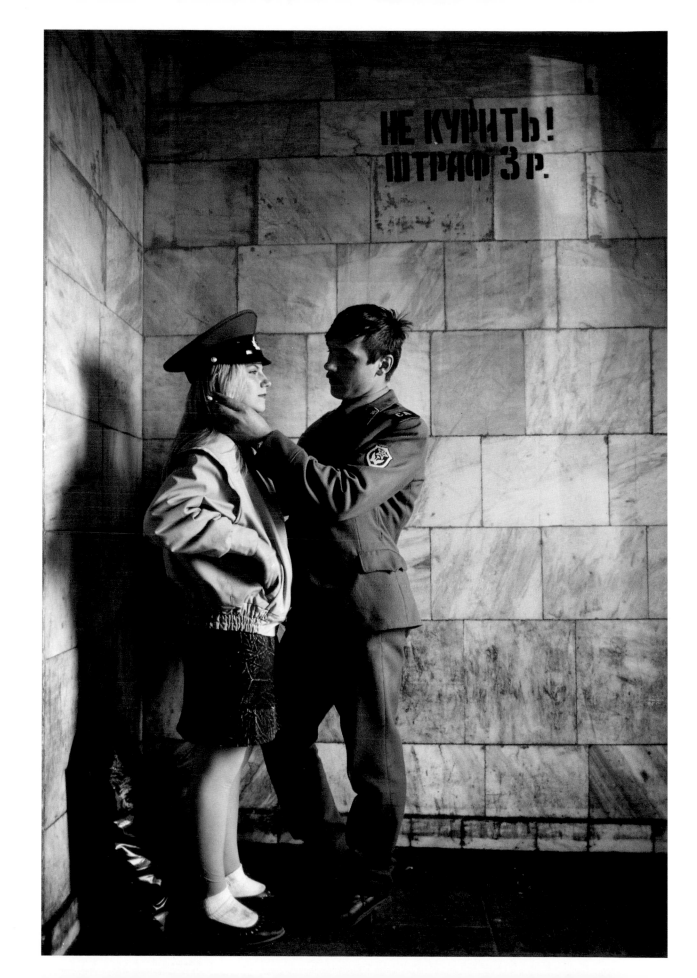

A military conscript says goodbye to his girlfriend at the Norilsk airport.

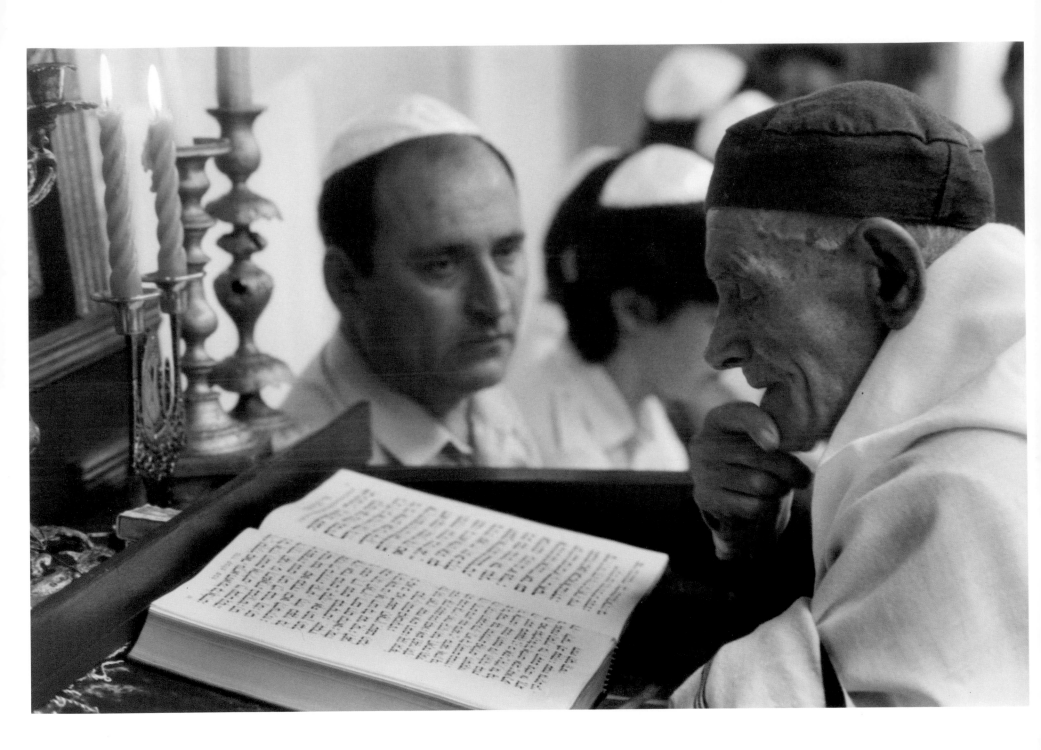

Birobidjan, Siberia
In the late 1920s and '30s, Jews from around the world migrated to Birobidjan, a Jewish Autonomous Region created by Stalin. Once they arrived, the Jews were not allowed to leave, and were prohibited from practicing Jewish traditions.

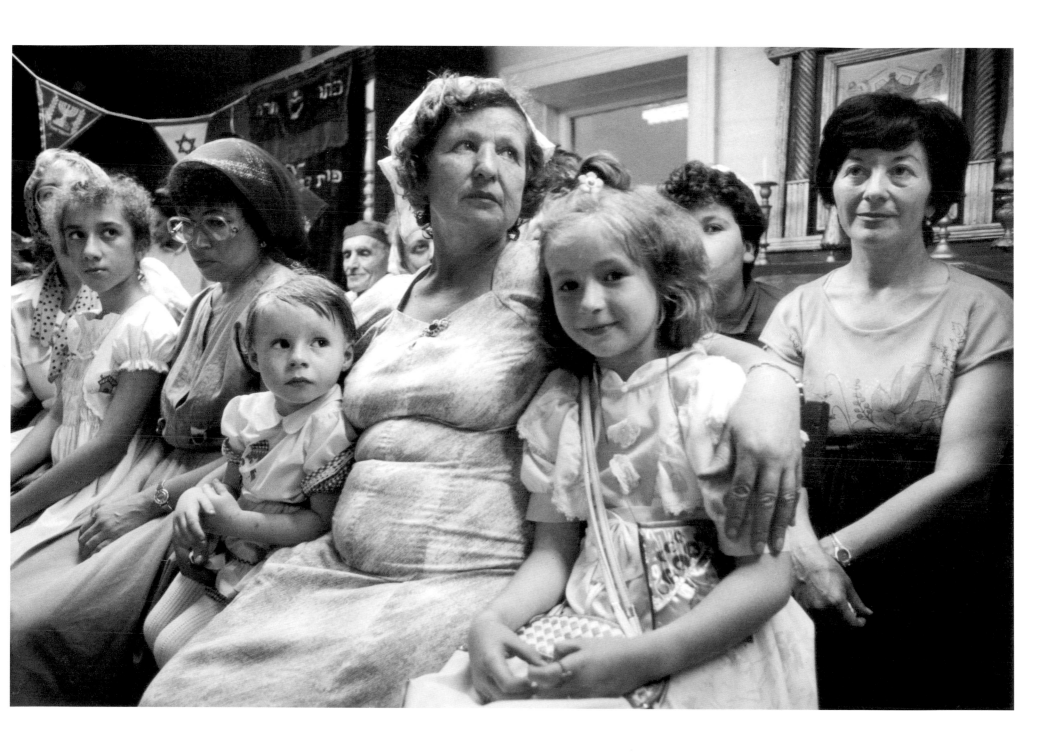

In the only surviving synagogue,
Jews in Birobidjan are taught about
Judaism by a group of young
Israelis.

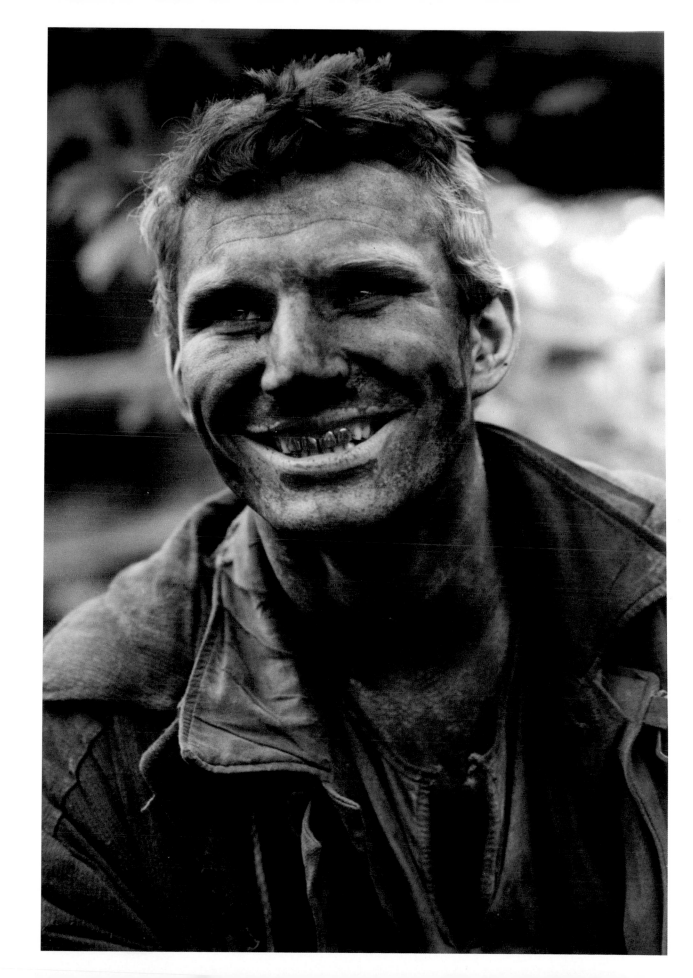

Miner Nikolai Rossoka earns almost
$60 per month, manually digging
coal in a space three feet square.

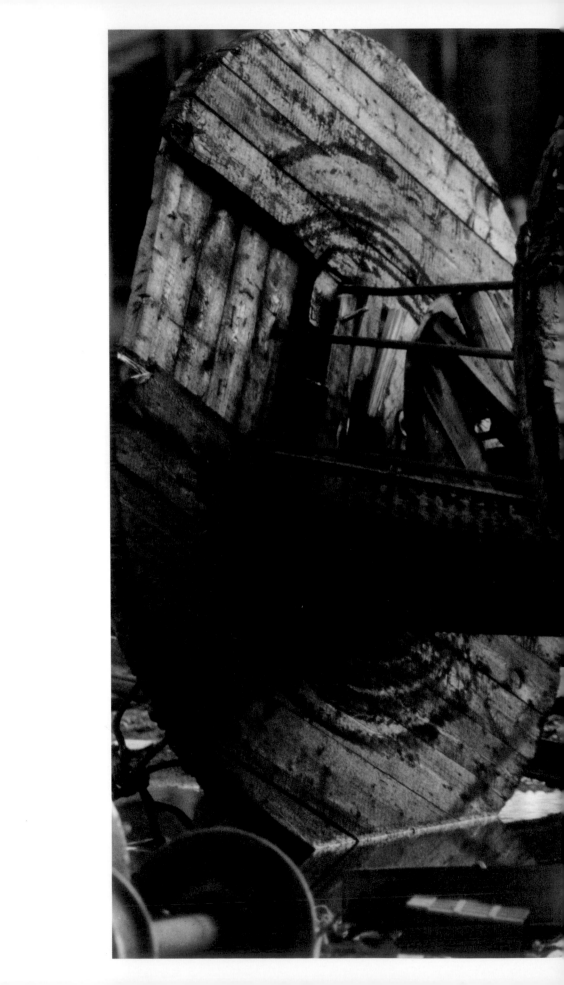

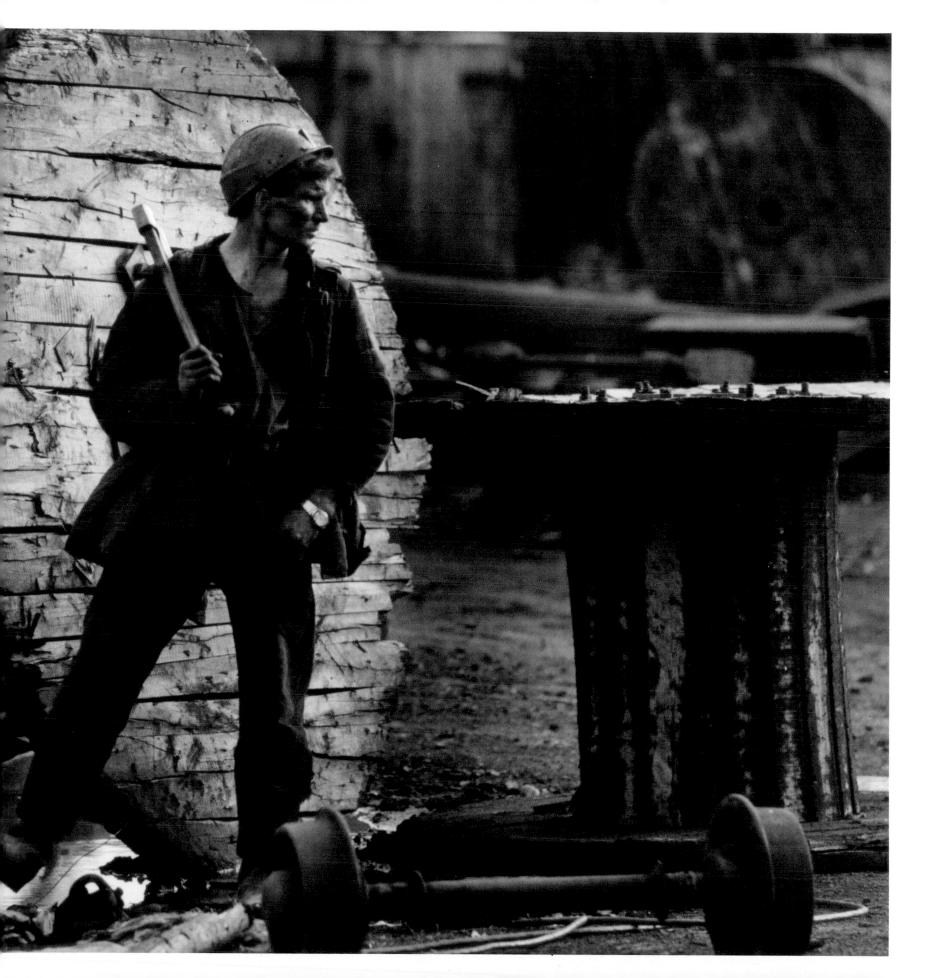

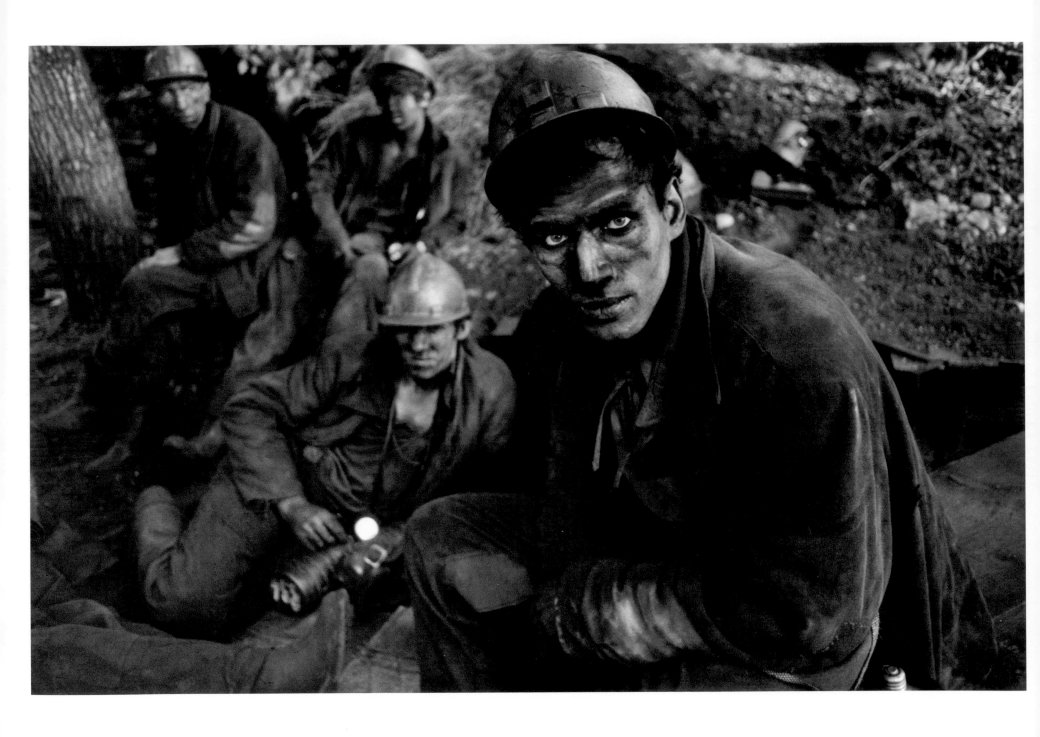

Miners who have finished their daily
quota wait out the rest of their
workday behind the mine's main
shaft.

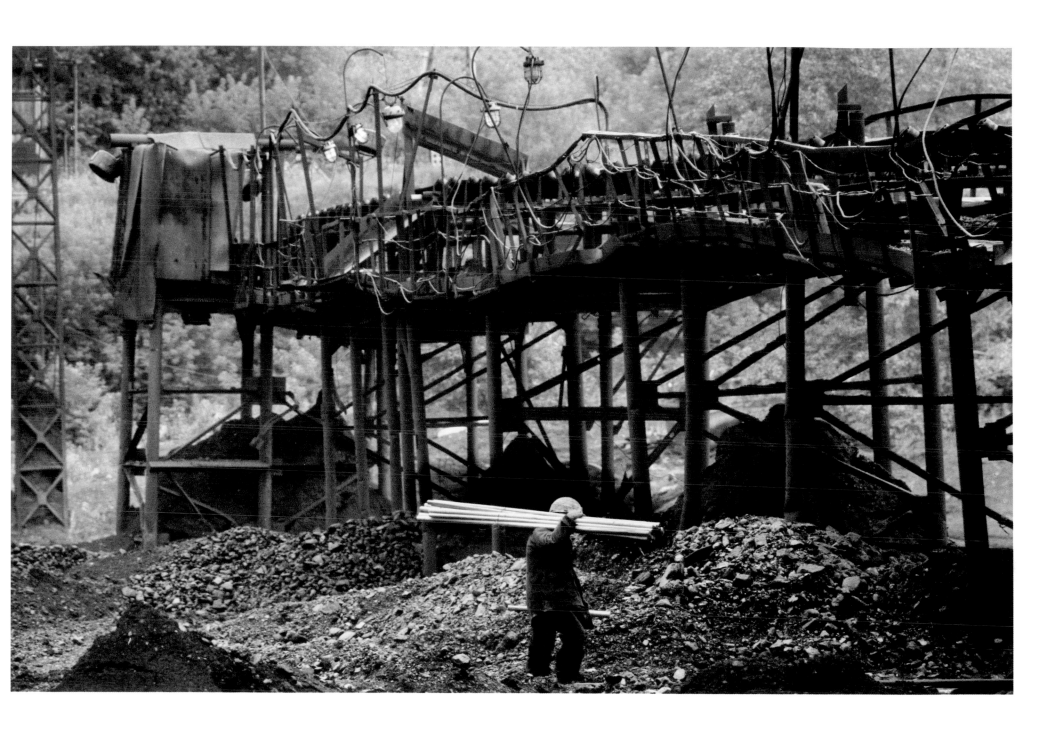

A miner carries supplies near a conveyor belt on the site of the Prokopyevsk Centralnaya mine, where two thousand miners excavate 900 thousand tons of coal every year.

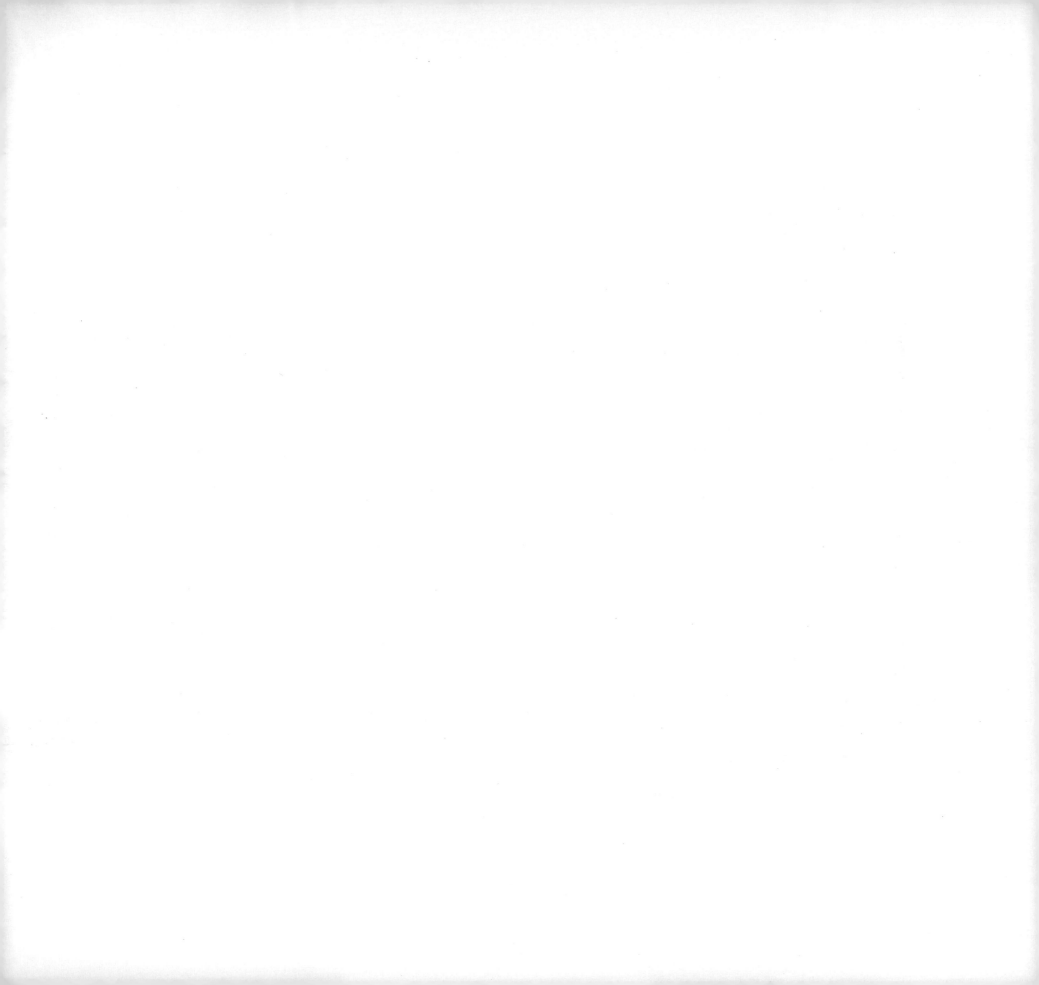

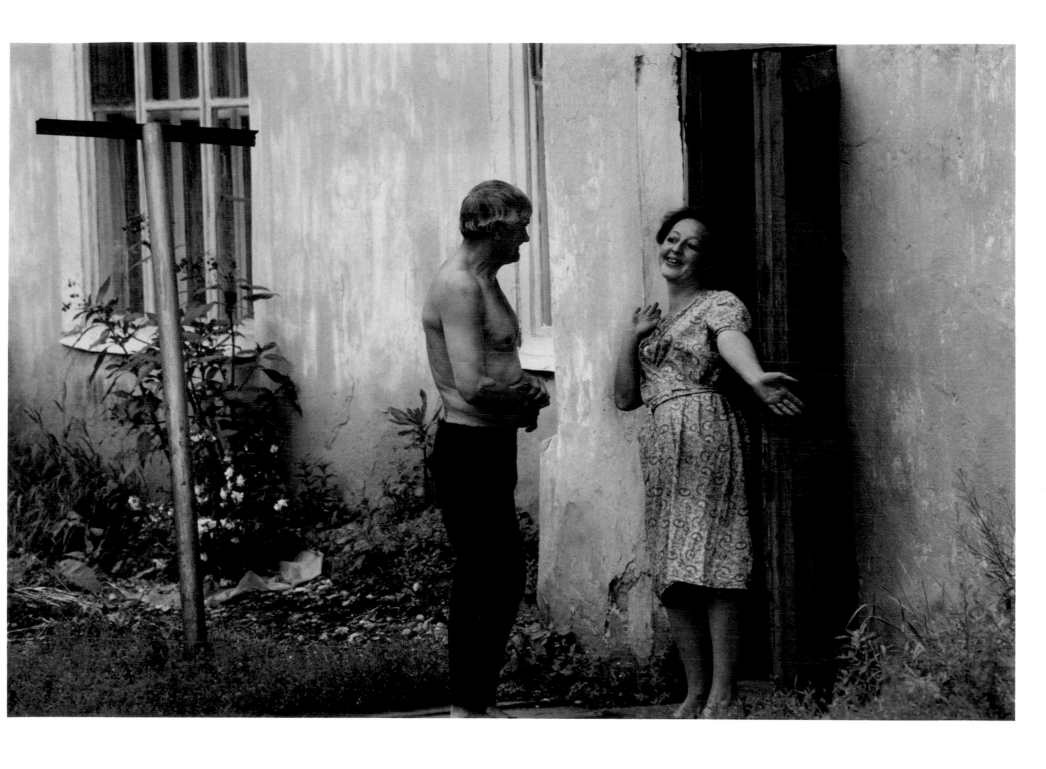

A coal miner in Prokopyevsk visits
a woman friend after his shift
underground.

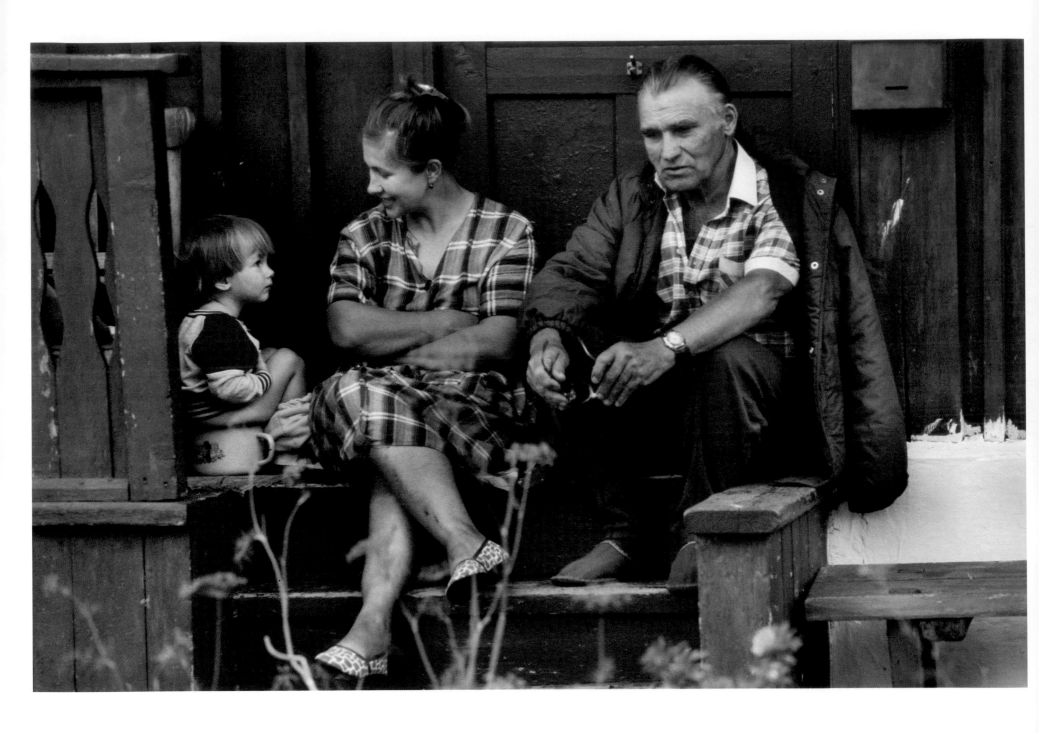

Retired coal miner Feodor Frolikov
sits on his porch with his daughter
and grandson.

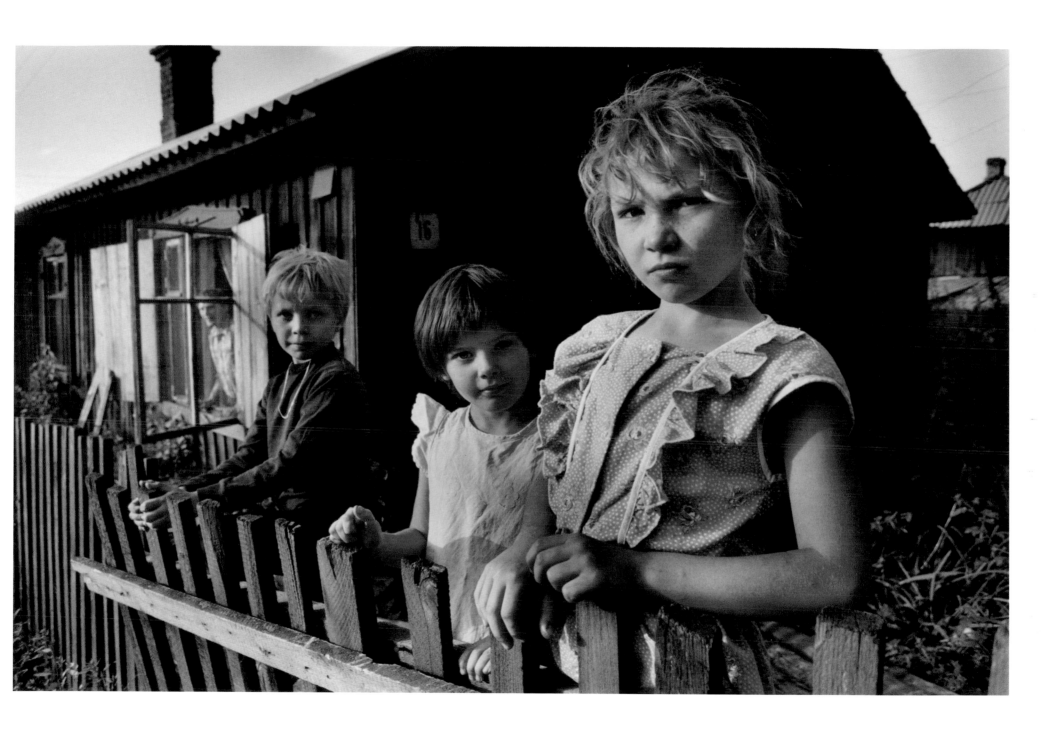

The children of Prokopyevsk coal miners wait outside their home.

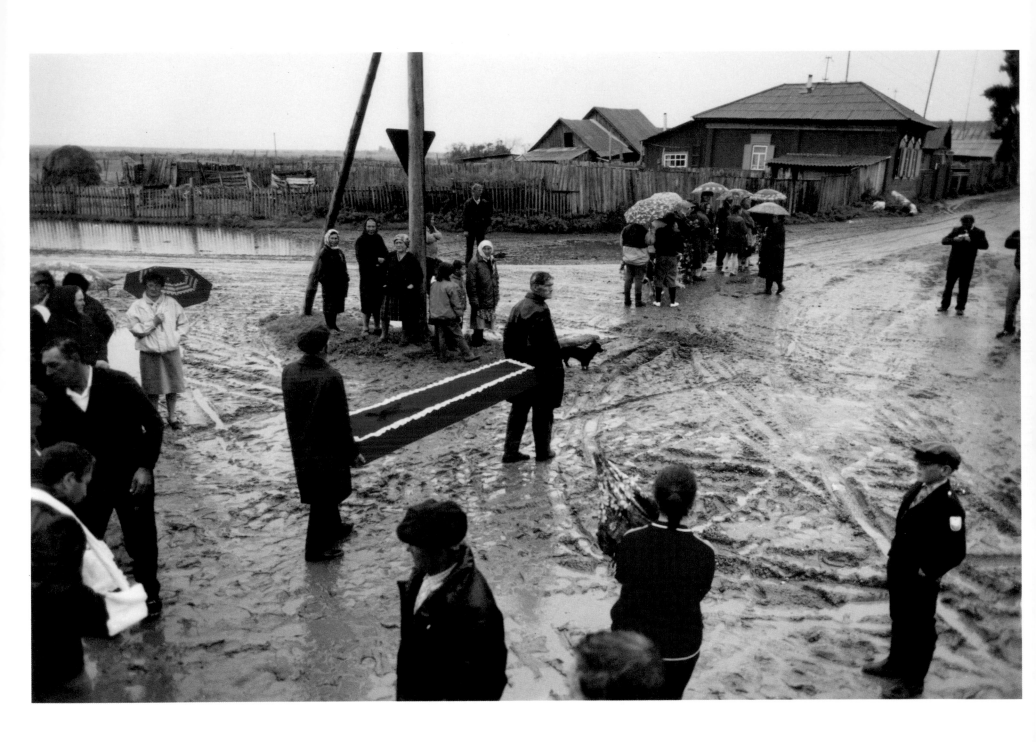

Lake Baikal, Siberia
In the fishing village of Kolesovo, the family of Leonid Vlasov mourn his death from a heart attack, and lead his funeral procession through the village.

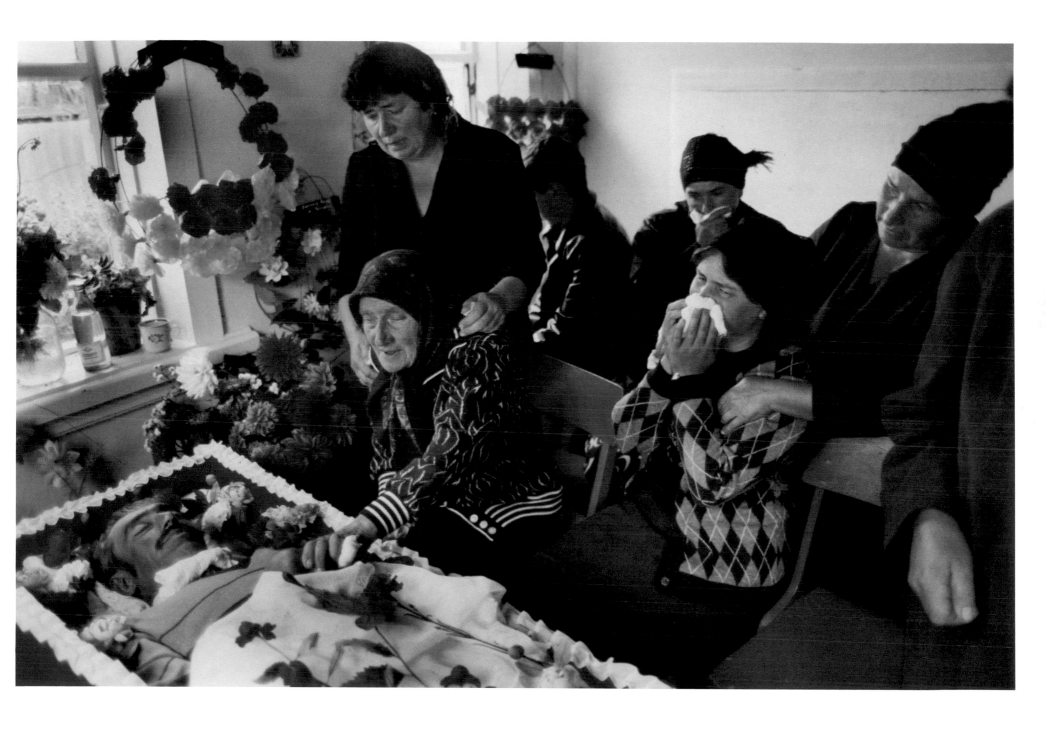

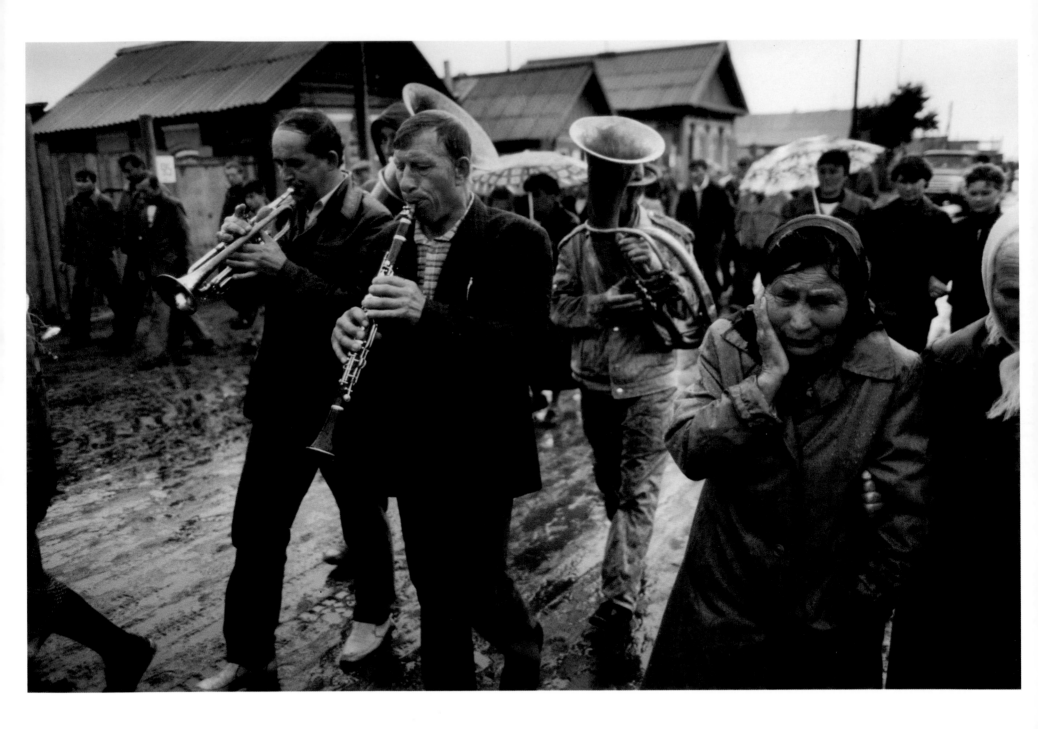

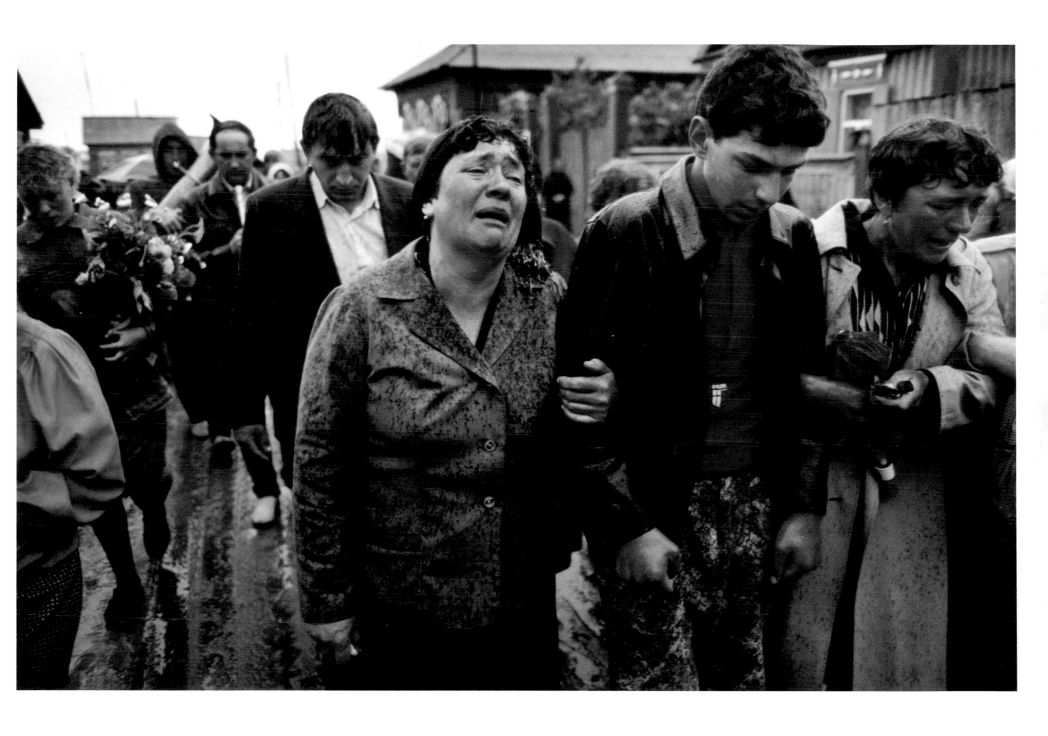

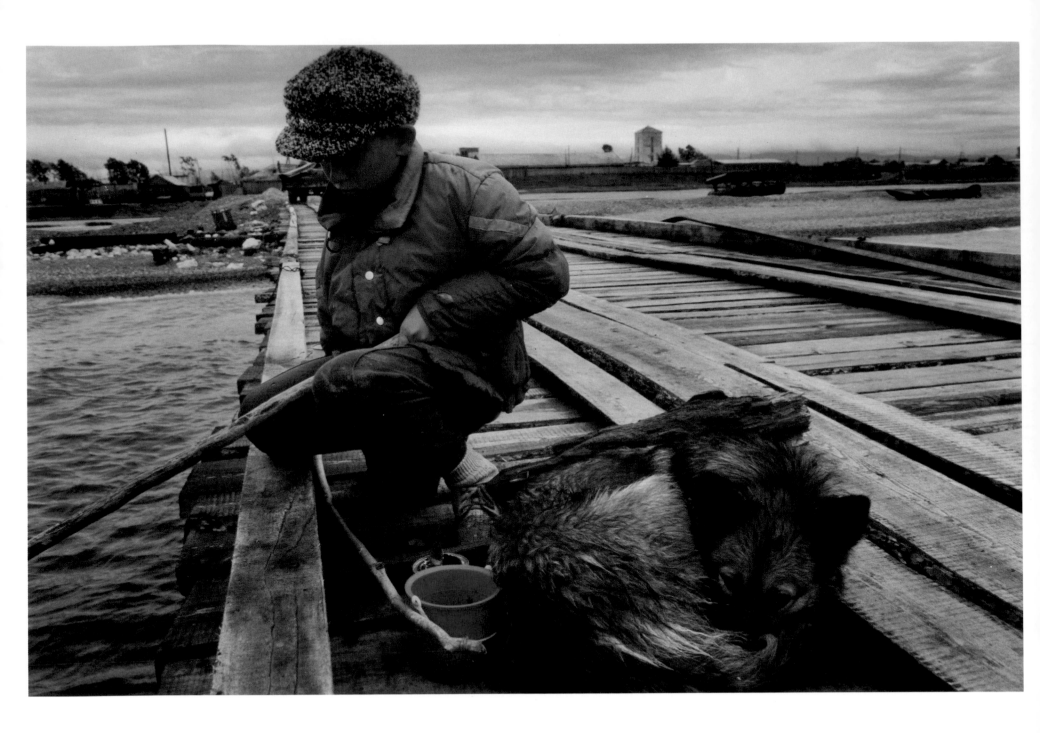

Dimitri Pivovar fishes for perch in Lake Baikal, the world's largest freshwater lake. The lake's ecosystem is in serious danger from industrial waste. As a result of the pollution, the fish processing plant, which until recently was the principal employer in the area, now has to import fish from the Baltic and Caspian Seas.

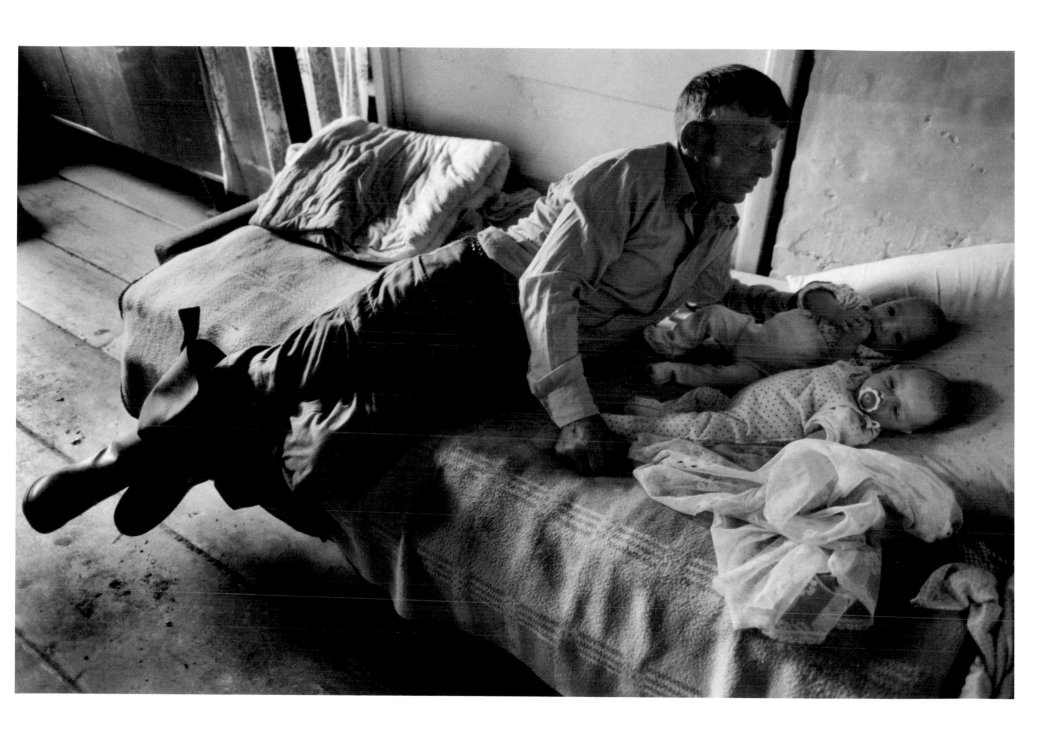

Fisherman Mikhail Khlystov, who
has 11 children, plays with his
recently born twin sons.

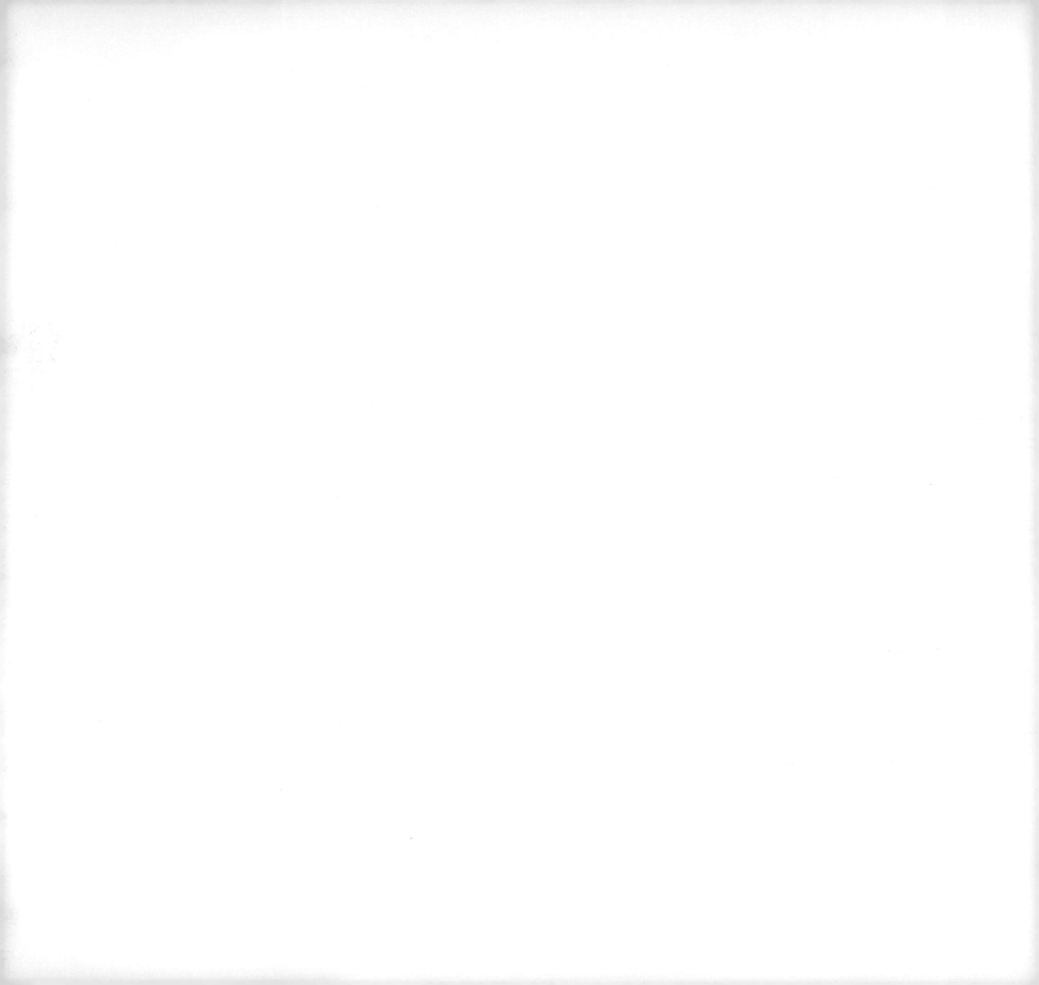

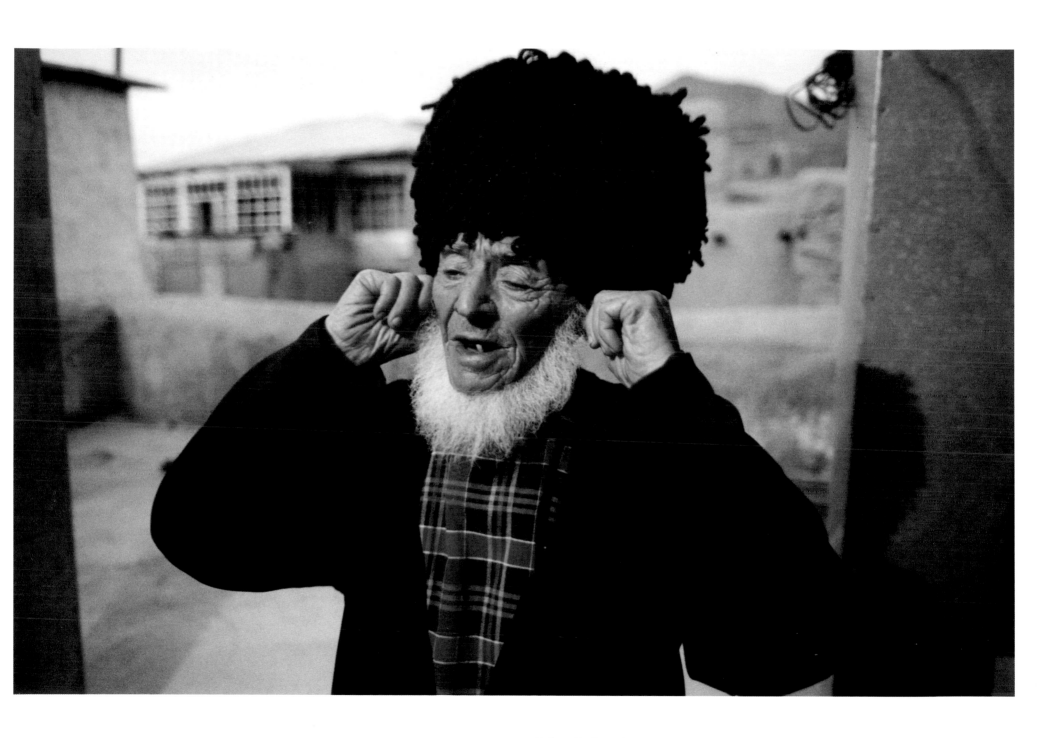

Nohur, Turkmenia
In the mountains on the border between Turkmenia and Iran, Turkmenian Moslems have retained their ethnic traditions through the centuries. Nouri Nourzallev, assistant to the imam, calls the village to prayer at the village mosque.

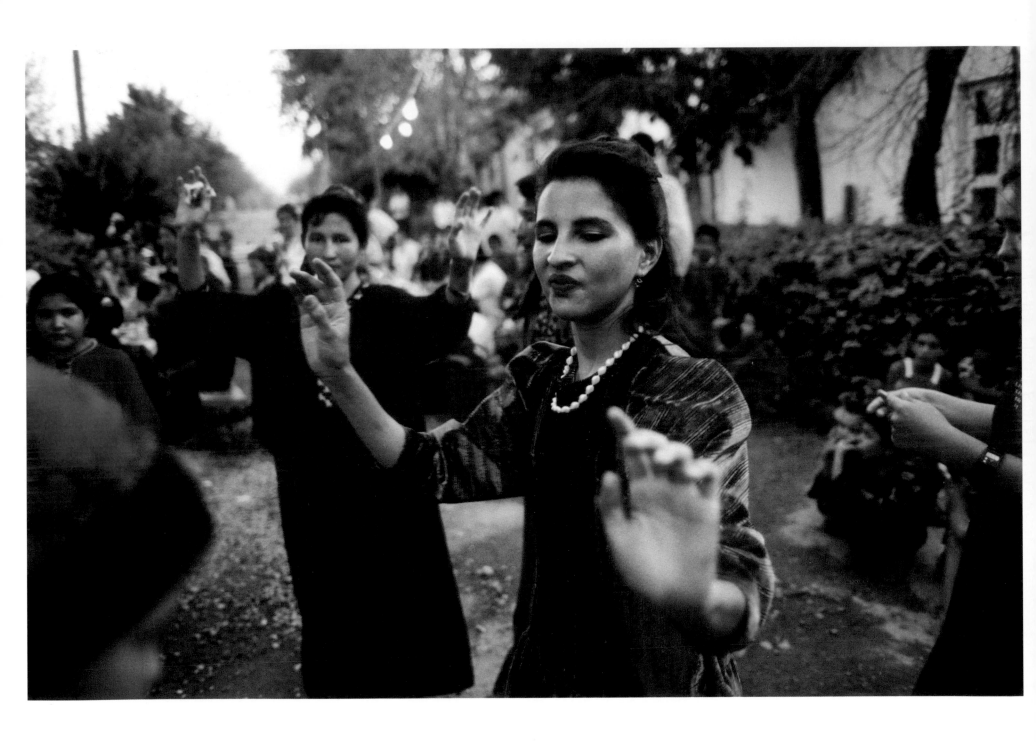

Islamic women dance a traditional
Turkmenian dance at a wedding.

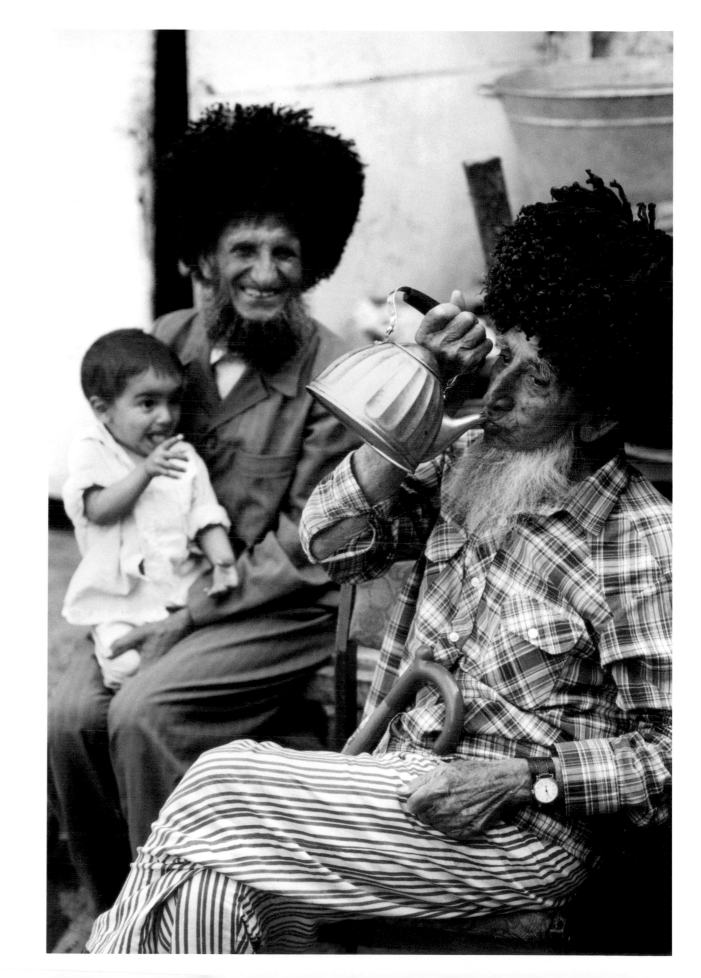

Wearing traditional wool hats,
Turkmenians share an afternoon
sip of tea.

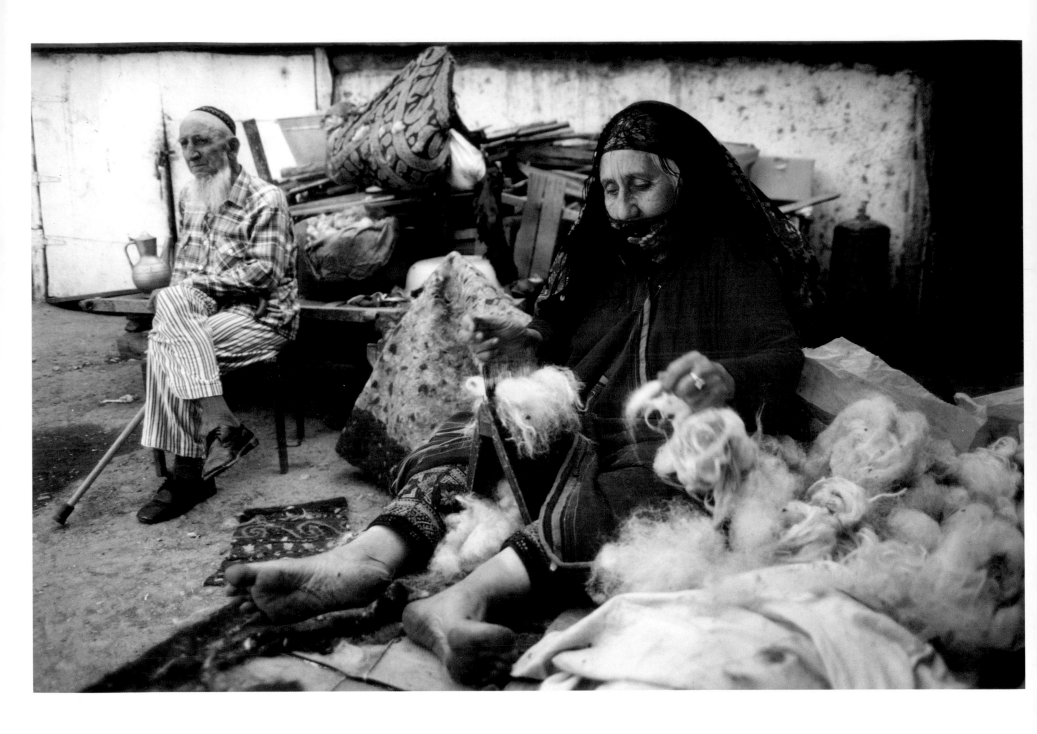

Ashgui Husseinawa works on a
Turkmenian rug. Weaving is a
centuries-old tradition in this
mountain region.

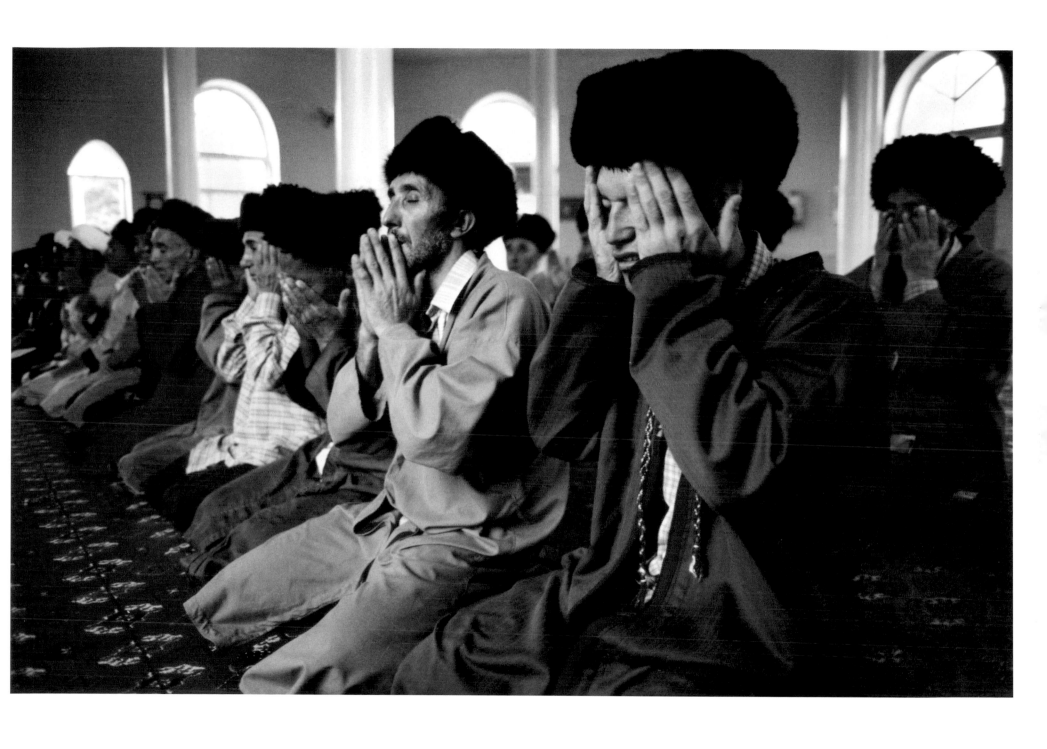

Sunni Moslems answer the call to
prayer in the village mosque.

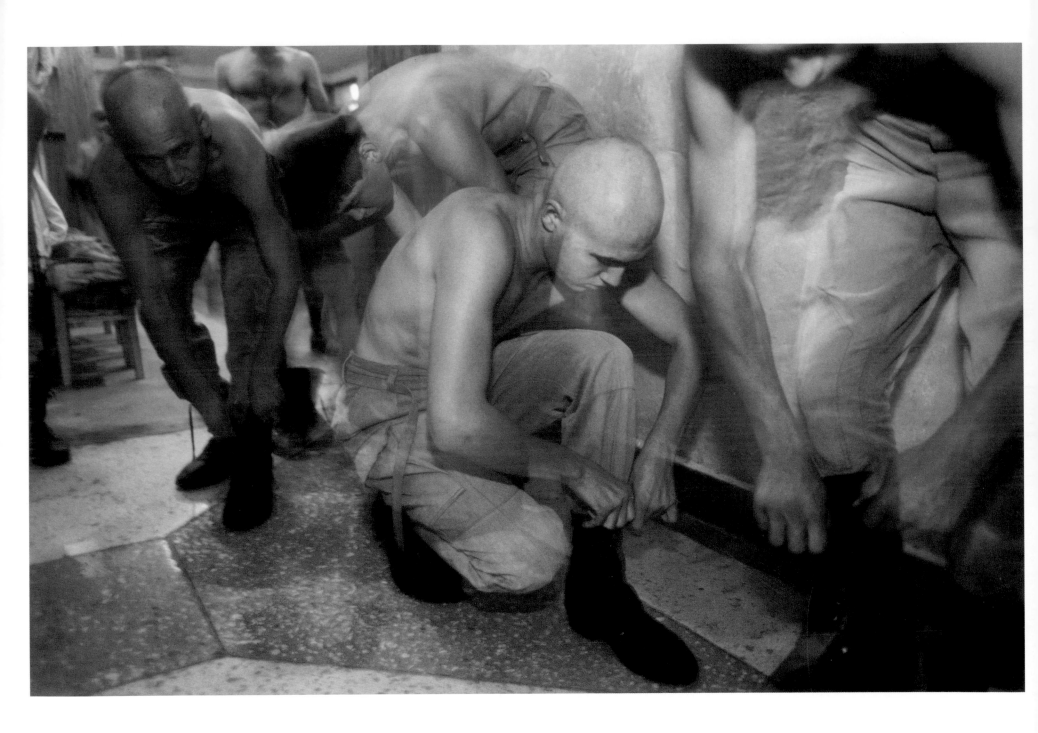

Ashkhabad, Turkmenia
In Ashkhabad, at a military training camp, Soviet Red Army conscripts rise at 6:00 A.M. to begin their physical exercise.

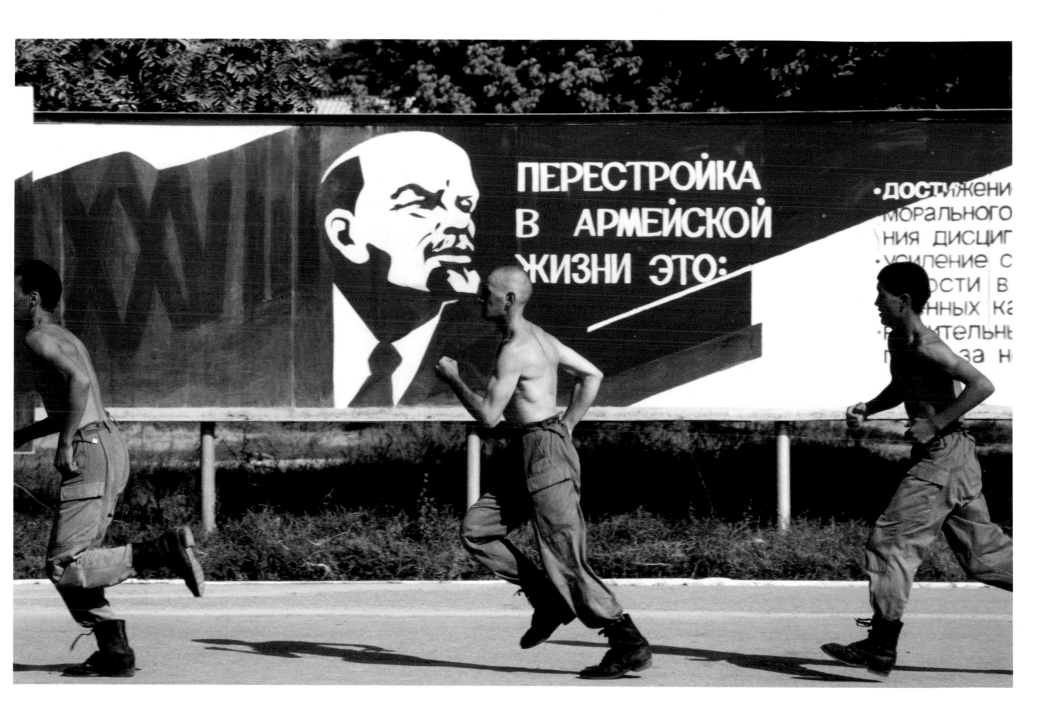

Coup D'Etat, Moscow

On Tuesday, August 20, the day after a coup d'état was announced, and Soviet President Mikhail Gorbachev was removed from power and held with his family at their dacha on the Crimean Sea, Soviet soldiers and tanks barricaded the streets and surrounded Red Square and the Kremlin.

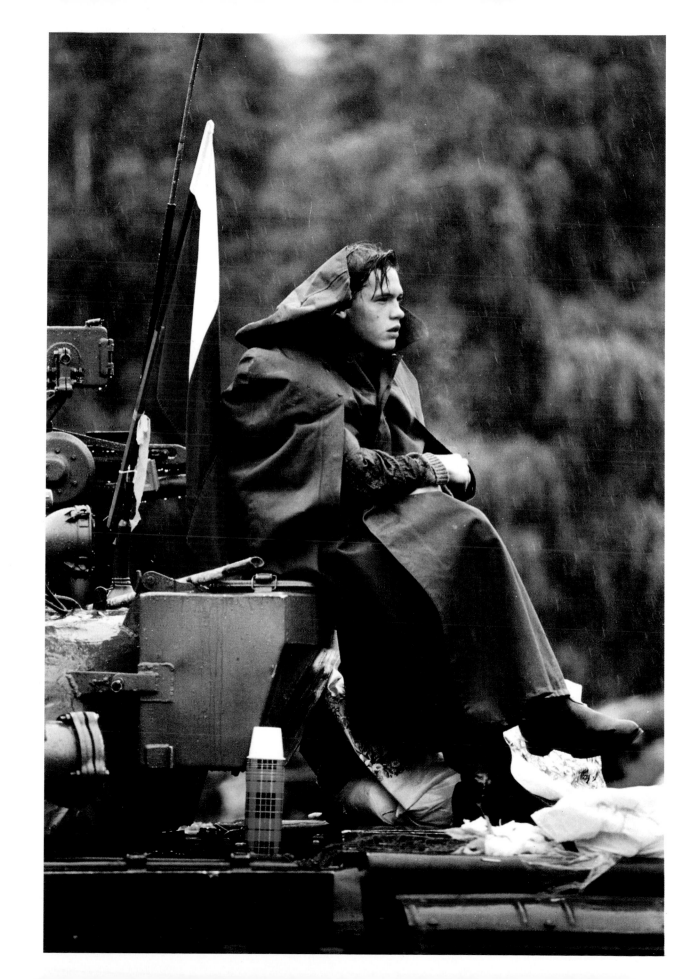

A young Soviet soldier, who had been sent to occupy Moscow, and who has defected to defend Boris Yeltsin and the Russian Federation Building, sits atop a tank.

After the attempted coup had failed, Soviet soldiers and their tanks, who defected to protect President Boris Yeltsin and the Russian Federation Building, were cheered as heroes by civilians as they left the city to rejoin their army units. Had the coup d'état succeeded, these soldiers would have faced possible execution for their defection.

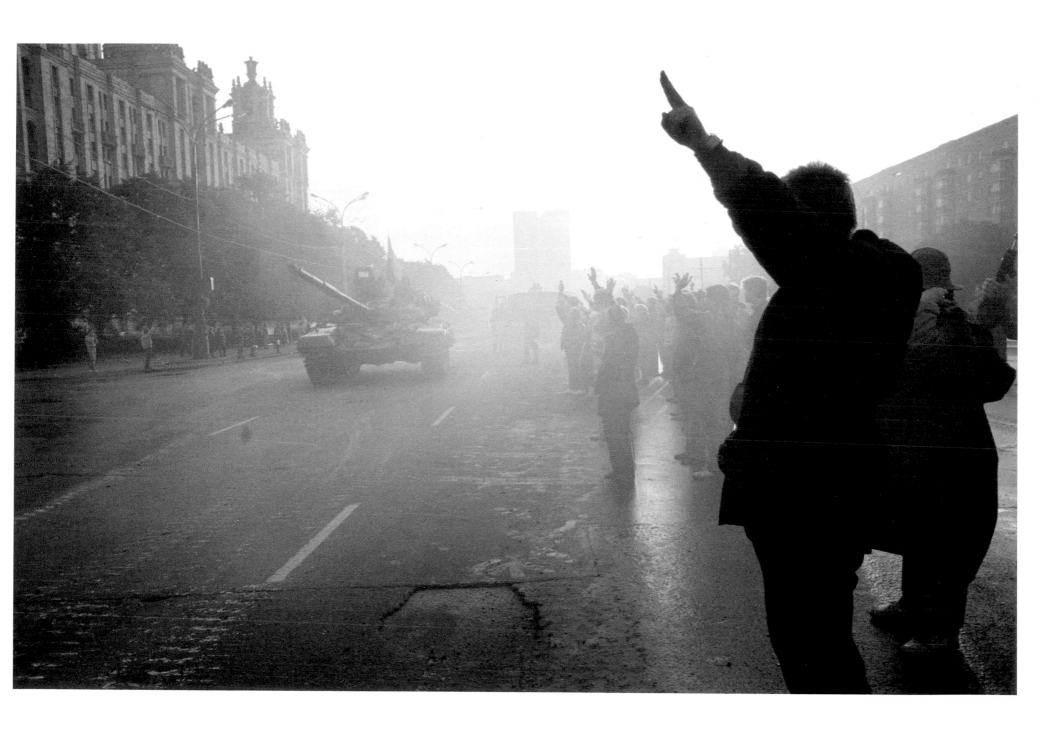

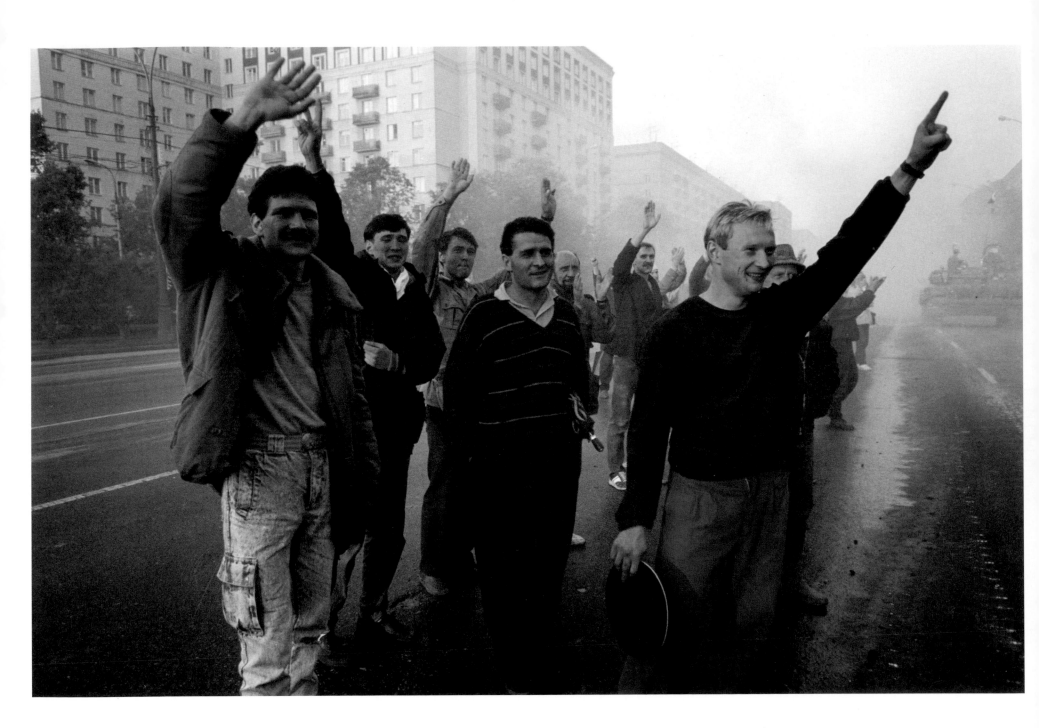

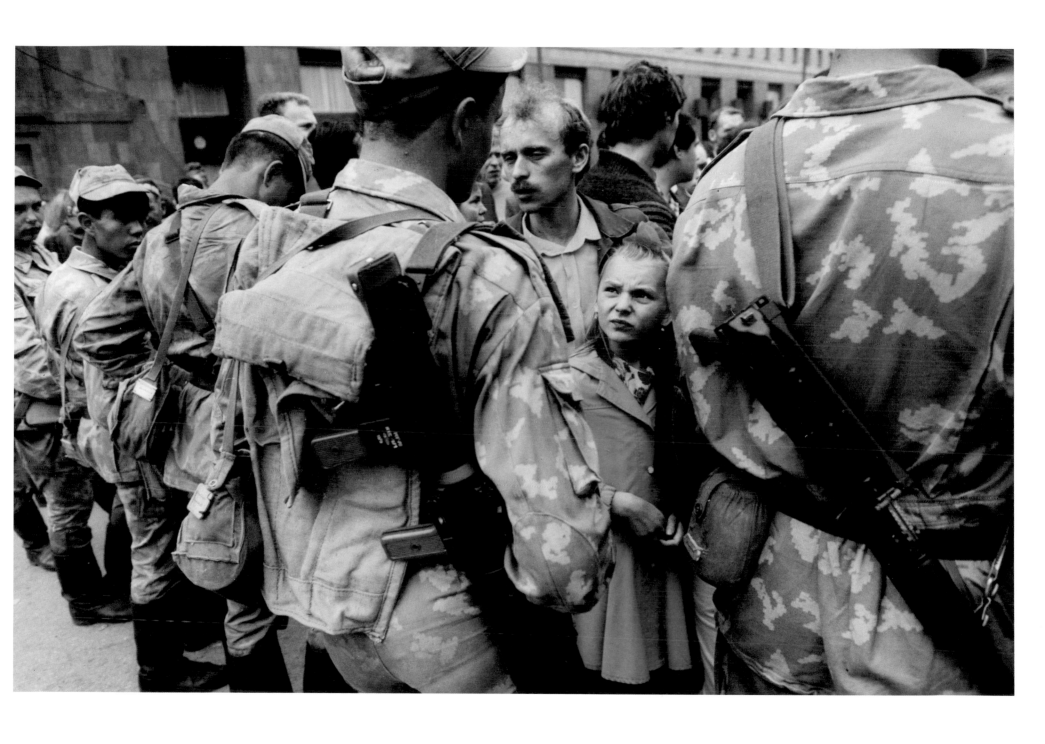

As Soviet troops barricaded Red Square and the streets of Moscow, citizens came out to witness this epic event. A young girl stares at a soldier.

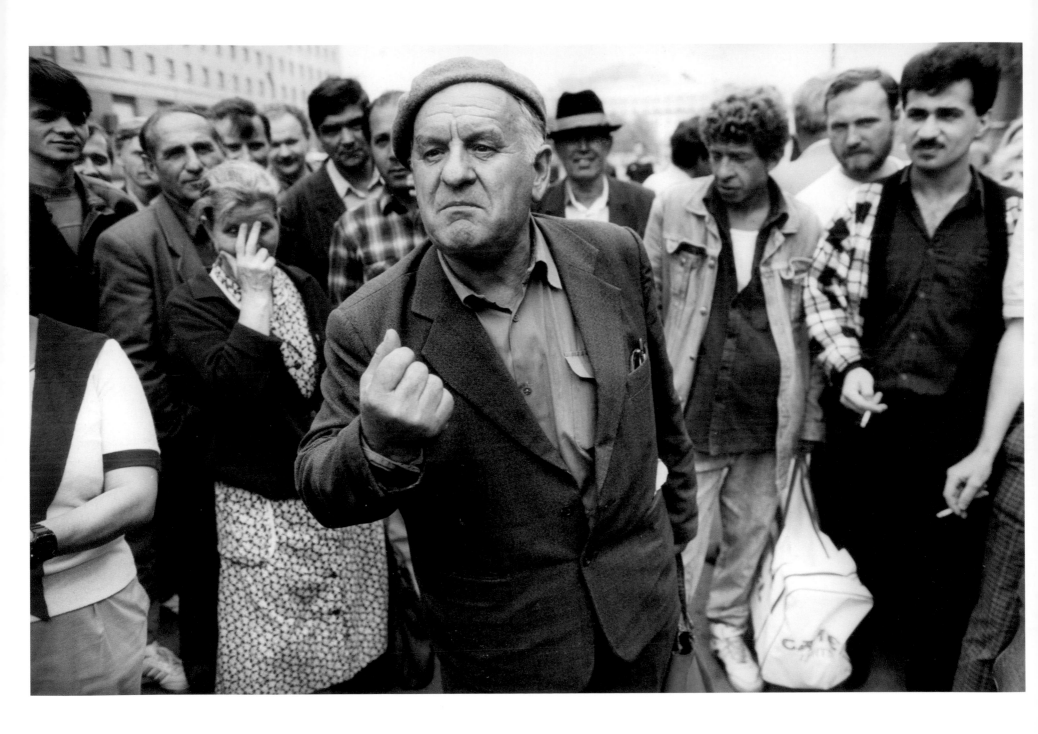

Soviet citizens gather in the streets,
where they publicly debate the coup.

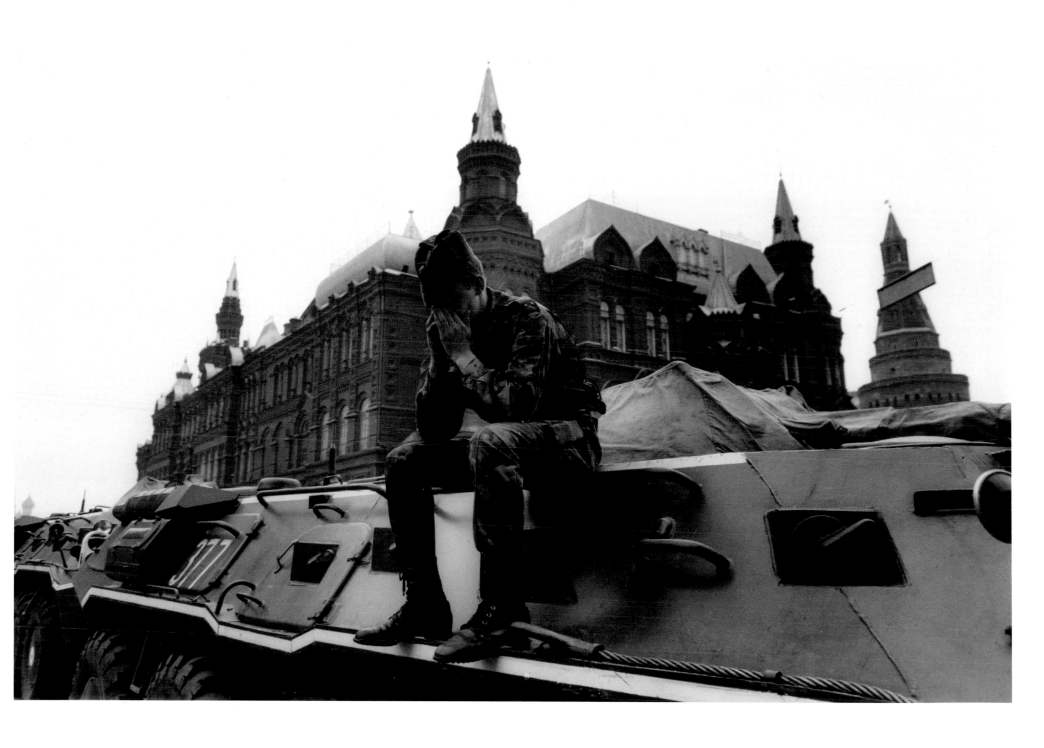

A soldier, atop a tank barricading
Red Square, buries his head in his
hands.

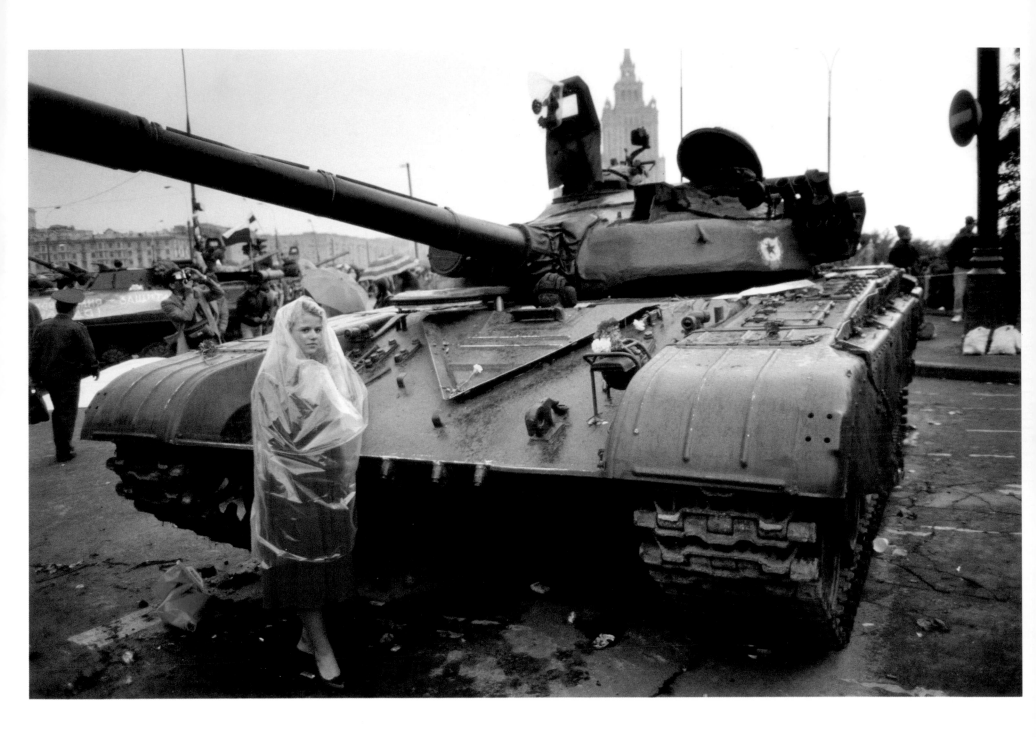

A young woman who had come to
the Russian White House to help
barricade it against possible attack,
stands in the afternoon rain.

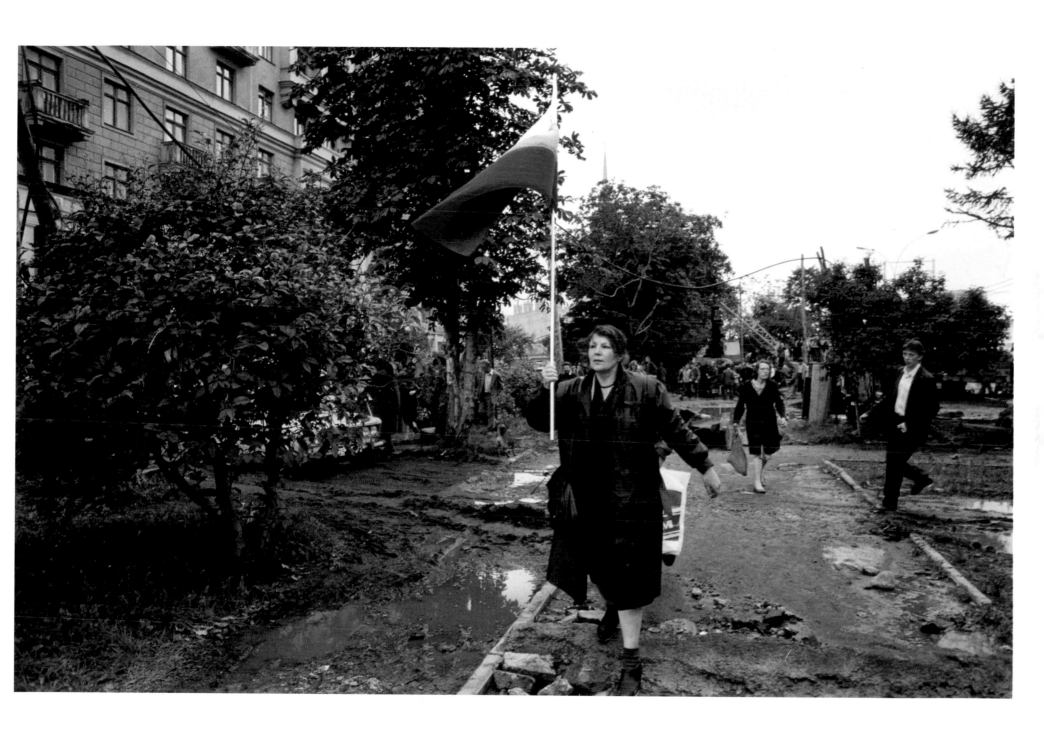

A woman holds the Russian
Republic flag across the street from
the Russian White House, as the
coup d'état fell apart.

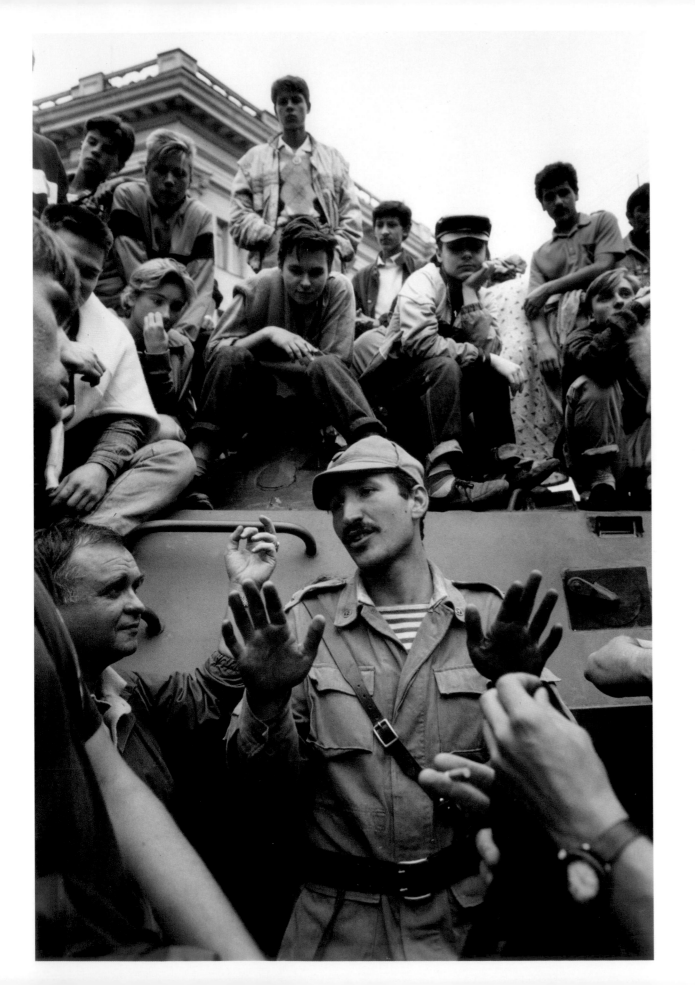

Surrounded by angry civilians, a Soviet soldier assures the crowd that he would not raise his weapon, even if he were ordered to do so.

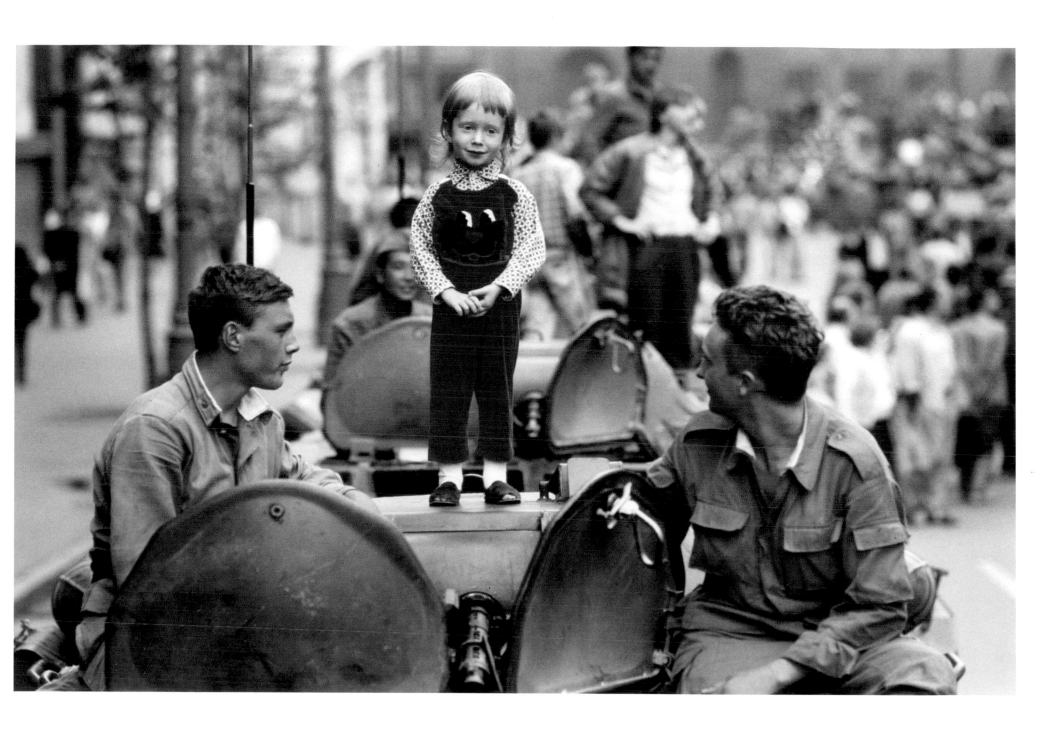

In a gentle moment that defied the gravity of the coup d'état, a young girl climbed atop a tank occupying Moscow.

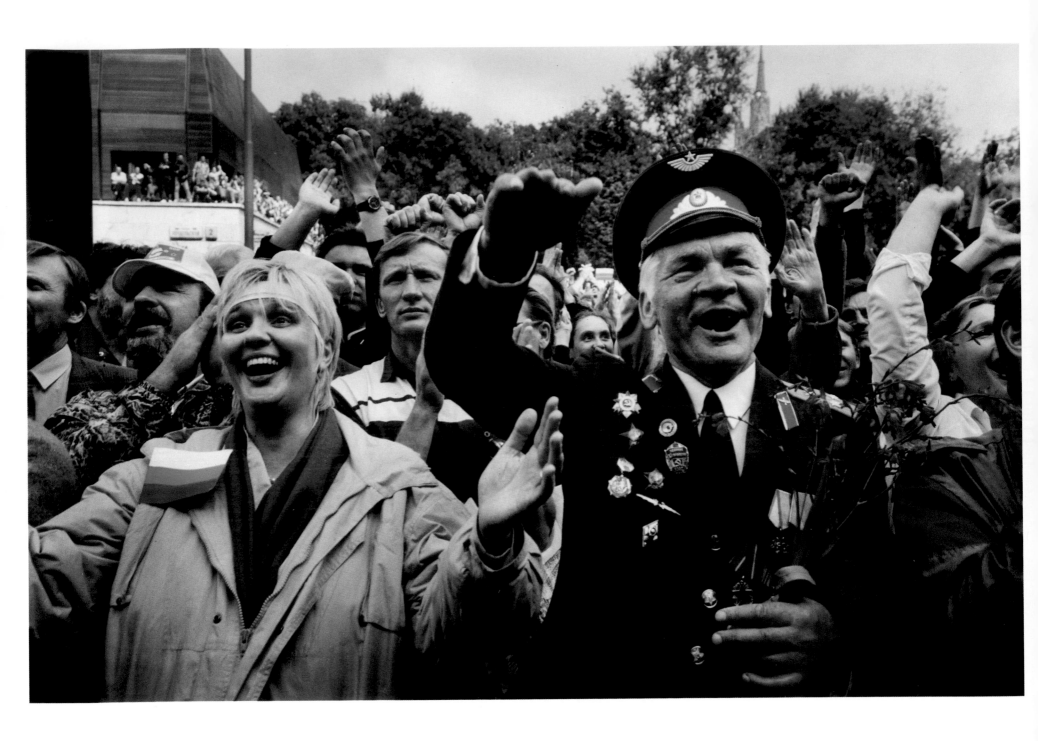

Tens of thousands of cheering ,
Russians embraced Yeltsin for his
courage and leadership in putting
down the coup.

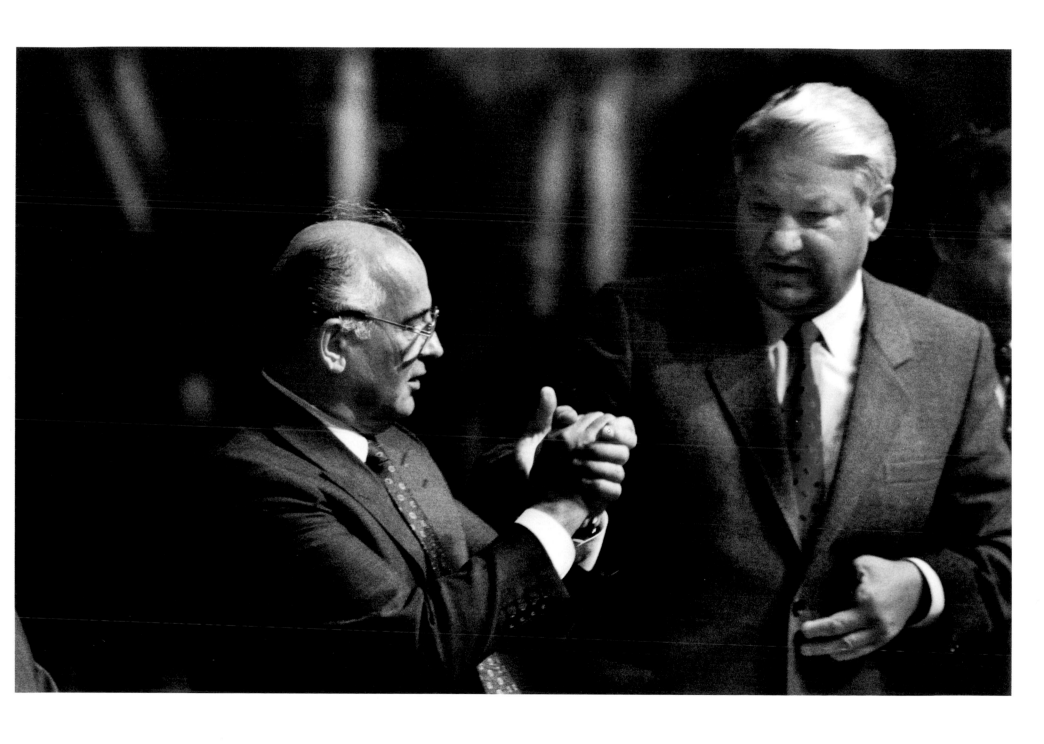

Soviet President Mikhail Gorbachev came to the Russian Federation Building, where he acknowledged and thanked Russian President Boris Yeltsin for his role in putting down the coup.

Citizens outside the Russian White House cheered the failed coup d'état. The next day, Soviet President Mikhail Gorbachev and Russian President Boris Yeltsin led the country in a state funeral for three young Soviets killed during the night on August 21. A state funeral is the highest honor in the Soviet Union.

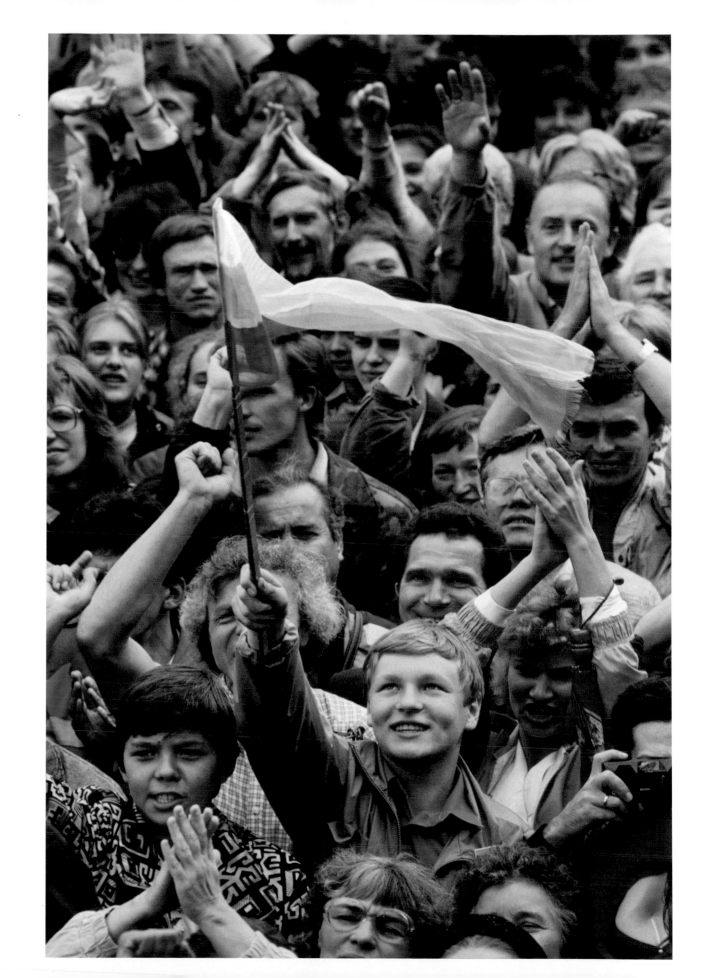

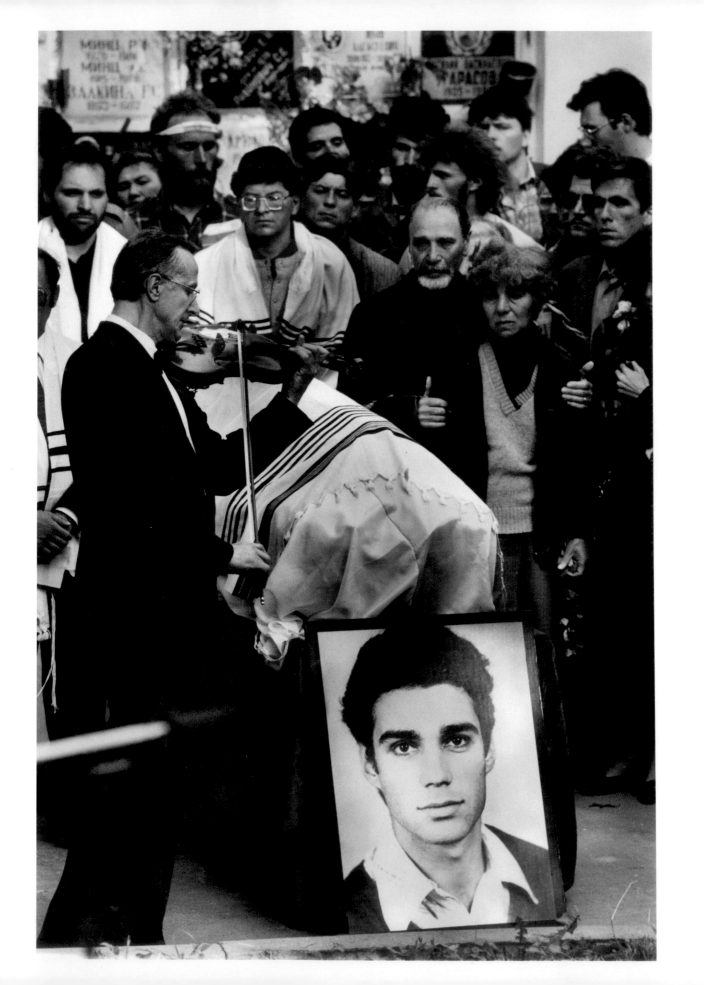

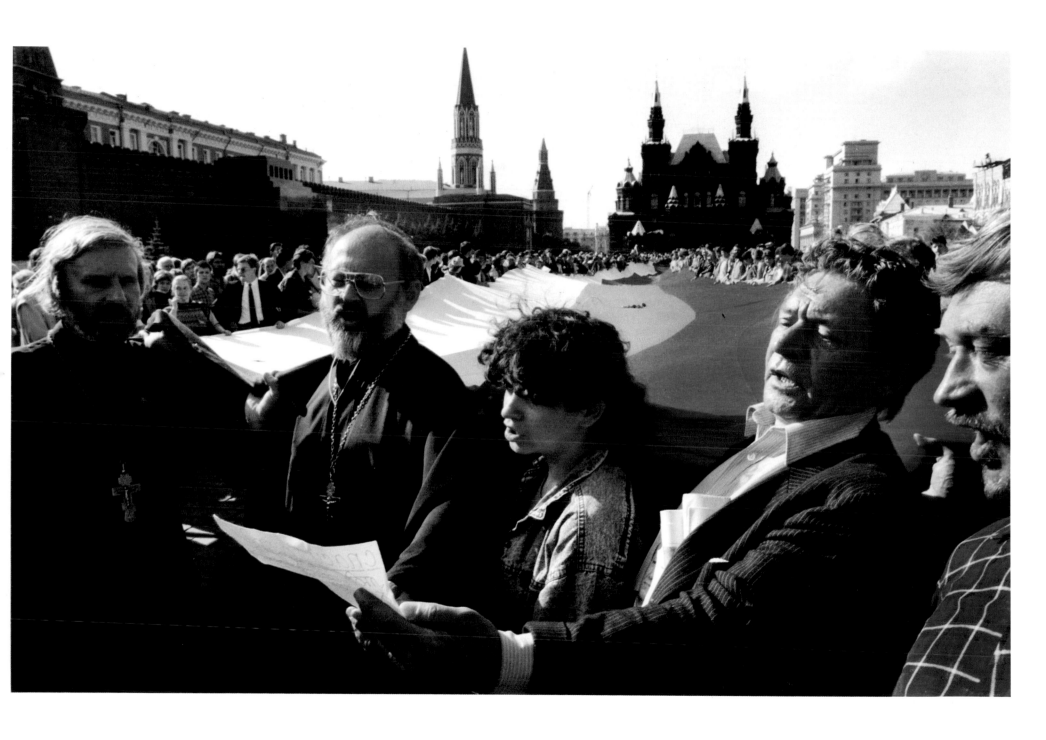

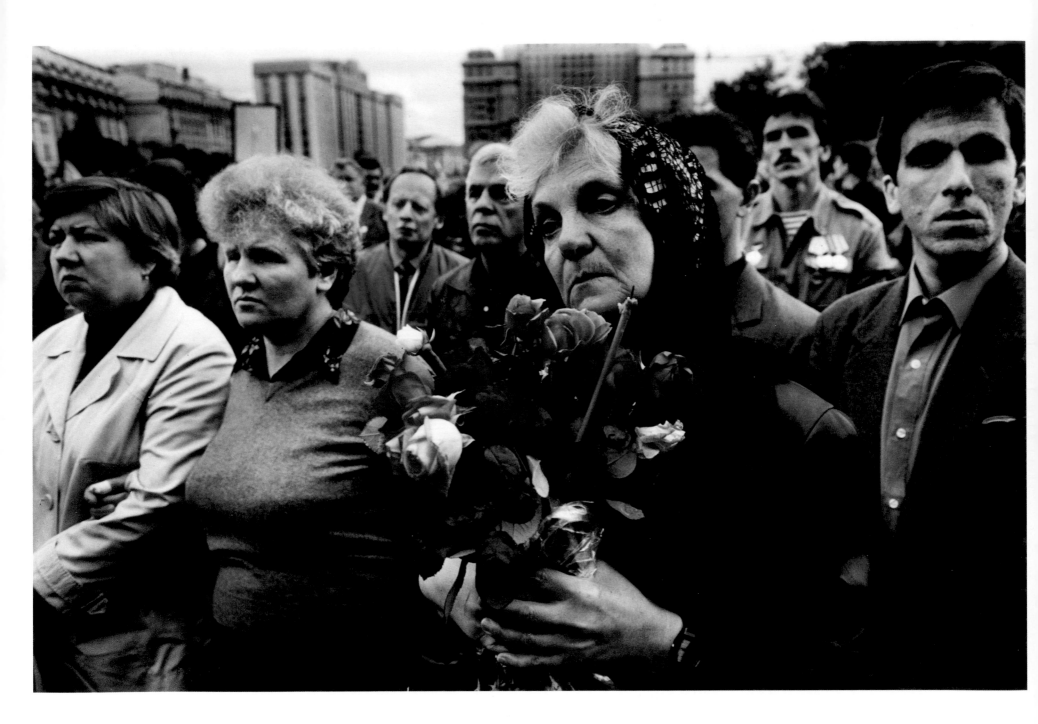

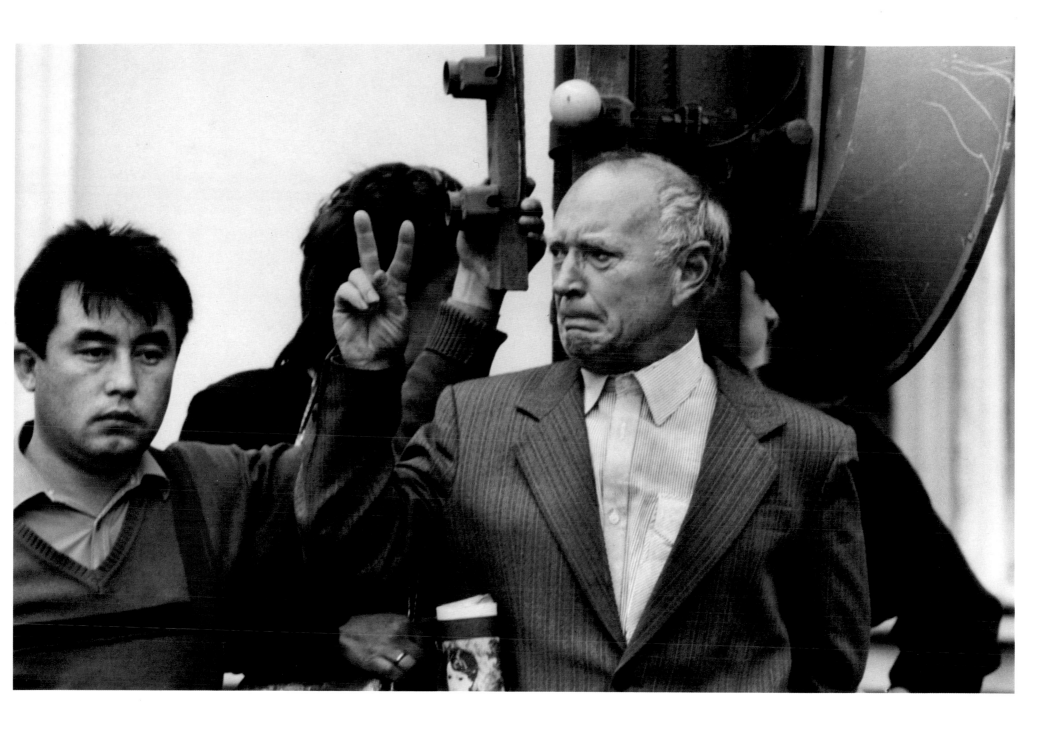

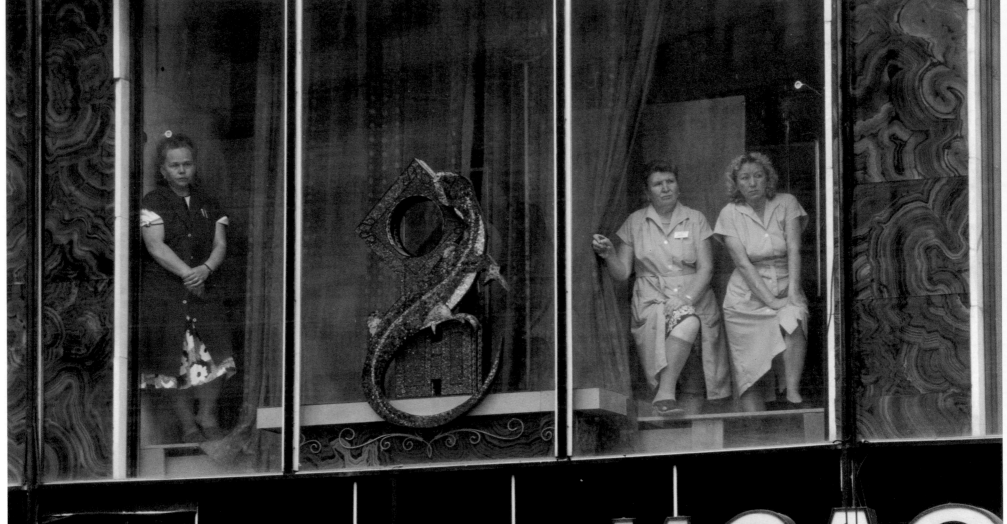

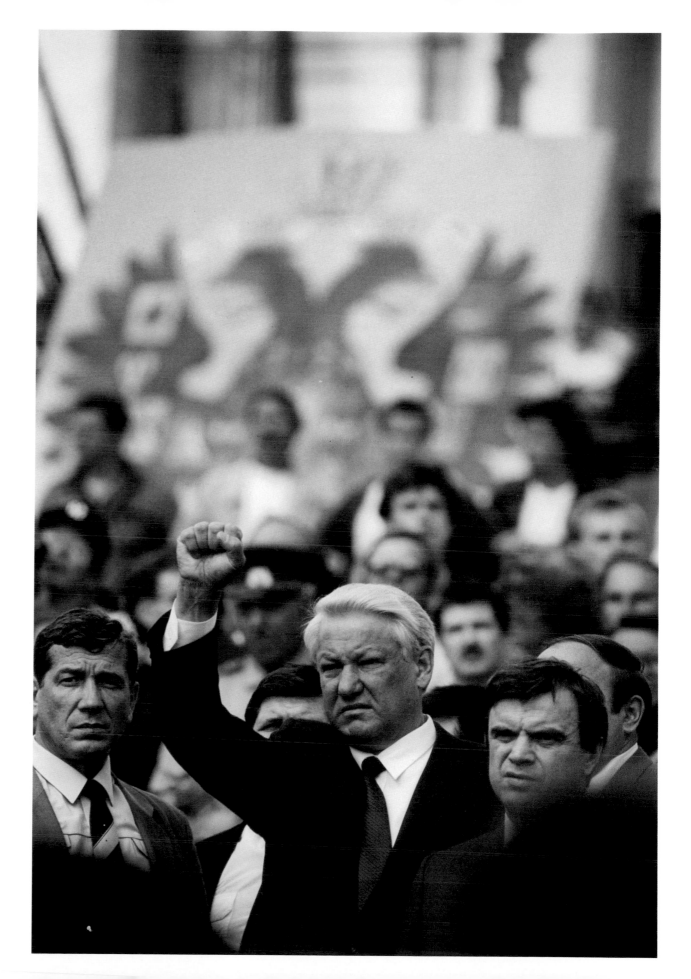

On Sunday, September 1, thousands of Muscovites came out to celebrate "Moscow Day." Young and old, wearing roller skates or dressed in costumes, they danced and rejoiced in the possibilities of reform and anticipation of the future.

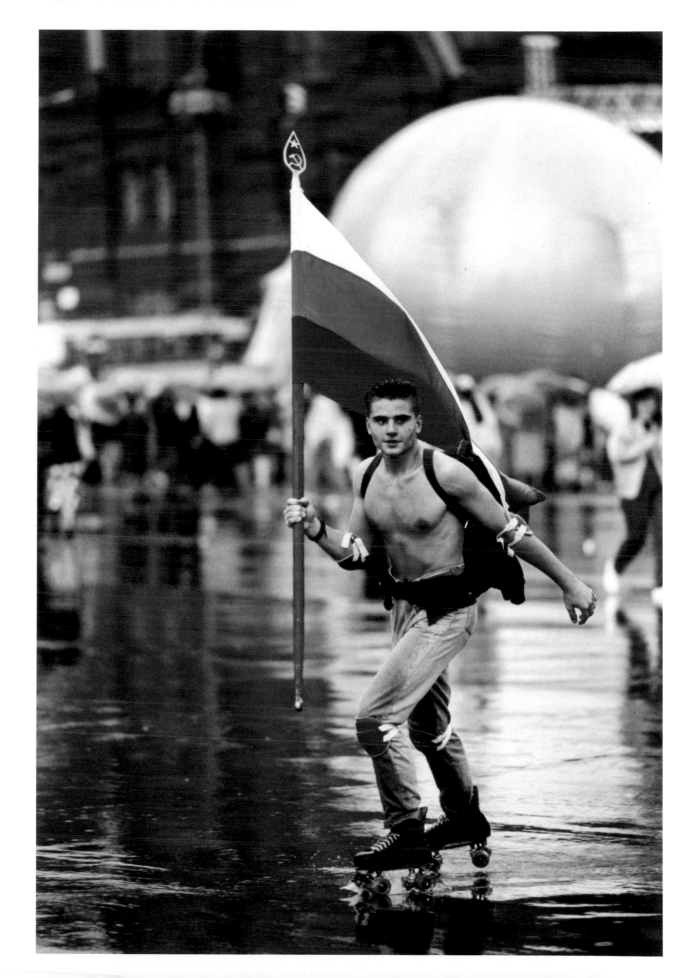

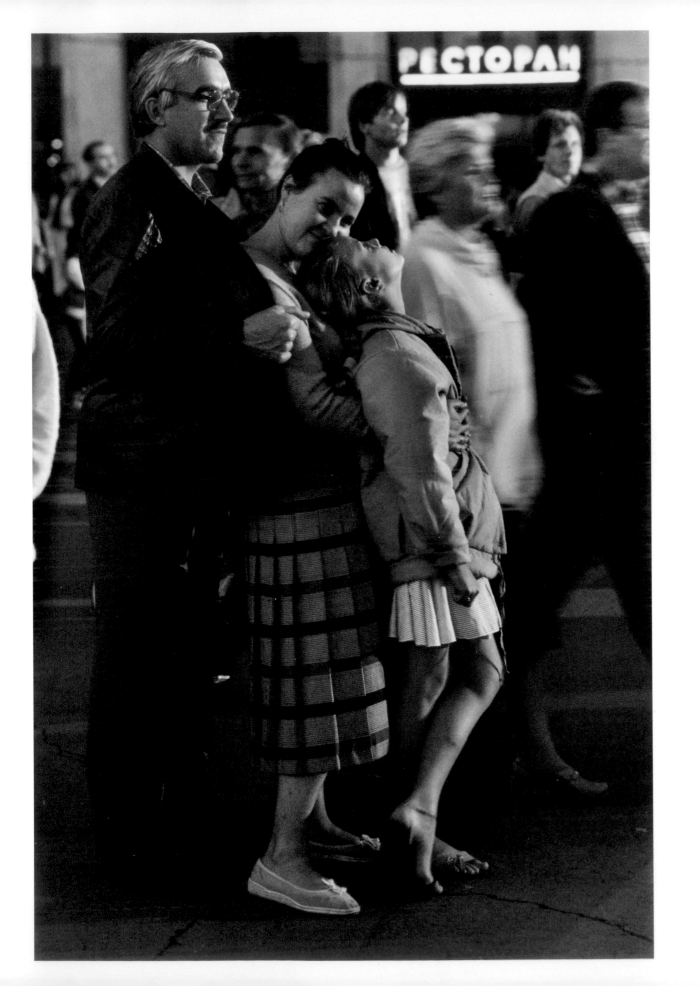

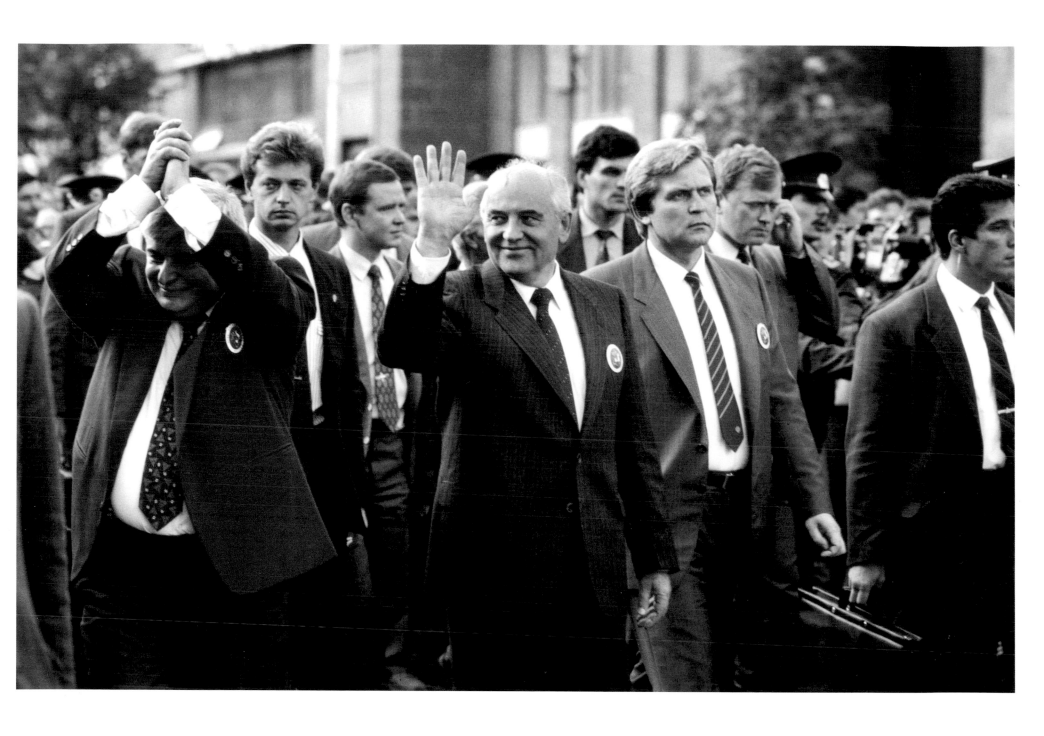

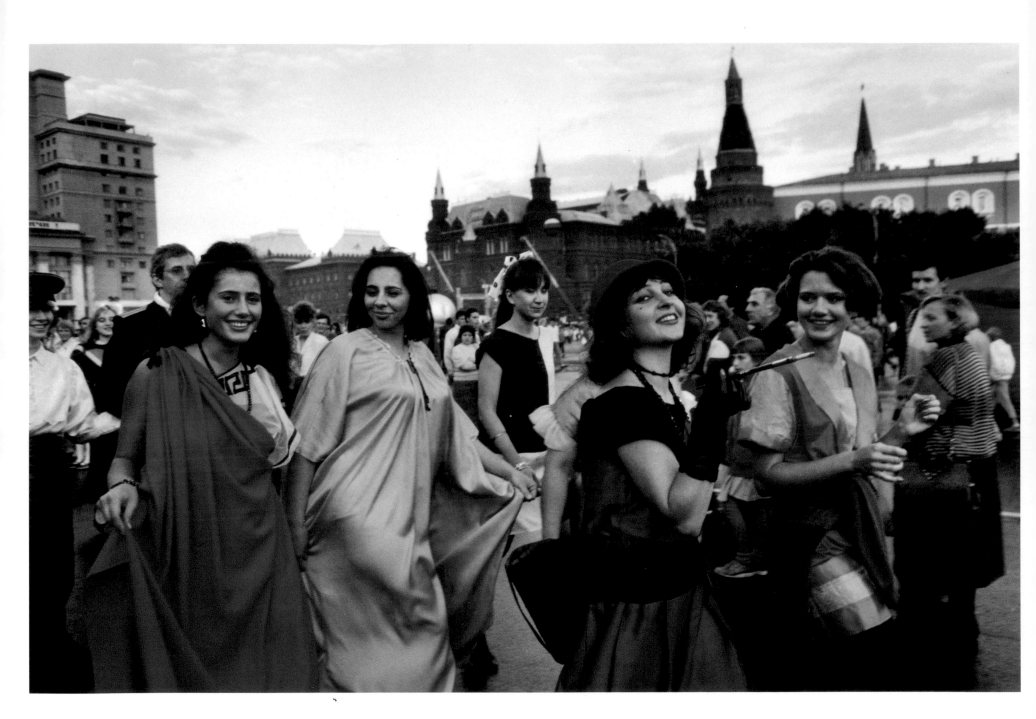

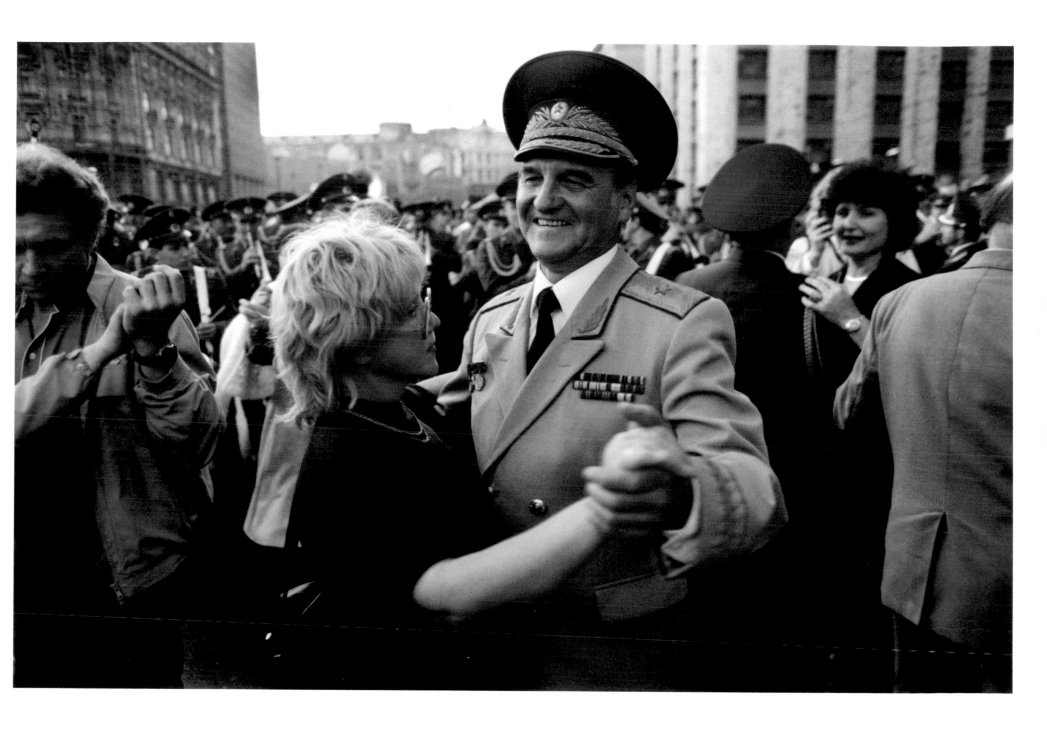

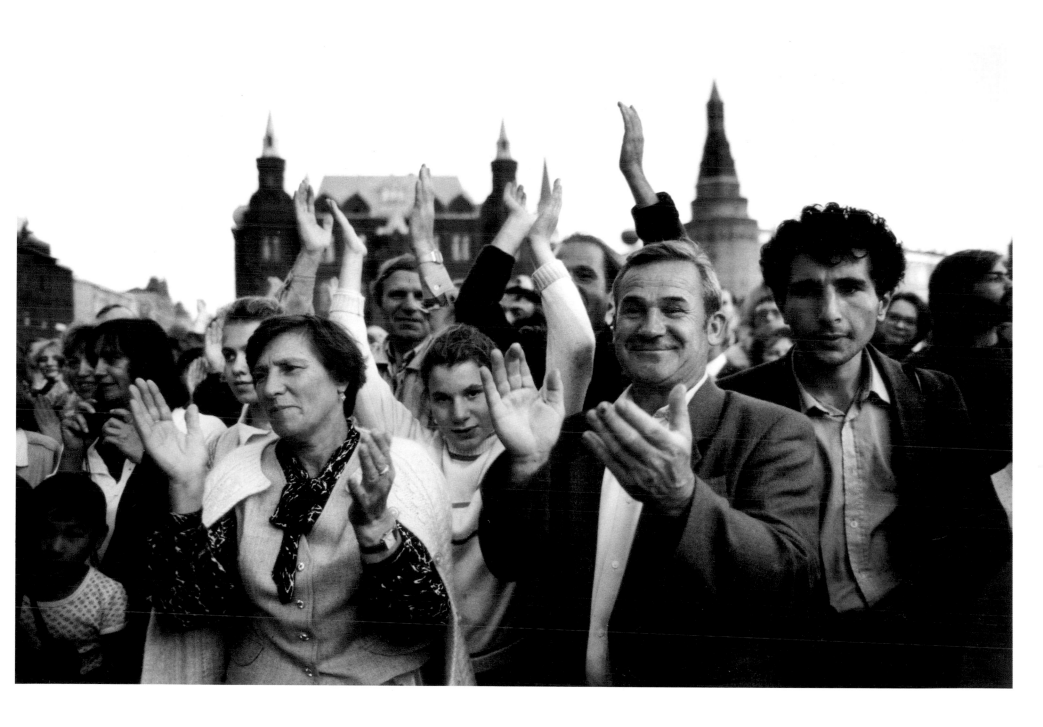

JOURNAL

DAVID C. TURNLEY

June 24, Moscow

Arrived on AF 2982 at 14:05. Weather hot and humid. Was met at airport by interpreter Natasha Lebedeva, who organized a taxi and drove us to the Intourist hotel, where she had managed to check us in as guests of a Moscow business magazine. Porter who delivered bags to the room asked for two packs of cigarettes rather than a dollar bill for his service.

Sat with Natasha and came to terms on our work agreement—$400 a week for ten weeks, with the option of a $1,000 bonus. Talked about themes for project and reviewed our itinerary. At 25, she is very savvy at how to work this system and more than once she sighed, saying how tough one has to be to survive here. The Intourist hotel is crawling with prostitutes offering themselves for $100.

Karin, my wife, and I went with Natasha to see friends who live in an apartment near the center of the city. They would like us to stay in their apartment for $40 a night. Over vodka, strawberries, cheese, lettuce, and tomato hors d'oeuvres, we discussed the Soviet Union. Veronica is a cultural attaché in the Soviet diplomatic corps, her ex-husband a cameraman, her son Sergei a finance and marketing employee with a Soviet magazine. His wife Anna is the assistant manager of a Pizza Hut. Conversation ranged from the Soviet economic crisis to *perestroika*, the Gulf War, Afghanistan, the KGB, and the Communist Party. Veronica said, "We are economically worse off, but spiritually better than ten years ago. The crooks are doing well economically in this society currently. I was in Italy some time ago, which is a beautiful country, but I feel spiritually happier here. . . ."

My first impression on this trip is that Moscow—the cars, the dress—reminds me of the 1930s and '40s. The Stalinesque architecture is overpowering. Economic woes are always the first subject of conversation, but the Russians love to talk about it, and while they are very distressed, one rarely senses that they have given up, or that they would really like to live anywhere else.

June 25, Moscow

Reorganized the itinerary and collected ideas with Natasha and her friend Sergei, who explained how his friend makes a fortune laundering money. He starts with collective farmers who sell their goods for rubles, and then sell back the money for hard currency. He then takes the hard currency and buys computers in the Far East and sells them in the Soviet Union for much more money. To start this process he has to bribe someone on the Soviet Farm Board.

Walked to Red Square—not only tourists, but Soviets flock here from everywhere—Mongolians in traditional robes, grannies carrying babies on their shoulders. Walked along the Moscow River to one of the seven huge apartment buildings Stalin had commissioned in Moscow—very much symbols of that period. Was looking at pictures of Marx, Lenin, and Engels in the lobby when a woman in her early thirties stopped to pose for the camera, then said in English, "Would you like to visit my flat?" I followed her up to the 11th story, as she explained that she and her husband, the financial director for the Savoy Hotel—Moscow's newest, fanciest hotel for foreign businessmen—had been handed down two apartments, originally from her grandfather, who had been a trade minister with Stalin.

The apartment was spacious by Moscow standards—but not fancy—with a great view of the river. She immediately brought out two tins of caviar, salmon, and a bottle of Georgian wine. She was heading the next day to her family's country dacha, where her mother was taking care of her child. She said her husband would be arriving home soon in his Volvo. She described him as a consummate businessman, who makes a fortune by Russian standards and stands two meters tall.

As I left, I couldn't help but notice the coincidence of the building's heavy Stalinesque architecture, and the system which allows only privileged bureaucrats to live there. Outside, fruit vendors were selling rotting Bulgarian grapes for five rubles a kilo. Five rubles is half the daily wage of the average Soviet worker.

Ate dinner with Natasha, her friend Andrew, and his wife Alla, at a new Jewish cooperative restaurant. Andrew was very upset by the bill—450 rubles—which is more than the average monthly wage of a Soviet. Alla told the joke about the Belgian competition in which the first prize was a ten-day trip to the Soviet Union, and second prize was a twenty-day trip.

June 26, Moscow

Went with Natasha to organize tickets at a place called Intourtran, the office where Soviets go to book and buy international and domestic flights. Met a black couple from Benin—students—who had been waiting two days to talk to someone about tickets to Berlin, and finally were told that there would be no more seats available for the rest of the summer. They said they found Russians to be very racist. I was originally told that it would not be possible to book all of the tickets I would need at the same time, but when I suggested that I could make the lady's life much happier, she dropped everything and proceeded to help. Eventually I offered the woman $25: she explained that she would prefer video cassettes, which I bought the next day in the hotel's hard-currency shop.

June 27, Moscow

The Soviet State Sports Committee sponsors a training facility for national and Olympic gymnasts and swimmers. These athletes live at the facility throughout the year. They are selected during competitions that take place annually throughout the country's 15 republics. The training center is located about an hour outside Moscow in a rural environment surrounded by a lake and a forest. While the training is completely professional and disciplined, the facility is rudimentary and the dormitory conditions sparse. Though the food is much better than that available to the general public, it is, by Western standards, very basic.

An American girls' team was visiting; apparently, in order to get more hard currency, the State Sports Committee has been receiving visiting delegations who come to train next to the Soviets. The contrast in character and training methods is dramatic. As one American coach put it, "What the Soviet team is doing in the first hour of training is what we try to work up to by the end of the day."

Svetlana Boguinskaya, the Olympic gold medalist, is currently training for Barcelona. The Western image of the high privilege awarded such a Soviet champion is spoiled by her example. Svetlana is paid 250 rubles—less than $10 a month. Unlike most Soviet citizens, she was able to buy a 20-square-meter apartment and a Volga car without waiting in line for years—but only after winning an Olympic gold, silver, and bronze medal. Her father is a construction worker, her mother a housewife, and their socio-economic condition has not been improved in any real terms by her success. Svetlana, probably one of the most visible representatives of the Soviet Union, an Olympic gold medalist, has two rotting front teeth that need to be capped.

"One of the big motivations for being an athlete," she said, "is obviously because it provides me with conveniences that I couldn't have otherwise—even if these conveniences are meager by international standards. I realized this

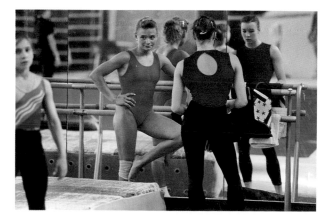

concretely two years ago when I dropped out of gymnastics, and went back to Minsk to live. One day I was standing in line waiting to buy chocolate, and the line was so long I was going to have to wait all day. I realized what the life of normal Soviet citizens is like. I came back to Moscow to resume gymnastics."

June 29, Moscow

Visited the Mozhaysk Prison #163/5. about 100 kilometers from Moscow, situated in the country in an area heavily forested with birch trees. The buildings on the complex are very old—the facility had been originally constructed as a military prison camp during World War I. The prison houses women—first-time offenders. There are no cells; the entire complex has the feel of a very old and austere boarding school or antiquated hospital. The dormitory rooms have iron-framed bunk beds, placed next to one another to accommodate 25 women in a rather small room.

They wear blue-patterned dress uniforms, and during inspection are obliged to wear white scarves. Although the minimum age in the prison is 18, when girls under 18 are pregnant, they are treated as adults. This prison has a house for prisoners' children under three years of age; currently there are 50 children in the facility. The presence of guards is minimal, and prisoners seem to go about on their own. Women watch television, or sit outside smoking cigarettes during their free time. Women with children in the children's home are allowed to visit them in their free hours. The women are given bowls of soup and small loaves of bread to eat.

With a capacity for 1,500 women, the prison holds 800 currently. Since *perestroika*, 200 women previously charged with political crimes have been released. The sentences for very serious crimes, including murder, seem short—usually no more than three to five years, though the death penalty is still an option in the Soviet system. Prisoners serving sentences for all types of crimes are integrated among one another; I met one woman who was serving three years in prison for having stolen 50 rubles—less than two dollars—and

another woman serving three years for having been an accomplice to a murder.

I spoke with Lidiya Pustovoit, a prison warden who has worked at the prison for the last 20 years. She says the changes in the prison system under Gorbachev have been dramatic: no more political prisoners for insulting the government; women not forced to work as hard; 12 vacation days a year; five days home leave every quarter for women with children under 18. Previously, aggressive, problematic prisoners were put in very severe solitary confinement for up to five months; now

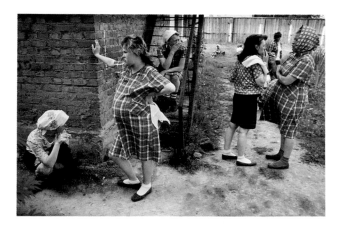

a discipline case is isolated in cells of up to four women with the possibility of reading, watching television and listening to the radio, for a maximum of 15 days.

The warden says she believes the system needs harsher punishment for certain cases. Prisoners now get more vacation than the prison staff. But at the same time that rights are increasing for prisoners, Warden Pustovoit says, "*Perestroika* and *glasnost* have brought about an increase in crime, and particularly an increase in Western-style crime, such as gang violence and the use and selling of drugs. With the availability of books and films from the West, people want more money, but they do not want to work for it. Watching movies with beautiful people, beautiful clothes, and housing, the point is never made that people must work for this, and the youth supposes that these things should be easily gotten."

Warden Lidiya Pustovoit is paid 210 rubles a

month with a 100-ruble bonus for being a major, and another bonus paid for her 20 years of service. She has two children, a daughter finishing high school, and a son serving his army service in Lithuania, and on this salary she has a hard time supporting her family. She is a Communist Party member. When she started working in the prison, this was obligatory. Under Gorbachev this has changed, and now it is no longer necessary to be a party member. She said that the fact that a foreign journalist was allowed to visit the prison was a reality that would never have been conceived of before Gorbachev.

Lidiya's son serving in Lithuania wants to become a businessman. She said, "This scares me, because the whole idea of becoming a businessman is new, and I still have a hard time accepting the concept. I am accustomed to a society where everything is handed down from the top. Something inside of me is suppressed. But I think that my son is completely free in his mind, and knows how to get around in this new society. When we visited him where he is based near Poland, he took us to a kind of black market and I was amazed at how he knew how to negotiate."

Photographed an attractive woman with Slavic cheekbones, wearing lipstick, who was sitting outside waiting to be inspected before she would go to work in the sewing factory. Unlike many of the women—who turned away when I pointed my camera at them—she accepted my photographing with an open face and gentle eyes. I spoke to her. Her name is Larisa Belyaiva, from Perm in Siberia. She is serving the last six months of a two-and-one-half-year sentence for robbery and pickpocketing. Her child, named Cyril, was born since she entered prison. "I grew up in an orphanage as an abandoned child," Larisa said, "and when I got out at age 15, I wanted more for myself. I found that I could pick pockets with great facility, and this was an easy way to live. Now, with the difficult economic situation, and a baby, I don't know how easy it is going to be for me to survive when I get out. I could have been released earlier if I had committed to never stealing again, but in all honesty, I do not know what I will do, faced with the conditions that I will

be released to. And on top of that, I am afraid that I will have a black spot on me with this prison record for the rest of my life, and that it will be difficult to find someone who will employ me."

June 30, Leningrad

Took the midnight red train from Moscow to Leningrad, arriving at 8:00 A.M. On the Baltic Sea the temperature and humidity are much lower than in Moscow. The conditions on the train—a sleeping car express meant for Soviet bureaucrats—were excellent, commensurate with any European first-class train. Moscow is a city with very Stalinesque architecture; Leningrad, on the sea, with two rivers, and dozens of canals, is a romantic and sensual city, European in its diverse architectural styles, with monuments, museums, and palaces that were the homes for centuries to the Soviet czars and royal families. In World War II, the Germans bombed every third building, killing between 500 thousand and one million people. Since that time the city has been rebuilt, preserving the style of historic buildings that were destroyed or badly damaged.

Drove by the St. Isaac Russian Orthodox Church, which had been the patron church to the Soviet Navy before religious worship was condemned by the Bolshevik Revolution in 1917. There I bumped into an historic ceremony, where a graduating class of cadets from the Soviet Navy had come to the church to consecrate their swords—a centuries-old tradition, during which a priest blesses and sends off the naval officers to their missions at sea. This was the first time since 1917 that a navy class had returned to worship and celebrate this tradition in the church, and many of the cadets took advantage of the occasion to be baptised. One cadet said of the experience, "I am very happy today to be reconnected to my motherhood and the tradition of my ancestors and of my country. I also feel, on a subliminal level of my consciousness, a renewed sense of confidence in my connection with God."

Despite this newfound freedom, the Orthodox priest presiding over the ceremony banned me

from taking pictures in the church until after my interpreter and fixer returned with a forged official letter from a Soviet business magazine, and pleaded with the priest that she had been baptised in the church 25 years earlier. He then asked the cadets how they felt about my photographing their service, and they all proclaimed that they wanted me to take pictures, and I was accorded permission.

Given the Third World dynamics of the economic infrastructure of the Soviet Union, it is easy to have the impression of a highly undeveloped country. But in Leningrad, it becomes very clear that a significant dynamic in the Russian psyche is pride in the historical, cultural, and architectural grandeur that this country once knew. It would be a mistake to misinterpret the disaster of the communist experience in the Soviet Union as a statement of the entire history of this country, or to interpret the Soviet people as a simple people. To understand the Soviet people, it becomes clear that one must know Soviet history.

July 1, Leningrad

The Kuznetsky Market, near the old home of Dostoyevsky, features private farmers who drive or fly their fruit and produce from Moldavia, the Ukraine, and Georgia. Produce was plentiful, but the prices were exhorbitant and unaffordable for the average Soviet citizen. One kilo of cherries costs 20 rubles, 10-20 rubles for a kilo of tomatoes, six rubles for a kilo of potatoes. On the other hand, most of the produce and fruit sold in this market is not available in the state-managed stores. Why? Natasha Lebedeva says, "In the state system there is colossal mismanagement at every level along the food chain. There is no incentive to grow the food, to pack it well so that it is not damaged or rotted by the time it arrives in the stores; there are not enough crates available to pack the food, because there is no incentive for the people who make the crates; the trains that deliver the food do not arrive in time, or sit in train stations for days before the food is unloaded and thus is rotten. Before Gorbachev, the best job one could have was a job that gave the worker the most free time and required the least amount of work, because everyone receives the same wage regardless of how hard they work."

Went out to the airport in the late afternoon to meet the mayor of Leningrad, who was returning from Moscow. Mayor Sobchak, who ran his mayoral campaign as a "democrat," won the first "free" election in this city since the Bolshevik Revolution. I spoke to his assistant, Vladimir Putin, who told me that the Leningrad City Council had been disbanded following Sobchak's election, and that the city is currently without a government. He explained that the priority of this mayor is to reverse the balance of employment in Leningrad from 70 percent of the employable population working in some capacity in the defense industry, to 70 percent employment in the private sector, producing commodities that the society desperately needs. But Putin said that this effort is difficult; it is hard to reemploy highly skilled laborers in the defense industry to manufacture things like frying pans, that are so needed. It is also difficult to transform a society that has been completely dependent on the state to control their lives. Transformation will require heavy assistance and investment from the West, but until now all foreign investment must first fall in the hands of the state, which has been very corrupt and inefficient in handling these funds. "We must solve the problem of communication, if we would like to join the world economy. It now takes one week to book a call to the States, which makes doing business impossible."

July 2, Leningrad

The shipbuilding yard "Almaz" builds high-speed hydrofoil navy ships that can do 70 knots—compared to 40 knots of a comparable American Navy vessel—as well as private yachts and fishing boats contracted from this state-owned plant. The general director of the shipyard, Anatoly P. Korolev, said that they currently are seeking joint-venture contracts with the American Coast Guard. They are also building ecological monitoring ships. Demonstrating the pride that the Soviet

defense industry has had, Korolev said, "We suppose that everything we build in this plant must be the best of its kind in the world." Workers in the shipyard earn between 500 and 1,000 rubles a month, as much or more than a surgeon makes in this country. A general laborer in the yard earns more than an engineer—a country-wide phenomenon, which he thinks soon will undergo a transformation.

Walking through the shipyard's milling shop where propeller shafts are lathed, I met the shop trade union leader, who shed some light on the realities of trade unions in the defense industry. "We are called an independent trade union, but how can you be independent in a defense industry factory? We don't have enough solidarity. If I begin pressing the administration, I won't get great support. Why? Because they are afraid that the administration will fire them. We have a law in the Soviet Union that the defense industry cannot go on strike. Often we talk about going on strike but we can't. Here we have to try persuasion to improve conditions, but it is difficult without the possibility to strike. But the difference here with the States is that the manager is not the owner of the factory—it is the state; if he was the owner, we would strike immediately. We do things for the defense of the country. If we were building private yachts, then we could strike. But I think we need the defense industry. We have many borders. I would not go to the US with a gun—but I think we must have defense. I don't think the Cold War is completely over. I'm not sure that Americans are helping the USSR free of charge without their own agenda. Perhaps if I could visit the United States, I would change my mind."

July 3, Leningrad

An abandoned building, labeled "The Peace House" by its inhabitants, has been occupied by squatters—mostly young artists and musicians.

On the way to the building, Natasha explained, "To get an apartment officially here, you have to have the right conditions. You can get on a waiting list, which can take from three to ten years, but to qualify for the waiting list, you have to currently

be living in less than five square meters of living space. It is almost impossible to get an apartment alone. You have to share with your family, including your parents or your in-laws."

The Leningrad of Dostoyevsky is an area with old, partially dilapidated, beautifully detailed buildings of several architectural styles in the heart of the city. This particular building had been abandoned; then when squatters took it over and protested, the city turned on the water and electricity, and has given the occupants until September to get out.

"The Peace House" is a seven-story, mustard-colored building with broken windows, without an elevator or banisters along the staircase. Tanya, newly arrived from Alma-Ata in Central Asia, took us into an apartment; a young man sat on a mattress with four others playing the guitar, while another slept on the floor in the corner. Dina, who had been here for three months, wore a t-shirt, jeans and a headband—the uniform that had been inherited from their '60s bohemian predecessors in the States. Alexei, a guitarist in a rock group, explained his living situation. "Approximately 50 of us live here, and we have also taken in approximately 25 abandoned children whom we try to educate. If you feel free inside, it is hard to live in many of the districts in this country. If you don't conform, but stand out, people don't accept you. It is not like in the US where you can do what you want. This house is the only place where you can feel free both inside and outside. We play music in the street, in the subway, and in the airport, to make money. In the States, if a person is talented, they can find a manager that will help them to find work, but here because we don't conform to the system, we must stay underground. We feel currently as if we are living through the depression period in the States. And rock music is always most creative during problematic periods. My band is called Christmas."

Alexei, his friends, and two other members of his band took me to the rooftop of the building, where the view of Leningrad is spectacular. From this perspective, it is the sense of time, history, and the grandeur of Leningrad that is most dominant, not the daily struggles that are required just to survive.

While Alexei and his friends sang songs, other squatters from the building sunbathed on the tin roof, referred to as the *plage nudiste*, or nudist beach. Later Alexei went on to explain. "There are some 10,000 rock groups in Leningrad alone, and many more completely underground. We don't have a serious drug culture mixed with this rock culture, because first of all drugs are very hard to get, and those available are mostly handmade and consequently very lethal. And secondly, the punishment here if you are caught is very severe." Nevertheless, on the rooftop, Alexei and his friends passed around a hand-rolled joint of marijuana that they had bought from someone in the local subway station.

Back inside, I opened an apartment door and found an 11-year-old boy, wearing only a pair of pants, crouched on the floor amidst a pile of rubble, in his room with only a bed and his little pet dog. Vitaly Taranyk, an abandoned child, has been living in the building for the last two years. Alexei told me that this young boy had been found in a cellar, having escaped from a state orphanage.

In another apartment that serves as a painting studio, an artist named Aslan paints impressionistic mosaics that look something like cartographic landscape maps. "There is a dramatic shortage of materials, paints, canvases. When we succeed to sell one of our works, we must use the money to buy more materials. And no one buys canvases in the Soviet Union. I give my paintings to a middleman, a gallery owner, who sells my works overseas. They are all over the world, but I don't know where, and I don't know how much he sells them for."

July 4, Leningrad

The Hermitage Museum is known for having perhaps the greatest collection of art in the world. The contradictions in this country never cease to amaze me. The grandeur of this museum is greater than any I have ever visited in Paris or elsewhere. The pomp, opulence, and power of this country is never more obvious than in the shrines of Leningrad's monarchs.

In the evening, driving down Nevsky Prospekt,

I stopped to make pictures of people reading newspapers posted on a wall. A young man in a black outfit with a kind of royal necklace around his neck confronted me for having photographed

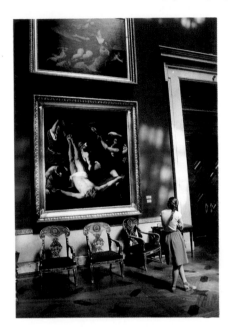

him. When I suggested that this was no longer a fascist state—not thinking that he understood English—he reacted to the word fascist. "I am not a fascist," he said, "I am a monarchist."

In the evening, I visited a jazz club, featuring a group playing Dixieland jazz, with pictures on the wall of many great black American jazz performers. I was reminded of the absence of blacks in this country. On two occasions, I have encountered black students from Guadeloupe and Benin, and have joined them in conversation. After the second time, my interpreter wanted to know why I like blacks so much. I told her I like people.

July 5, Leningrad

Around the corner from the Maly Opera Theatre, where the famous Kirov Ballet performs, stands the second-largest Jewish synagogue in Eastern Europe. Before 1917 and the Bolshevik Revolution, services at the synagogue would attract and seat up to two thousand Jews. But until Gorbachev, the communist government effectively

wiped out any sense of Jewish identity for Soviet Jews. These days, the synagogue congregates about 20 people for a typical Sabbath service. But with *perestroika* and *glasnost*, there is nevertheless a slow but sure revival of Judaism and Jewish traditions.

A group of young Jewish students from the Yeshiva University in New York have come to the Soviet Union to teach Judaism. They are conducting summer camps for young Jews in five cities, including one at the synagogue in Leningrad.

Sharon Beres, 21, lives in Southfield, Michigan. "When things started to change, we saw an open door to come here and teach Judaism in the Soviet Union itself," she told me. "Some of the children who come here to study with us speak Hebrew already and many do not; some know about Jewish traditions such as Passover, but most know nothing at all. We teach them Hebrew so that when they get to Israel they can go to a store and ask for bread and butter. I worked with Soviet Jews in Israel outside Haifa last year. It is very hard for these people to get jobs, because they are educated as physicians, scientists, and engineers, and the competition for these positions is high.

"Most Jews know songs that we sing during services on the Sabbath. We have taught these children three songs and we sing them over and over again. And then we taught them—as a joke—a song with the lyrics "Ay, yi, yi, yi, yi," and the next thing we knew, everyone in town was singing this song. The children can ask the craziest questions—like are Jews allowed to wear makeup? When we asked them to draw pictures of what a Jewish holiday meant to them, many drew Christmas trees with a star of David on top. We realize we have a long way to go.

"We have not been directly affected by anti-Semitism during our visit here. I have almost been upset by this, like I have been missing out on the whole experience. But when I was on a bus the other day, talking to a woman about who makes money in this country, she said people who work for the communist government make money. I asked her if any Jews work in the government, and the bus driver turned around, glared at me and said, 'Jews started communism in this country.' It is interesting, because in the passports of Russian Jews, under 'nationality,' it does not say 'Russian' but rather 'Jew.' We want to teach these people what that means, and we would like them to move to Israel, because we are afraid they will lose their identity here."

Later that evening, at a get-together sponsored by the young American Jews from Yeshiva University, Russian Jews were led through the traditions of lighting candles, breaking bread, reciting prayers and singing songs that celebrate the Sabbath. There was an interesting mix of people, some who appeared euphoric over their renewed sense of identity and community, and others who seemed hesitant—even anxious—with this new sense of freedom of expression.

July 6, Murmansk

Took a plane this morning from Leningrad to Murmansk, which is situated above the Arctic Circle, bordering Finland and Sweden. Discovered today that my interpreter—a wonderfully clever and capable interpreter, fixer, and survivor— is absolutely terrified of flying. Convinced that there is a lack of maintenance and spare parts for "Aeroflop" planes, she awakened at 4:00 A.M. to take five calming pills for our 8:00 A.M. flight. White-knuckled the whole two-hour flight this morning. It will be interesting to see how she manages the next 13 flights that will crisscross every corner of the Soviet Union.

The change in geography is accompanied by a change of climate and light; it is cold here in the middle of summer, and apparently the sun never sets. A city known for being a naval seaport on the Barents Sea, and for being the most important fishing port in the country, Murmansk was almost completely destroyed in World War II by the Germans, and today there are only two buildings standing that leave any trace of prewar architecture. The rest of the buildings, housing some half-million people, are entirely postwar, prefab, concrete apartment buildings, as found throughout the Soviet Union.

On the way into town, a line of cars that stretched a mile and a half waited to buy petrol.

The taxi driver explained that it is typical to spend an entire day waiting in a queue to fill one's gasoline tank.

A young photographer, Sergei Yeshenko, who works for the local newspaper representing the Young Communists League, told us that the local economy is supported by the fishing and cargo industries, and is the port for atomic icebreaking vessels that lead ships through the North Sea. He said that recently there has been a movement by Greenpeace to relocate the repair facility for these atomic vessels further from the city, in case of accident. Also, emissions from the many nickel foundries have completely destroyed the ecology that surrounds them. Last year, a foundry that had been situated outside a town in such a way that the winds would blow the emissions away from the city, had its poisonous emissions blown into the town when the winds changed direction. Most of the people in Murmansk either work in fish processing factories, or are sailors or sailors' wives.

Drove through the town in the late afternoon, along the port, and visited an area where families, mostly fishermen, live in small wooden houses. Vitali, age 24, works as a fisherman on a state-owned boat and is at sea for four months, and then comes home for four months. He is tall and strong with a gentle bearing, and his wife has an unpretentious, open and enthusiastic character. The couple welcomed us into their home, after just returning from having spent from 11:00 A.M. until 6:00 P.M. in town, standing in lines trying to find food to bring home.

Anna insisted that we sit down; she prepared coffee with concentrated milk, and put out a plate of salami and brown bread. "I'm Russian. All my grandmothers and great-grandmothers were Russian. In our history there were a lot of talented and intelligent people who created a very rich culture. How can one not be proud of this? Our main problem in this country has always been government. I only appreciate Peter I and Gorbachev."

Back at the hotel, the only dinner available was in a restaurant accompanied by a disco, which played American contemporary pop songs to a crowd of Russians, and the many Finns who come to the Soviet Union to drink cheaply and find inexpensive Soviet prostitutes. One young Finn who joined our table explained that he had employed the services of one of these local ladies for $30 for the night. He said that he did not blame the women for their acts; they were victims of the Soviet system.

It is now nearly 1:00 A.M.—and Murmansk is still covered with daylight.

July 7, Murmansk

The single purpose for the town Monchegorsk is a state-controlled nickel foundry used in defense. Workers in the factory have life expectancies of 50 years, maximum. From the road one can see for miles, the entire sky covered by the nickel gas emissions from the multiple chimneys of the sprawling, mammoth, decrepit foundry. In an otherwise forested region, there is practically no vegetation. Permission to visit such a state foundry —operating in the defense industry—is almost impossible to acquire. And moreover, as I later discovered, the entire city of Monchegorsk, two hours south of Murmansk, is off-limits to foreigners without a special permit.

Determined to witness work conditions in such a Soviet foundry, Natasha and I hired a taxi and simply drove to the foundry and entered the grounds without these prerequisites, on a Sunday workday, when the number of security personnel and management were minimum.

Inside the foundry huge furnaces melt nickel ore, stoked by workers with long poles. Liquid nickel is then pored into iron vats which are transferred by crane to be again poured into iron casts. Cans connected to rubber hoses, through which the workers breathe when they are working near the poisonous fumes of molten nickel, hang from the workers' necks. Having spent three months experiencing gas masks while covering the Gulf War, I could easily tell that these quasi-gas masks are anything but efficient. After 30 minutes of photographing near these melting furnaces, I felt a burning in my lungs and nose.

At that point, a management official insisted

we follow him to his office. He interrogated my interpreter: How had we gotten access to the foundry? The police were called. My film was taken—the real film had been hidden in my underwear during a visit to the bathroom—and we were asked to leave, and to return with a visa to the city and permission to visit the foundry. Everyone seemed a little embarrassed. Once outside, the two policemen took us to the police station, where their superior returned the dummy film.

We then asked if we could visit the local hospital and the policemen enthusiastically escorted us.

Therapist Emma Drafkina, 28, grew up in the town, and her father, like practically everyone else, works in the foundry. She volunteered that the hospital deals principally with lung disease, cancer, and from problems stemming from weak immune systems. She seemed reluctant to go into further detail, and went to the telephone to call the head physician of the hospital.

While she was gone, Natasha explained that people in this region, largely cut off from the outside world, are still suffering from a mentality fearful of being critical of the country. In her own life, through her last year of high school—the year that Brezhnev died—she and her fellow students were told that the Soviet Union was the best country on earth. There were no problems with the ecology. She remembers reading in Soviet newspapers about homeless people in the United States during that period, and being told that poor people could not breathe any more, because capitalist industry was destroying the ecology.

Then the head physician arrived. Dr. Anatoly Morozova invited us to his office, where he agreed to talk with complete frankness about local health problems. He explained that he came from a region near Chernobyl in the Ukraine.

"Our principal job is to accept that we cannot close this foundry, so we must find medical treatments to solve the health problems it creates. We are making advances in this area that are not being used elsewhere. The principal health problems here result from heavy concentrations of nickel toxins, as well as a mixture of other noxious gases in large concentrations, inhaled over a long period of time. This seems to cause a depression of the body's normal immune system, leading to all kinds of illnesses, including allergies, pulmonary disease, and cancer. It also seems to have created an unusually high occurrence of birth defects in children, and a high infant mortality rate of 35 in 1,000. All of this—the polluted ecology, combined with a poor economy, lack of good food and vitamins, high stress—makes for serious health problems."

At that moment our taxi driver entered the office. Two new policemen had arrived, demanding we leave the city, because we did not have proper visas. Once outside, the policemen, huge in stature, seemed to be more curious about us than anything else. We agreed to try to get visas to return tomorrow. As we got in the taxi, one of the policemen reached in the car and handed Natasha his phone number.

July 8, Murmansk

The fishing port in Murmansk is the largest fishing port in the Soviet Union; approximately 30 thousand fisherman and some nine hundred vessels trawl in waters all over the world. One ship has just returned from 45 days at sea off the Norwegian coast. A van with mounted loudspeakers played the national anthem for the returning sailors. Lubov Ritkov and her daughter Lena were there to greet the father of the family, who has been working at sea for the last 19 years. He earned approximately 3,000 rubles for his last 45 days of work, will be home for eight days, and then will leave again for 102 days to fish off the coast of Canada.

It is ironic, says Irina Hobofova, who strips off fish gills in one of the port's processing plants, that most of the fish that she and her co-workers process never reach the shelves throughout the country. Most of it—particularly salmon, caviar, and other precious fishes—is sold to foreign countries for desperately needed hard currency. "When I was a child, I could eat caviar and everything I wanted. Now it is hard—even for us who work in the plant—to find fish in the stores."

After walking through the fish processing plants, we were invited to partake in a huge feast of various kinds of fish that the state was testing, but had not yet been made available to the general public. We were joined by one of the plant's assistant managers, Gennady Kuzmenko, a short man with blue eyes and an Albert Einstein hair cut. Until six years ago he worked as a "propagandist" for the state inside the plant.

"I am for drastic reforms in this country overnight, and Gorbachev doesn't offer them fast enough. And I don't trust that Yeltsin has a clear vision of what direction the country should take. If it were up to me, I would like to completely privatize industry and create a free market. We were taught that the capitalist system resembles a carrot, with the rich at the top and the poor at the bottom. We were taught that a similar drawing of the system in the Soviet Union would resemble a lemon, with all the population in the middle class. The reality is that the capitalist system looks more like a beet root, with a large middle class, a small lower class, and a small higher class in the economic bracket. The Soviet Union still looks like a lemon. I would like us to look more like a beet root."

At the visa office/police station where we tried to obtain visas to Monchegorsk, we were handled by a heavyset, gray-haired commander, who scolded us for having gone there in the first place. He said we would need an official letter from the foreign ministry or a newspaper inviting us, before he could issue visas. We called a contact in Murmansk, a photographer working with the Young Communists newspaper, and asked him for such a letter. After consulting with his editor, he was told that the editor would be scared and therefore unable to give us the document. And so we decided to try again in the morning to acquire an "official" letter.

In the Arctic Hotel—where I have listened to disco music with my meal of cucumbers, tomatoes, and shish kebab, with the same dozen hookers sitting at the same tables with the same drunken Finns—a group of policemen confronted a drunken Russian near the elevators. An argument ensued, the drunk could hardly stand, and one of the policemen hit him in the stomach. The man fell to the ground, and two more policemen gave him kicks with their black boots. Natasha says that in the Soviet Union, police brutality is without recourse.

July 9, Murmansk

Called the president of the local journalists' union in Murmansk, and asked if she could help us acquire visas to return to Monchegorsk. She agreed, typed the letter, and we were given visas—with the condition that we be accompanied by another journalist from the union. Enter Sergei, a photographer for the Young Communists newspaper, who drove with us back to Monchegorsk.

We returned to the hospital where we spoke again with the head physician, Dr. Anatoly Morozova, before visiting patients suffering from maladies caused by the pollution from the nickel foundry. "When Monchegorsk was built in 1936, the nickel foundry was situated so that the poisonous gas being emitted would blow away from the city. But the lake, from which we get our drinking water, is directly in the path of these blowing gases. For two months of the year—when the snow melts—the concentration of nickel in the drinking water is one-and-one-half times what it should be. The bottom line is that the foundry has to be demolished or reconstructed, and this is not being done. And there are 46 other towns in the Soviet Union with ecological problems worse than ours. At least here we have winds.

"One of the problems in our culture is that the health system is entirely free, and when people come to the hospital they receive extra compensation—so it actually pays to be unhealthy in this country. You get the same money and you don't work. To explain the paradox: a truck driver is fined 800 rubles for drunk driving. But if he causes an accident while drunk, and requires hospitalization for three months, he receives the best treatment free of charge."

Dr. Morozova's associate, Dr. Alexander Minin, gave us a tour of the hospital. We visited Olga Zemerova, whose eight-month-old son Eugene is the third child in her family to be born with serious birth defects. We saw Kiril Krigin, who visits the hospital every year with a chronic respiratory allergy. Lying in the intensive care ward was Valentin Potemkin, who is convinced that his ulcerated stomach is a condition of the gas he inhales every day. When asked if he knew others who had suffered ailments from the pollution, he laughed, and with the respirator tube sticking up his nose, said, "There isn't a family in this community who has not had someone sick as a result of that foundry." He then asked the interpreter if he could get in trouble for what he told me.

We left the hospital and drove back to the factory—where we had been refused access—to make pictures of the conditions from the car. As we drove by the administration building, a man came running out and wrote down the number of the license plate. Five minutes later, we were surrounded by four racing police jeeps with blue lights flashing. At the police station, we were met by the local KGB official, who asked me to explain our visit. I told him in no uncertain terms that we were simply trying to do our job, and that I thought that the real criminal was the state that allowed a foundry to emit such poisonous gases that had adversely affected everyone in the community. He seemed to appreciate my answer, but our photographer escort, showing his true colors, stuttered that he had called in the morning to inform the KGB of our visit, and that things had gotten out of hand. The KGB official berated our photographer friend for poorly assuming his escort duties, and kindly said we could be on our way back to Murmansk.

July 10, Murmansk

Mid-afternoon. Sitting in the airport in Murmansk waiting for a delayed flight to Vilnius that was to have left this morning. Apparently, a plane meant to take off earlier with people who had been on board since 5:00 A.M. was cancelled due to technical problems, and the passengers refused to leave until the airport found another plane. Thus, the plane meant to fly us to Leningrad was used.

A young woman who works in the room reserved for foreign passengers speaks excellent English. After trying to help me find other routings to Vilnius, she shared a few details of her life. She married when she was 18 and has a four-year-old son. Her husband, a sailor, goes away for five months at a time to sea, off the South American coast, and is paid $700 for his five months' work—an enormous salary in the Soviet Union. I asked her how she copes when he is away, and she told me that she has a boyfriend whom she sees when he is gone. She doesn't want to divorce because of his job, their son, and because, "As a Russian man he has deep feelings for his wife, and I don't want to hurt him." She uses birth control—pills imported from Hungary that she says are extremely rare and difficult to buy. She acquires them from her friend who is a pharmacist. On the black market they are very expensive for the average Soviet citizen. Despite the hardships of her life, she would never leave Murmansk. She likes the pace and the values of life here.

Airports are places where people have long faces, but here there is a particular Soviet variety, a face of self denial worn every day by the Soviets. Seventy years of repression—with at least 27 million people being sent to gulags in Siberia—taught one lesson: The system is more important than the individual. But what is more impressive is that people do cope somehow, and moments of interaction become very special. A conversation is heartfelt; a visit is always accompanied by food and drink, no matter how meager. Wealth is shared around the table. The Russian soul, while beaten down, is profound, and still very much alive.

July 11, Vilnius

This morning I saw a line of people buying newspapers in the early morning light. I began making pictures. A distinguished, middle-aged man with a long beard and blue eyes looked up from buying his paper, and asked where I was from. I told him, and he smiled and said, "It is such a pleasure to meet a free man from a free press." We sat down on a park bench, and Donatas asked if he could help me with my mission in Vilnius. He is an architect who would like to start his own firm: Could I send him a handbook on opening one's own business?

"This is a very exciting time," he said. "We have prepared for our free life for the last 40 years. This is a revolution of information. Under the Iron Curtain we had to go through the wall to get information. We used short-wave radios that we built ourselves. As a student I taught myself English, French, German, and all the Slavic languages so that I could listen to the BBC and the Voice of America to have a window on the free world. A lot of people died in darkness in this country without freedom. For many years during the time of repression, my wife was singing openly in churches in Vilnius, and I was persecuted for this, pushed out of my job many times. Every third or fourth man was either sentenced to jail or sent to Siberia. My grandfather died in prison for his beliefs. My son served in the Soviet Army for half a year before escaping and going into hiding. He came out of hiding after Lithuania declared independence.

"We say in Lithuania that Gorbachev is standing on the Empire State Building yelling, 'I'll jump if you don't help me.' It is a communist lie that we Lithuanians hate the Russian people, but if someone openly says here now that he is a communist, you will see wide eyes open up. As far as my role is concerned, President Landsbergis, a musicologist, is directing a symphony for Lithuania all over Europe. I, an architect, am helping to draw the blueprints of a visual symphony for the future of our country."

Following dinner, and before saying good night, I apologized to Donatas that our conversation had had to compete with disco music in the restaurant. Donatas smiled one of his huge smiles. "We are in a state of war here. Disco music we can handle."

July 12, Vilnius

Was awakened this morning in my hotel room by a loud explosion at 3:30 A.M. My architect friend Donatas called at 8:00 A.M. to tell me that someone had blown up a huge cross in Lenin Square that had been erected two weeks ago to commemorate the Lithuanian uprising against the Russian

occupation of Lithuania. After visiting the site of the explosion, went to the television tower where the Soviet Army put down a demonstration on January 14, killing 14 people. The Russian Army still has a tank stationed behind barbed wire surrounding the TV tower.

In the Vilnius cemetery, where the January 14 victims were buried, hundreds of Lithuanians had come to bury the bodies of a family who had been exiled and killed in the 1940s under Stalin. I met a young Lithuanian-American from Chicago—a

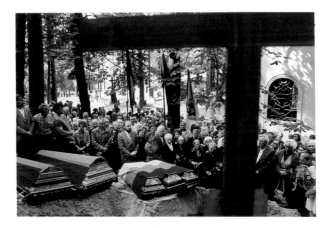

student at Brown University who has come over to do a film documentary on his homeland. He pointed out that one of the assets in the Lithuanian revolution is the strength Lithuanians derive from their devout Catholicism.

Late in the day we went to the Parliament building for an appointment with Lithuanian President Vytautas Landsbergis—a former musicologist. I was accompanied by Natasha, the Russian translator, but at the president's office, his associates said he would refuse to speak Russian—even though it is his second language. An English translator was recruited to help me. Our meeting was brief. He arranged for a car to pick me up in the morning at 7:30 A.M., to accompany him to a village outside of Vilnius.

July 13, Vilnius

A black, Soviet-made Volga picked me up at 7:30 in the morning, and drove to the home of President

Landsbergis. With his wife, Grazina, and an entourage of bodyguards, we headed off into the Lithuanian countryside—not to return until 2:00 A.M. The bodyguards said this was a routine day for Landsbergis, who frequently finishes his meetings at 3:00 or 4:00 in the morning, and who can survive well on three to four hours of sleep with occasional catnaps.

Our first stop was at the family's country home, where the presidential couple visited Landsbergis's father—also Vytautas—a former architect, who served both as an officer in the Czar's White Russian Army before World War I, and in the Lithuanian Army, following the Bolshevik Revolution. Landsbergis sat down alone with his father on the porch to confer about current events in Lithuania. His father is, at 98, still completely lucid and one of the president's most important confidants and advisors. This was followed by play with his grandchildren, coffee with his father and his economic minister, and a showing of pictures from recent trips overseas. As the president helped

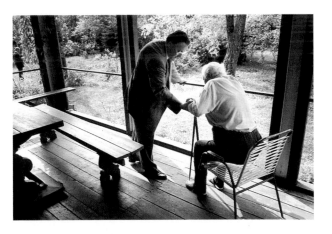

to change his grandson's diaper he commented, "There is a famous Lithuanian poet who wrote a poem to the effect that even the children of lords wet their pants."

A drive through the Lithuanian countryside revealed a rich land sprinkled with birch forests and small subsistence farms, principally cultivated with non-mechanized farm implements. Since Chicago is home to 800 thousand Lithuanians—the largest Lithuanian city in the world—it is not surprising to see enclaves of American-style suburban brick homes in this countryside, too.

The president visited town meetings in two collective farming communities. He laid wreathes at gravesites of Lithuanian independence fighters, and visited with crowds at town meetings. What became clear is that the Lithuanian people—at least in the countryside—are still not completely sure what is happening to them, and thus how to react to Landsbergis, or to the idea of democracy. There was very little applause, but enormous curiosity. Landsbergis seemed to be genuinely interested in the thoughts and concerns of the people; his patience for conversation—lunches, dinners, coffees—was endless.

As we left the home of an elderly woman, given the Soviet government prize for the best home on a collective farm, she took President Landsbergis aside. In front of the director of the collective farm, who was very proud of this Soviet-style scheme, the woman angrily protested that the director had not allowed the people on the farm to erect a church.

July 14, Vilnius

Visited the oldest cathedral in Vilnius, St. Ann's, as well as the huge cathedral in the center of town, where thousands of Roman Catholic Lithuanians attend Sunday Mass. Was joined by Donatas and his wife Stella, on a stroll after Mass through the center of this sensual city, with its sidewalk cafes and mix of Baroque and Renaissance architecture. Donatas brought along a bouquet of flowers for my wife Karin, who was back at the hotel. Donatas, an architect and a married man for 30 years, sat me down to counsel: "It is important that you learn to play the game of diplomacy, to mix work and personal life so that your wife always thinks that your work is oriented to serve her." I was a bit overwhelmed that this man and his wife, whom I had known only briefly over the last four days, seemed genuinely concerned for the well-being of my marriage. We agreed to meet later for strawberries that Stella had picked in the countryside.

We all finished the day by celebrating interpreter Natasha's birthday. A proud Russian, her experi-

ence in Lithuania had not been very pleasant. A number of Lithuanians, including President Landsbergis, had refused to speak Russian to her; one young man, upon learning her nationality, made it clear he thought all Russians should be killed for what they had done to the Lithuanian people. Generally very progressive and nonnationalistic, Natasha finally shared her view—after a couple of glasses of lousy Russian champagne—that Lithuania could never be entirely independent of the Soviet Union, because it lacked economic infrastructure and important natural resources. She also was most miffed that these people refused to speak Russian.

July 16, Kiev

Today is the first anniversary of declared independence in the Ukraine. A holiday was celebrated throughout Kiev tonight, with traditional folk-dancing, singing, and fireworks. The festivities were not unlike a typical Fourth of July celebration anywhere in America. Given the fact that Ukrainian independence was declared only a year ago, one would have expected a fervor in the celebration; instead, it felt casual, more like a holiday than testimony to a dramatic victory of independence. And no one here could actually tell me what independence means to the Ukraine.

It becomes increasingly clear that no matter how many miles I chart around this country, history that dates back decades—if not centuries—has created a mentality among the Soviet people that I will never fully comprehend. The greatest example is the docility of the independence movements here. Although the system clearly is not working, the people of the Soviet Union, unlike Czechoslovakia, East Germany, or even Romania, by and large do not take to the streets and demand change in any urgent or vehement tone.

July 17, Between Kiev and L'Vov

Drove from early morning until 1:30 A.M. from Kiev through the Ukraine to L'Vov, once a part of Poland on the far western border of the Soviet Union. The landscape is very much like the American Midwest—vast, flat plains of wheat

and vegetable fields—until we reached the region surrounding L'Vov, where it becomes much more rolling. The difference between an American farming landscape and the Ukraine has more to do with the physical structures and farm machinery. Here farming is done principally on collective farms—small villages in which each member is responsible for only one particular function of the large farm. An employee goes off to work every morning and comes home at night with his job finished for the day, much like any factory job. Farmers on collective farms are awarded bonuses of small tracts of land for their own private

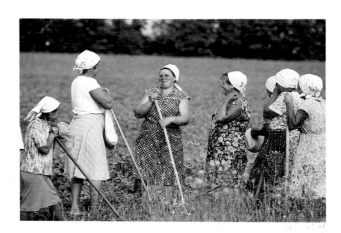

production, and thus it is common to see farmers leading one or two cows to pasture, or hoeing a small field, while nearby hundreds of cows are herded together, or combines work vast fields of wheat.

The few people I encountered along the way seemed more suspicious and less familiar with foreigners than in other parts of the country. We went through the routine police check and interrogation outside a small town where I had stopped to photograph a woman who lowers and raises the barrier at a railway crossing. She had immediately run into her little guardhouse to notify the local authorities of an alien. An old man, very much in his own tranquility, sitting in a pile of hay while his cow lazily grazed nearby, enjoyed having his picture taken, but refused "on this first visit" to divulge his name. He suggested that we might be successful in this regard on a second visit.

July 18, L'Vov

L'Vov is probably the most interesting Eastern European city I have visited—including Prague, Budapest, Gdansk, and Kraków. This city takes one back 50 years; it was never bombed during the World Wars, and it is possible to see the architecture and remnants of civilization under the rule of the Austro-Hungarians, the Poles, the Germans, the Russians, and finally the Ukrainians. For anyone wanting to understand what Eastern Europe was like before the Germans destroyed centuries of soulful development, this city is a hidden secret.

July 19, L'Vov

Spent the day with Stepaniya and Yaroslav Popovich, preparing for the 10,000-ruble wedding that their son Roman will celebrate tomorrow with his 17-year-old bride from an adjacent settlement. In this village, Gidzivka, the Popovichs and approximately four hundred more families farm collectively on some of the richest agricultural land in the Soviet Union. A dozen women—family and friends—spent the day preparing cakes, sausage, salads, and other delicacies that will accompany the two hundred bottles of vodka that have been procured for two hundred guests. Yaroslav drives a tractor on the farm 12-15 hours a day, seven days a week, earning 200 rubles a month. He has saved for 40 years and borrowed money from relatives to afford a wedding that will meet the expectations of Ukrainian tradition. His wife Stepaniya works in one of the two factories on the farm making cardboard boxes, and is also responsible for the production of one hectare of beet roots. Roman, their son, has a job as the chauffeur for the collective farm manager.

The collective farm at Gidzivka uses approximately 1,300 hectares of land to grow corn, 250 hectares to grow wheat, and another five hectares to grow vegetables. The farm grazes two hundred milk cows and three hundred cows for meat; has one school for all grades; a medical clinic with a general practitioner, a pediatrician and a nurse; a post office; six food shops and one general store; and one policeman.

The Popovich family lives in a home that they have built themselves on one-half hectare of state-owned land, the largest plot a collective farmer can live on. They have two cows and three pigs. I asked Yaroslav Popovich about his thoughts on the privatization of collective farms. He said that though the idea was attractive, he still found it abstract, having been brought up on a collective farm. And although the state recently offered to lease farmers five hectares on which they could do their own farming, this is very impractical because Soviet farmers can neither afford, nor have available, the necessary machinery, spare parts, petrol, or fertilizer to make a go of it privately. While he has been driving a tractor for 40 years, he still could not afford one of his own. As far as the small private farming he does on the side, he must sell his meat to the state for four rubles a kilo. At the state-run market, he would have to pay 12 rubles to purchase back the same meat. "We had more to eat before *perestroika*. But now that the Soviet Union is selling all of its agricultural production overseas for hard currency, we have much less. No one knows where our production is going."

Later in the afternoon, standing in a wheat field being worked by five large combines, I spoke with fellow collective farmers Roman Ovshanik and Mikhail Dzeva. "We would all like to own our own farms," Roman said. "Farmers, I think, are like farmers anywhere: We don't like government control. But this idea here is still an abstraction, and it will be 15 years before it becomes a reality." Mikhail went on, "The Soviet Union would have no problem feeding itself if we could be our own farmers. But as it stands, there is no incentive to work hard—we are being paid so little. I will work more than 12 hours today and will earn only ten rubles for my work."

Back at the Popovich farm, Yaroslav, Stepaniya, and their friends—in the midst of these severe economic realities—were in an entirely different spirit. They labored with great enthusiasm to prepare for the big wedding tomorrow, where the bonding of two human beings would be celebrated with dignity and festivity.

July 20, L'Vov

The wedding of Roman and Luba commenced today at about 1:30 P.M., when five "ambassadors" from the home of the bride appeared with a basket at the home of the groom. After greeting Roman and conducting a mock negotiation with his best man, the group exchanged shots of vodka. Roman was presented with a traditional Ukrainian shirt, which symbolized the acceptance of the bride's family. This was followed by a "snack" for this original wedding party—the first part of a feast that would last for two days. Roman's mother and father sat with two loaves of bread on their laps—a symbol for all that the family had done to raise their son. Roman, in front of the rest of the family and relatives, bowed on his knees, kissing first each of the loaves of bread, and then each of his parents on the lips, three times. This touching ceremony symbolizes the passing of the son from his status as a child who has been provided for, to an adult male who will now assume responsiblity for his own family with his new wife.

With this completed, Roman, friends, and family members loaded themselves into a small school bus adorned by flowers, and with the white Soviet car that Roman asked to borrow from my driver, headed to the home of his fiancée, Luba. Along the way, farmers in the fields stopped cutting hay to wave at the passing wedding party. At Luba's family's house the same ceremony was celebrated, with her parents and grandparents and four more loaves of bread. As people from both villages joined together, the wedding moved to the local Ukrainian Catholic church. There, following tradition, Luba and Roman in their wedding clothes visited first the gravesite of her father, who had died in a farm accident. Then they entered the church, to be married by the priest.

From the church, the wedding party returned to the Popovich house, where eating and dancing continued all night and the following day. If anyone ever questioned the energy or diligence of Soviet workers, it would only require the experience of a Ukrainian wedding to witness the inner depths of the Soviet spirit and zest for life. Men and women, women together, twirled to

Ukrainian polka music at a pace that would make most people seasick, even without vodka.

In an effort to take our leave, we approached the groom's parents to thank them for their hospitality. Stepaniya would not allow us to depart without an enormous doggy bag filled with sausage, meat, cake, and vodka. As we walked to the gate, the band struck up a Ukrainian anthem in honor of the departing Americans. The wedding guests surrounded the car in the darkness, the groom's brother and father kissed me on the lips, and we said *dosvidaniye*.

July 21, Moscow

Flew today from L'Vov to Moscow. A brief moment of alarm when smoke started rising from the airplane floor at takeoff. It turned out to be dust rising from the carpet, as the plane pumped ventilation into the fuselage.

Arrived in Moscow to be picked up by Natasha's friend Andrei, an ex-military officer/interpreter in Vladivostock, who may take the baton from Natasha and help me on the rest of the trip.

Checked into the Hotel Metropol, next to Red Square—a newly renovated joint-venture hotel with all the trappings of a really grand hotel, except that the city of Moscow has turned off the hot water in this district for ten days—a trick they seem to do routinely.

July 22, Moscow

Organizing here before being "sent" to Siberia tomorrow morning. Saw my brother Peter this morning, who arrived to photograph the Bush-Gorbachev summit on July 31. Coming here for *Newsweek* magazine since the beginning of Gorbachev's reign six years ago, he used to dread his trips in those early days, because there was so little real contact with Russians. In contrast, he relishes his trips now.

At Alphagraphics, the first computer graphic shop in the Soviet Union, I was able to get a laser print from my portable Apple computer. Spoke with an American designer who has come to Moscow to work in graphic design for brochures, billboards, advertising, and books. Strange to walk into such a shop in Moscow and be counseled in how to use Cyrillic software in my computer by this employee from New York. Several more American businessmen came in to use their services, and it occurred to me that this kind of flow in and out of the Soviet Union from the West is becoming the norm, and not the exception.

Went to the Office of Internal Affairs to procure permission to visit a maximum-security prison—a gulag, as they used to be known—in the northernmost part of Siberia. The Minister of Prisons told me of visiting maximum-security prisons in the United States last summer, and how American authorities told him, when organizing his trip, that a Soviet journalist would never get access to such a prison, and an American photographer would only be granted permission here with difficulty. After a cup of tea, and the presentation of a bottle of brandy, my visit was promptly organized.

July 23, Norilsk

Norilsk, the Siberian city above the Arctic Circle, is the northernmost point of civilization in the Soviet Union. Home to 500 thousand people, it was established in the 1930s to mine and process metallurgical resources, and as an area in which to exile thousands of Soviet dissidents. Officially closed to foreigners, the view from an aircraft provides a glimpse of thousands of miles of barren swampland and tundra. Permanent permafrost, a layer of ice, lies beneath the ground in this region where snow falls ten months of the year, and where the temperature plummets to minus 55 degrees centigrade.

Arriving at the airport, it becomes obvious that this location in the middle of Northern Nowhere is both an important strategic base and industrial center, with silver military jets sitting on the runway, train wagons loaded with oil, satellite antennae, and missile launchers sprinkling the landscape. The airport has the surrealistic feeling of a warehouse that processes people between civilization and another realm. Descending from the airplane, one is immediately surrounded by a herd of notorious Siberian flies and mosquitoes.

My new interpreter, Andrei, explained to me a kind of de facto apartheid system that exists in the Soviet Union, which makes people hostage to the city and address marked in their internal passports. Officially, a citizen cannot change residence without finding someone in another city to trade residences, or without marrying someone who agrees to share their domicile with their new spouse. Consequently, millions of people around the Soviet Union, including former gulag prisoners in places like Norilsk, cannot migrate.

Our taxi driver from the airport, Efrim Federov, came to Norilsk 14 years ago to make "big money"—a state salary for driving his taxi, augmented by a "polar bonus." He said this decision had been the worst mistake of his life; he will leave the day he puts in his 15 years next August, and can collect his pension. Conditions here are particularly difficult—scarce food, pollution, isolation, and a severe climate.

Foundry after foundry line the road into the city, emitting huge amounts of smoky gas into the atmosphere, the fumes covering the sky and blowing in the direction of the city. When asked why people don't strike, since they are obviously angry over these conditions, Efrim said, "Are you kidding? With the large military presence here, they would simply crush striking foundry workers like mosquitoes. They would close the airport and install a curfew. And here there is only one way out—the airport. There are no roads to anywhere." When we stopped to photograph the pollution, an angry female guard came running out to reprimand me. Efrim fumed in the taxi, "She is just a dog of Soviet bureaucracy. She's living in shit, and yet she doesn't want anyone else to learn of these conditions. If I had a gun I'd shoot her—she is like an animal in a concentration camp, and 50 percent of the people here are like her."

The city is one huge prefabricated town, perhaps the ugliest and most decrepit I have ever seen. Efrim said a Hollywood crew had been visiting to do a fiction film about a CIA agent living in

Siberia. In front of the hotel, disco music blared, "Welcome to the Hotel California."

At 10:30 P.M., in full daylight, we went to the restaurant, where a woman led us to a private room and said that although the kitchen was closed, she would prepare us a meal. We were served chicken, champagne, and tomatoes—a gourmet meal for this region. She said food for the hotel restaurant was a constant problem; she had to barter for it every day. When I asked if our chicken had come from a local source or from Moscow, she said, "Oh no—it came from America." I asked in surprise how American chicken could make it here; she did not have a clue about the route it had taken, and laughed that this was just another one of the absurdities of northern Siberia.

July 24, Norilsk

The Bogins live in a prefab apartment building similar to every residence in this town, in a relatively spacious three-room apartment with all the amenities of a middle-class family—color television and a modern kitchen. At noontime, to honor our visit, Sergei, a Norilsk copper-foundry worker, brought out a bottle of brandy from which he had four shots before our lunch was over. The grandmother, Lidiya, set a table for the first American ever to visit their household. Sergei and Tatiana, his wife, originally came to Norilsk for only three years, and have now been here for 15. They, too, are looking forward to the day when they will leave: "Before it is too late."

Sergei earns 1,600 rubles a month for being the chief on his shift in a very dangerous job. Seven thousand workers are leaving the city a month, replaced by four thousand new arrivals, but it is the skilled laborers who are leaving. The state would have to pay these people at least double and maybe triple the salary not to leave. Conditions in the foundry are severe. When asked whether his friends had lung problems from the poisonous acidic gases, he said, "Of course, but the administration does not recognize lung problems as professional-related diseases unless you die."

Tatiana, who works in a bank, wanted to know if people in the West have to wait in queues for everything. She said that the situation here is so absurd and illogical that, "Four tons of money is delivered to our bank in an old bus, because they don't have a special armored car."

"I suppose anyone who had worked in Alaska for 15 years would be able to afford a nice house," Sergei said. He continued in laughter, "I'm even surprised by the patience I seem to have to deal with this. In your country there are not so many problems because you can buy guns. If they were available here, we would have done away with these people a long time ago." Tatiana added, "We have had 70 years of having to be patient, and it has affected our mentality. It is only now that the young generation is more free to consider other options."

Returning to the "Hotel California," we passed three former gulags for political prisoners, and I observed that this must be the ugliest city I have ever seen. Our taxi driver said, "Every time someone starts digging into the ground around here to build a building, they find human remains. This city was built by the hands of political prisoners, thousands of whom perished in the process."

July 25, Norilsk

In the 1930s and '40s, Stalin sent more than 300 thousand political prisoners to gulags in Norilsk, as far north in Siberia as human population can exist. Although these gulags and the incarceration of political prisoners officially ceased following Stalin's death in the early '50s, one of these prisons still remains—#288/15—now called by prisoners inside, "one of the most repressive severe-regime prisons in the Soviet Union."

I was picked up at 7:00 A.M. with my interpreter Andrei by the prison warden, Gennady Marinitch, a huge, dark-haired man in uniform with knee-high black boots. We were driven in his chauffered Volga to Prison #288/15. The day before, over the telephone, he had suggested that I come some time late in the morning. I wanted to follow the prisoners' normal routine from the time they got up to the time they went to bed. A compromise was reached, and I was told I could begin my visit from the hour the first prisoners left their barracks in the morning to go to work. Preparing for the inevitable, I expected to be escorted during my visit by a prison official.

The prison is 35 years old and controlled by 250 guards and officers. It sits inside the city limits, surrounded by two rows of 15-yard-high barbed-wire fence with razor tips, guard towers, and soldiers patrolling with German shepherds and Kalashnikov machine guns. Inside, the warden—sitting under a portrait of Lenin in his office—got busy on one of many red phones. Before long, the entire prison hierarchy—eight men—prepared to escort me on my visit.

The warden explained that the prison is called #288/15, because the maximum sentence in the Soviet Union is 15 years or the death penalty. He said, "People criticize our country for human rights. With your country's life sentences, what about your human rights?"

In the prison yard, several hundred prisoners in black uniforms and caps with shaved heads marched to a checkpoint from their barracks,

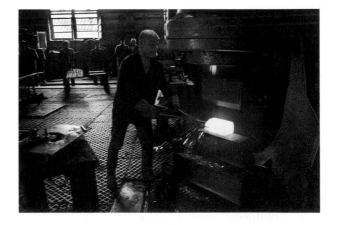

where they were counted and dismissed to hard labor inside one of the prison's many workshops.

Finally, I was taken into an almost empty barracks, where several prisoners, who had worked a night shift, were sleeping on some of the 60 cot-like beds. As I moved into position to photograph or to speak to a prisoner, several of the officials would stand beside or behind me. As we walked down the hallway, it became clear that the officers were carefully directing me to see only certain rooms. They wanted to hurry me through my visit; I would have to use my persistence and "official permission from Moscow" to assure I got anything like a true picture of life inside this prison.

I walked through the prison workshops, where prisoners build wooden furniture and construct heavy metal containers to be used in the local foundries. In every area, prisoners with emaciated, tight-skinned faces and deep, hollow eye sockets went through the motions of their routines in silence, with little expression, while prison guards stood by.

In the last of the workshops, with a bellowing furnace roaring in the background, a man with huge arms and gold front teeth took molten steel from a fire. He held the steel under a giant hydraulic hammer until it was pounded into bricks, one after another. I photographed him, and stopped to ask his name—Victor Bubnov—serving seven years for his second offense of major theft. I was told that Victor worked the most severe job inside the prison; he had chosen the job himself and had done it almost since his arrival.

After asking to be left alone, I spoke with Victor for several minutes. He said he had had a drinking problem, which led to his criminal activity. He had been in solitary twice in seven years. Officially, a prisoner can be confined for 3-15 days, but unofficially, prisoners are often kept up to six months with food only every other day, a wooden plank to sleep on, almost no light or ventilation, and a hole for a toilet. "When I first came into prison, they would put you there for anything, including not having one of your shirt buttons buttoned, and it was still completely at the officers' discretion to isolate prisoners for anything as small as looking at them in the wrong way." Victor, who will get out next May, said, "I have a hope that I will be able to earn my living when I get out, but I'm not sure. I would like to have my own piece of land and be a farmer." He receives 300 rubles a month for his work, but most of that

goes toward his food, and he will have only 2,000 rubles ($65) saved when he is released after seven years.

At that point, I pulled out a Polaroid camera and gave Victor a Polaroid of himself. This novelty took all the prison officials by surprise and before I knew it, the officials asked if I could also photograph them, in front of the prisoners, and then next to them.

I asked to see the solitary confinement cells. Major silence and deliberation. Finally, I was told that there were only one or two prisoners in

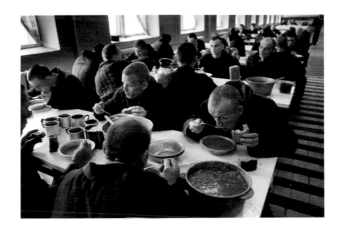

solitary, and the area was quarantined; I would not be able to see it. My interpreter Andrei, an experienced journalist who knows Soviet bureaucracy extremely well, stood by in his KGB-like black leather coat. Andrei and I agreed that our priority was to get into the solitary-confinement area, and to stay until the end of the prisoners' work shift.

In the lunch hall, prisoners sat at tables of six men with one loaf of bread, one large bowl of soup and porridge, and one vat of black tea, from which each prisoner poured into his own tin cup and bowl. The room smelled like kerosene. With a guard standing at each table, the men were given 15 minutes to eat before being led back to their barracks.

From there we were led into a room where we sat down to eat with the warden and his associates. On the table was a feast of potatoes, sausage, salad, and bread. After champagne toasts to

perestroika, question after question about life in America, and the status of prison officials and their salaries in the West, the officials seemed to relax their suspicion and enjoy meeting someone from a far land.

Still, it became clear that they hoped the day would end there. Back in the warden's office, we pulled out the trump card, and told the warden that we would be seeing the Minister of Internal Affairs back in Moscow, and would like to give him a glowing report of our visit. This inspired more internal phone calls and deliberation. It was agreed I could see two prisoners in one of the solitary cells, accompanied by a guard, for two minutes.

Several dozen cells were closed by iron doors with one small window, approximately six by ten inches, and locked with large iron padlocks. Screams emanated from several of these cells. I was allowed to look through one window. In almost total darkness inside the cell, I made out two figures, and slowly one of them made his way over, putting his face to the window to peer at me. Protesting that it was impossible to photograph through the window, the padlock was unlocked and the door opened, still leaving an iron-barred door between me and the prisoners. The prisoners first hid their eyes from the light, then stared at me. Their skin was pasty-colored. The air and smell stood still with no ventilation. As the guard relocked the cell, I asked what these two men had been imprisoned for. He told me it was for quarreling with the administration.

From the solitary confinement block, we asked to photograph the prisoners' shower, where they wash at the end of their work day. We were again told to wait, and finally were told the prisoners had already showered. At this point Andrei, who intentionally dresses and behaves to give the impression he might have an association with the KGB, exploded. "All right comrades, who do you take us for? We're not here for our pleasure but to do our jobs. Either you take us to see the prisoners shower now, or we will wait until the next shift is finished at midnight." Officials jumped into action, and we were instantly led to a shower facility where dozens of prisoners were still showering.

On my way out of the prison, another prisoner,

who looked as if he must be in his late fifties or early sixties, but is in fact 37, called me over. He said, "These people will never show you what really happens in this prison." I began to speak to him when one of the officials arrived and told the prisoner to stop dramatizing things. I told the official I wanted to talk to the prisoner privately, and the official nervously agreed. We were led to an office where we were told we could speak for five minutes in private.

Vladimir Diomin, in prison for three years for robbery, said, "This place is famous for the repression against the prisoners, and for the severe regime the prisoners are put through. They talk about *perestroika*, but here it never changes. The administration is still from the old days and they're the same. Instead of improving conditions, they are inciting fights between prisoners, to divide and conquer by giving some privileges to some prisoners who will work for the administration for a pack of cigarettes or a cup of tea. I was in a general regime colony before being moved here, because I am always speaking out. Literally, there are no political prisoners here, but there are many people here that the state finds controversial. Any kind of small infringement is treated with maximum punishment. I am not afraid to talk to you, because the way I'm living my life here, I cannot live long. There is only one goal in the minds of all of these prisoners, and that is to survive and stay alive. We cannot have any contact visits from a woman unless we are married, so in fact the system breeds homosexuality. I have been put in solitary so many times I cannot remember. Officially, I can't be put in solitary for having talked to you, but I am sure there is better than a 75 percent chance they will find another reason to put me there in a couple of days."

The interpreter and I were then taken again to the same room in the administration building where we had eaten lunch, and presented with yet another table of food, two more bottles of champagne, and a bottle of brandy. I was given a wooden box of gifts—made by prisoners—that the officials wanted me to take back to America.

The following night, one of the officials—the accountant—arrived at my hotel door, delivering the box of gifts from the prison. We invited him to join us for dinner at the hotel, and after much deliberation, his wife Nadegda joined him, and we ate dinner together. He said that the prison officials had been in a state of shock, "like snow in the summertime," when they were given the call from Moscow that an American would be visiting the prison. Such a reality, he said, was inconceivable. Neither he nor his wife had ever met an American previously, and he asked if I could show him a dollar bill. They were both overwhelmed when I gave them a five-dollar bill as a gift.

Nikolai, the prison accountant, then insisted that we join him and his wife back at their apartment for a goodnight cognac. On the way to the apartment he pointed out that all of the buildings in Norilsk had been built by political prisoners, and that the architects who had designed the city, also gulag prisoners, were architects from Leningrad. The name Norilsk means "on face," and the story goes that these architects had designed the city so that anyone walking in any direction would be stung in the face by the freezing wind, punishment to all the bureaucrats who would live in the city they built. He also pointed out that Siberian Russian is a very precise Russian, because it comes from all of the exiled intelligentsia.

Upstairs, in the apartment built by political prisoners, Nikolai and Nadegda graciously offered sweets, coffee, and cognac, and a jam preserve made from a rare berry found in Siberia. They said that in the summertime in Siberia, when the sun never sets, it used to be customary for friends to drop in to see one another at 2:00 or 3:00 in the morning. Because the economic situation in the country has become so bad in the last two years, and food is rationed, they don't do it anymore. He produced a photo album of his family, and the evening finished with a dance that Nikolai proposed to my wife to the tune of prisoners' music that he had recorded inside Prison #288/15.

July 26, Norilsk

In a town of 300 thousand people, more than 100 thousand employees work at three foundries that export hundreds of millions of dollars' of copper, nickel, and platinum each year, as well as producing metal for the country's own needs.

Mikhail Steklov, an ex-weight-lifting champion, is the director of the Norilsk Nickel factory. Mr. Steklov represents the new generation—engaging, candid, and humble. He spoke directly about the ecological disaster of which his factory is at the center, and about his desire for a national transformation to a market economy. Steklov, whose wife is a doctor, said, "I'm very afraid for the health of my two children, who were born and raised here. Norilsk is a city of 300 thousand people; if you look at the wastes in the air, versus the number of people, it must be one of the most polluted cities in the world. This is not taking into account the climate, which is as severe as anywhere in the world. You'll see the problems for yourselves—acid gas, metal dust, and high temperatures inside the foundries, causing lung disease, a whole range of dermatological diseases, and cancer. Everywhere it is known that nickel is highly carcinogenic. The acid gas that our foundries emit is many times worse than the foundry that you visited in Montchegorsk. Besides, Montchegorsk is so close to Finland, Sweden, Denmark, and Norway—who have tough ecological laws—that their situation must be controlled. Here, we are so far away from any major population centers that the state does not pay so much attention to these questions. Like a lot of things in the Soviet Union, the laws necessary to improve the ecological situation are not being legislated."

Steklov, who earns 2,500-3,000 rubles a month as the factory boss, and who is not a member of the Communist Party, although this would have been obligatory five years ago, says he is in favor of privatization. He believes that this would allow the foundry to earn profits at a rate commensurate with the world market, improve production, and find more active solutions to ecological problems.

I ended my visit by offering my host a bottle of Kahlua. Mikhail said he hoped that our departure would be successful—unlike in wintertime, when planes get stuck here for up to three weeks. With an infectious smile, he said, "We

Russians here are optimistic, because if you're not, you'll never survive. There is nothing to make us optimistic, but we remain so anyway."

July 27, Norilsk

A Norwegian ecological expert visiting Norilsk said today that this city with its metallurgical foundries emits 2.3 tons of sulphur dioxide into the air each year, making it the most acid-polluted city in the world. The air in this region contains 2,000 micrograms of nickel per cubic meter—with 350 being the maximum number before conditions become dangerous. Inside the nickel and copper foundries, the number is 10,000. He said the only way that this situation could be improved would be to close the city.

July 28, Moscow

Walked today along Moscow's Arbat Street, where artists draw portraits, street musicians perform, vendors sell Gorbachev dolls, painters exhibit works satirizing the Soviet bureaucracy, sailors on leave dance and drink champagne with their girlfriends, and elderly men wearing World War II decorations walk in a daze. A few years ago, this whole scene would have seemed extraordinary in its festivity and animation.

July 29, Moscow

Just when I think that I am starting to understand the Soviet psyche, I have an experience that reveals how little I really know. Two years ago, when I spent a month working on a project focusing on life in Moscow, I met a couple, Vadim and Greta, whom Karen Schneider and I profiled, and with whom we became friends. At that time Vadim and Greta both spoke limited English, and both idealized—and dreamed about visiting and perhaps living in—the United States. Since that time, Vadim made his way to America. He was seriously mugged in the bus station in Manhattan on his first night, but went on to remain for a year, visiting 17 states and waiting tables in Cambridge for several months. Greta then followed and stayed for three months.

Both returned seriously disillusioned; both now feel completely disappointed by what they see as a country with wealth in the hands of a few, very little culture, and little real freedom of information and intellectual analysis of world events.

This experience has reinforced their belief that the best solution for the Soviet Union would be a czarist monarchy, returning to what existed before the Bolshevik Revolution. Both ferociously blame Jews for that revolution, and for the destruction of Russian civilization and culture.

Vadim and Greta, who were divorced for a time and then reunited, remarried officially in the Russian Orthodox church last year. They seem to be devout born-again Christians. Greta, whose parents are both Lithuanian and live in Vilnius, now vehemently denies these roots—unlike the majority of her compatriots—and prefers to think of herself as Russian. She says that the subjugation of Lithuania following World War II was a Soviet system phenomenon, and not the doing of the Russians.

Shocked by Vadim and Greta's blatant anti-Semitism, I recounted this to two more Russians—my current interpreter, an ex-journalist, and an ex-Soviet navy interpreter who drives us to and from the airport in Moscow. I was disappointed to find that they also embrace this vision of the Bolshevik Revolution, and the subsequent downfall of Russian culture, as a Jewish-inspired transformation.

July 30, Khabarovsk

Now flying seven hours east of Moscow to the Soviet Far East and the city of Khabarovsk, just above China, and one of the last stops on the Trans-Siberian Express. It would be possible to fly to New York from Moscow in about the same time. We are crossing seven different time zones on this flight, and heading into a region where one finds a mixture of Siberian and Asian culture and civilization.

Left hundreds of journalists behind in Moscow: the "pack" who have arrived to write about the Bush-Gorbachev summit, and who will be instant "experts" about life in the Soviet Union after their

visit of a few days. More and more I am becoming aware of the pitfalls of journalism. Few journalists actually speak the Russian language, which is fundamental to understanding Soviet views or contemporary realities. Am convinced now that the worst mistake and disservice that a journalist could make covering this country would be to put anything into a nutshell—because the truth is complicated, contradictory, always changing, and nuanced.

July 31, Khabarovsk

I imagined there would be a mix of Russian and Asian culture in this Far Eastern Soviet city, but this is not the case. It is entirely Russian, with no trace of Asian influence. Train and plane schedules are regulated by Moscow time—although the local time is seven hours in advance—a symbol of how the entire way of life is still completely Russian. The architecture is Stalinesque and functional, like most Soviet cities. The economy here is no better, and is, in fact, a bit worse than in other parts of the country. Food shops have even more meager supplies than elsewhere, and conversations always include the word "difficult."

Many people, in discussing the future, prefer a new order where each republic becomes independent and Russia looks after itself: Thus, Yeltsin seems to be the man of the hour. But it becomes clear that change is happening at a slow pace, and will take many years to radically overhall the economic infrastructures.

August 1, Birobidjan

Drove west two hours from Khabarovsk across the barren Siberian landscape to Birobidjan, a small town that was created in 1934 by Stalin to be the first Jewish state in the world.

Vladimir Belinker, editor of the *Birobidjan Star*, one of three Yiddish newspapers in the world, sat in front of a portrait of Lenin, with a yarmulke on his desk, and explained how this experiment had never worked. The early 1930s were a time of general hardship and starvation throughout the Soviet Union. More than 50 thousand Soviet Jews, as well as Jews from 14 other countries, came to this city to settle, following Stalin's offer to create a Jewish homeland in Far Eastern Siberia. At that time Yiddish was the only language spoken in these streets. The reality of this "Jewish homeland" began to fizzle in the late '30s, when Stalin's repression forced Jews to abandon their traditions and, ultimately, for many to leave the country. Today, approximately nine thousand people, or 4 percent of the population, carry passports in which the official nationality is Jewish.

It is difficult to observe any kind of Jewish tradition beyond the Hebrew language classes being taught to emigrating Jews, the Yiddish newspaper,

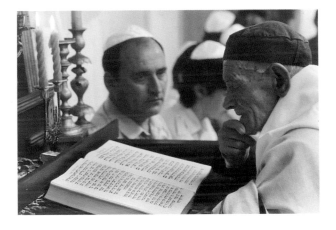

or the synagogue—which has difficulty assembling the necessary ten people for a quorum on any given Sabbath. I asked how this could be possible, given the fact that it was Stalin himself who had created the idea of this Jewish state. Vladimir laughed, and said the contradictions of state policy in this country are abundant. The Jews who came in the early '30s were religious, but subsequently all Jewish holidays were prohibited, and for that matter, anyone practicing any Jewish tradition became known—or arrested—as a "saboteur."

The pervasiveness of this repression became evident when two Jewish men, in response to my inquiry about kosher shops in this town, needed to have the concept of kosher explained. In the last 18 months, 1,800 Jews have left for Israel, and it is apparent that the pace of this emigration is accelerating. At a Hebrew and Jewish traditions

class for people emigrating, Klara Portnaya said, "Most of the Jews here want to leave this so-called 'Jewish state' as soon as possible. It could not be worse anywhere else in the world."

August 2, Birobidjan

I came expecting to see Jewish tradition being practiced in the world's original Jewish state. I have found two generations who have lost any sense of religious identity or culture, Jewish or otherwise.

David Waiserman, a local historian and the grandson of Leon Trotsky, helped me understand the process that has accomplished this phenomenon. He said, "Twenty-six of the 43 delegates participating in a congress of the Social Democratic Party in London in 1903, which led 14 years later to the Bolshevik Revolution, were of Jewish nationality. Given this association, a kind of systematic anti-Semitism took place under czarist rule, prohibiting most of the 3.5 million Jews living principally in the Ukraine, Moldavia, and Byelorussia from working in factories or farms, migrating to large cities, or attending large universities. Thus, following the Revolution in 1917, a Soviet Jewish commission attached to the communist government and financed by an American organization, set out to find a region suitable for a Jewish homeland. A decision was made to create a Jewish autonomous region in Birobidjan, following one of these expeditions in 1928. The area, 72 thousand square kilometers—later reduced to 36 thousand—was practically uninhabited at that time. By 1939, there were 28 thousand Jews living in this region. Most were either communists or members of the Komsomol Communist Youth League, and thus not religious. Although their parents and grandparents had celebrated Jewish tradition and culture, the idea was to create a Jewish state under communist orientation, not a religious state.

"Thus," Waiserman went on, "although Stalin did not create this state, he eventually buried it. Though the Jewish religion was rarely practiced and traditions kept very discreet, until 1937 there were 14 Yiddish schools, a famous Yiddish

theater, two Yiddish high schools, and two Yiddish newspapers and magazines. By 1948, following Stalin's decree prohibiting anyone from being 'cosmopolitan' or from practicing any ethnic tradition, all of these institutions were shut down. This repression almost completely wiped out any Jewish tradition—religion, language, art, and culture. We are only now trying to revive this 40-year abyss."

He continued, "This revival is very difficult however, with the current large wave of Jewish emigration, which will be impossible to stop. We are losing our best people—engineers, doctors, scientists. And not only Jews are leaving, but 27 percent of the entire population of this region, as a result of mixed marriages, giving non-Jews the right to move with their spouses and families. I laugh when they say that Jews represent only 4 percent of the population here. If you analyze the lists of people leaving, 40 percent listed their nationality previously as Russian. Now that they want to emigrate, they have found it very easy to find papers documenting that their grandmother or grandfather was Jewish.

"Before, it was very dangerous in the Soviet Union to be Jewish. By 1950, there was not a single Jew in the Soviet politburo. Still, out of 380 people serving on the central committee of the Communist Party, only two are Jewish. I could not study at the Academy of Political Science because I am Jewish. But today this status allows you to emigrate—a very expensive commodity. I just came from Leningrad, where unofficially it costs 45,000 rubles to have your nationality changed to Jewish in your passport."

Elisabeth and Isaac Belinker, whose parents brought them to this region in the late 1930s and early '40s, still speak Yiddish together, but must speak Russian to their children, who were prohibited from learning the language. Elisabeth said, "All Yiddish schools were shut down in 1937. Teachers were either imprisoned, killed, or left. There was total repression. It was a closed area—we were allowed to emigrate here, but not allowed to leave."

Today, with a crucifix bearing Jesus Christ

hanging on their wall, the couple admits that, like their fellow Jews in Birobidjan, they have lost practically all tradition or sense of religion. Elisabeth said, "We are only now trying to revive our roots. The concept of being Jewish means nothing to us. It is a formality. Maybe the new generation will feel something different." When I asked her husband Isaac what it meant for him to be Jewish, he said, "Nothing at all. I make no distinction between myself and anyone else—I don't believe in nationalism." Yet when I asked if he thought of himself as a Jew or a Russian, he said, "I am Jewish." Several of his children—some of whom will be leaving soon for Israel—began to laugh at both the confusion of his remarks, as well as the absurdity of what has become of the world's first Jewish state.

August 3, Birobidjan/Khabarovsk

Returned from dinner to hear on the news that in Gorky Park, Moscow—seven time zones away—there were major riots today between veteran paratroopers who had gathered to celebrate an anniversary, and police. Although the conflict seemed to stem primarily from too much vodka, it makes one wonder if this could be one of the first signs of general chaos that might occur as a result of the devasted economy and various nationalist campaigns.

Checking out of the hotel in Birobidjan after staying three nights, I was billed 110 rubles, or the equivalent of just more than three dollars for two rooms—one for myself and the other for the interpreter. We went to dinner tonight in Khabarovsk at a joint-venture private Japanese sushi restaurant and were charged $110 for two—the equivalent of 3,300 rubles.

August 4, Prokopyevsk

After an eight-hour flight, including three plane changes and a 50-kilometer taxi ride, we arrived at the Hotel Centralnaya, in downtown Prokopyevsk—the first foreigners lodged in this coal mining town, said by many to be one of the poorest in the Soviet Union. The hotel has no

bathroom, running water, or telephone in the rooms. In our room there is a television—without an electrical cord. But a team of four women who run the desk and clean the rooms, fascinated by us, have been running up and down the halls, bringing us cucumbers and tomatoes, tea, towels. Three women came in this morning without knocking to watch my wife get dressed, fascinated by a "Western" woman.

August 5, Prokopyevsk

Walking behind the sagging administrative and locker-room facilities of the Centralnaya mine—one of the oldest of the 15 mines in the Prokopyevsk region—I almost stumbled into a group of miners having a smoke after their shift. Camouflaged in black soot from head to toe, the group was almost indistinguishable from the coal-scorched earth on which they sat. Only the whites of their eyes, the gold caps on their teeth, and burning cigarette ends glittered through the soot.

I identified myself as an American photo correspondent. The group seemed a bit dazed,

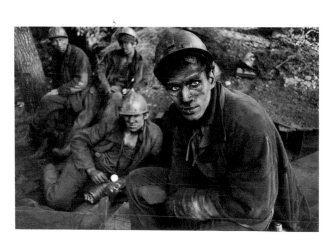

since I had appeared from nowhere in the middle of this provincial town in deep southern Siberia. I asked them questions about their work in this highly unmechanized coal mine. Years earlier, I had been down several gold mines in South Africa, and many miners had told me that they enjoyed their work; I asked this group if they enjoyed theirs.

Among the group, one young man stood out.

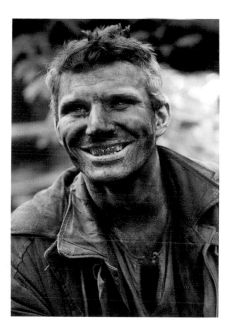

With blond hair barely discernable underneath the dirt, high Slavic cheekbones, and four shining gold front teeth, Nikolai Rossoka sat with an axe over his shoulder. "We have grown up in this town from where it is difficult to escape, and where there is no other way to make a living for our families than to do this work. None of us would be here if we had another choice."

Nikolai, who at 25 had already worked nine years in the mine, said practically his whole family worked there—one of his two brothers, his father, his wife's father, and his uncle—who had been crushed when the roof of a seam caved in. Nikolai, his wife Lena, and their three-year-old daughter live in a two-story miner's barracks in the middle of town. His mother and father live across the street in a two-room wooden dacha-like house, with white cotton-lace curtains. Removing two layers of black overclothes to wash off soot in the mine's grimy shower facilities, Nikolai invited us to visit his family at their home.

Although small, without a toilet or hot water, the apartment was immaculate, with freshly painted walls, a new JVC television, and wedding crystal glasses shining through veneered cabinets in the living room. News of our arrival quickly spread through the neighborhood, and we were joined by relatives and friends who stopped by to have a look at these foreign beings. Nikolai's family, delighted by this occasion, excitedly re-counted how all his friends called him "America," because of his lifelong dream to go there.

Proudly putting American music on the hi-fi system that he had bought with his meager salary, Nikolai turned the conversation to the reality of ever making a visit to the United States. With vodka having burned away some of the illusions, I looked around the group and could see sadness in Nikolai's sisters, who were convinced that none of them would ever have the means to go. In their eyes, one could see how the evening's festivities had temporarily transported them to another land, and had suddenly just landed back in Prokopyevsk.

More vodka, dancing, and finally the evening concluded early in the morning with Nikolai and Lena insisting that we come again for dinner the next night, and walking us back to the Hotel Centralnaya—which could have come straight out of a Soviet version of the movie *Paris, Texas*.

The next day I went to the mine to accompany Nikolai underground, after spending a day getting permission from the vice-president of the local miners' association. The director of the mine refused, saying conditions underground were extremely dangerous in this mine—one of the most dangerous in the Soviet Union. If anything were to happen to me, the first American in Prokopyevsk, it would trigger a scandal that would shut down the mine and leave the miners unemployed for a month.

August 7, Prokopyevsk

Am sad and nostalgic today. Last night, Nikolai and Lena—after both had spent long, hard days at work—served Karin, Andrei and me one of the nicest meals I have ever had. It was obvious how much care and preparation had gone into it, and what economic effort had been made.

As Nikolai and Lena walked us back to our hotel following dinner, we passed the elementary school. Nikolai pointed and laughed, "When I was young they taught us about how cruel the capitalist

system is, that it leaves young children starving without food. I was so stupid to believe this propaganda." I found myself caught between not wanting to disillusion Nikolai's dreams and hopes for America, and my grief that in fact there are children starving and homeless adults living in the streets of my country. I told him that I had also endured a brainwashing about the Soviet people while growing up, and tried to explain the huge disparity in the spectrum of living conditions for American people. We agreed that the truth about both of our countries is very mixed.

When we said good night, we said goodbye. We said we would see one another again, but underneath, we all had serious doubts.

As it turned out, our plane has been delayed today, and I am sitting at a table with a view to the rear of the hotel, looking down at the route that Nikolai takes every noon to his job underground. Nikolai just passed underneath my window, carrying his pink plastic sack that holds the soap he uses to wash off the coal. This happenstance sighting drove home the fact that Nikolai, with his dreams to be somewhere else, will still be here—God knows how many more years—slaving underground for rubles that have no value.

August 10, Ulan Ude

The Datsun Monastery is the seat of Buddhist training and worship in the Soviet Union. Buddhism suffered from repression, like every other religion during the Stalin years. The traditional religious faith of the Buryat, a tribe representing approximately 250 thousand people in this region and dating back to the ninth century, is undergoing a tremendous revival. The lamas, or religious masters of the faith, sit inside the temple involved in deep meditation, while worshippers come to pray to Buddha. Surrounded by holiness and religious statues inside this shrine, the first words to me from the acting Dalai Lama—momentarily breaking off one of his chants—were, "Would you like to change money?"

The value of hard currency, or *valuta*, as it is called here, has permeated all aspects of life in the Soviet Union.

August 11-12, Lake Baikal

It was perhaps not coincidence that we encountered a death as we arrived at the mouth of Lake Baikal. The ecosystem of the largest fresh-water lake in the world is under threat of murder from reckless pollution by Soviet industry.

Driving through the village of Kolesovo, we encountered a funeral for 35-year-old Leonid Vlasov. His body lay in state in the family's home; women, friends and relatives mourned around the makeshift casket, surrounded by wreathes of flowers and bottles of vodka. The men stayed outside until it was time to walk the body, in the pouring rain, to the cemetery three kilometers away. A four-piece band played funeral music. As the deceased's mother started to pass out from grief, one of her surviving sons opened a bottle of spirits, took a mouthful, and spit it on her face to revive her. The rest of the vodka would be consumed later, during toasts to Leonid, who died of a heart attack on a Friday night, one might suspect from excessive drink.

Along on our expedition was Anatoly Kuklin, a Buryat journalist who writes for the ecological magazine *Our Baikal*. Anatoly, who made love for the first time in a rowboat on the lake and who was married nearby, speaks about this natural treasure with great passion. Representing 20 percent of the globe's fresh water, it would take all of the rivers in the world two hundred years to fill Lake Baikal, which measures 1,640 kilometers at its deepest point, and has a surface size of 31 thousand square kilometers.

Anatoly summarized the situation confronting the lake, which locals call "the sea." "Although Lake Baikal has a tremendously efficient ecosystem that naturally purifies itself, paper mills and other industries alongside Baikal's tributaries have recklessly dumped their wastes, paying no attention to the fact that unless this is stopped, the lake will be completely dead in less than a hundred years." The seal population has been dying at an unnatural rate in recent years, and fishermen have been catching smaller yields than before, and of far smaller size.

As we drove through a fishing village on our

way to Baikalsk, we stopped to photograph an elderly man, Vassily Ubeev, of Buryat origin. His wife immediately invited us all for tea. Tea became a feast. Anatoly explained that the Buryats, of Mongolian origin with Asiatic features, are split today between Buddhists and Russian Orthodox. As Siberians, he said, this kind of hospitality, gentleness, and strength, is completely natural. "You have to remember what kind of people can survive here."

The fish processing plant in Posolsk was shut down, because there were no fish to process, either from Lake Baikal, or from the Baltic and Caspian Seas—from where the plant had been importing fish ever since the lake had become less fertile.

We stopped at the mouth of one of many small tributaries feeding into the lake. Until recently, one of the biggest problems confronting the lake's ecosystem had been the timber floating down these tributaries on their way to the paper mills. The logs got stuck and sunk; the eventual decomposition of this timber was swallowing high and unnatural volumes of oxygen needed by living organisms in the lake. This problem had been solved by using prisoners to keep the logs from jamming.

Reaching Baikalsk, we witnessed what has become a common sight during our journey across this country: a factory—in this case a paper mill—with stacks emitting clouds of billowing smoke that completely fogged the sky and could be smelled for miles.

Before my guide, Anatoly Kuklin, and I parted, we shook hands and I thanked him for his help and generosity. He said, "I am more than happy to help anyone who can tell the world about what is happening to our great lake. Please make people know that this lake does not belong to the Soviet Union—it belongs to the world, and we must all help to save it."

August 14, Moscow

A young girl comes home from school one day and asks her father for one ruble, because her class is raising money for the Communist Party in Angola. The father responds, "No, I won't donate money, because there is no Communist Party in Angola."

The daughter returns to school and tells her teacher, who sends her home that evening to tell her father that the class is raising money for the starving children in Angola. The next day, the girl returns to school with two rubles. The teacher asks what happened to change the father's mind and the daughter replies, "My father contributed two rubles, because he said there must be a communist government in Angola, if children are starving there."

August 17, Ashkhabad

Throughout my trip around the Soviet Union, the overwhelming presence of the military complex in this country has been ever-present. With a defense budget exceeding $180 billion a year, and more than four million men serving, the Soviet Union has the second-largest military in the world, trailing only China in terms of numbers. There are military bases in most cities. Men in uniform are seen everywhere. We saw missile silos in northern Siberia, a camouflaged missile battery in the Far East, and military radar and fighter planes at almost every airport.

The army training base in Ashkhabad, the capital of the Islamic republic of Turkmenia, 40 kilometers north of Iran in central Asia, is one of 13 bases serving the military regions into which the Soviet Union is divided. Currently 322 new conscripts are undergoing basic training, with a staff of approximately 160 officers. In the Soviet Union, every 18-year-old man is obliged to serve two years in the armed forces.

During my day at the base, these young men, representing approximately 40 different nationalities, but predominately from the central Asian republics, were awakened with reveille at 6:00 A.M. and moved immediately into a strictly disciplined, daily program. The soldiers, wearing khaki fatigues, a belt with the Soviet Red Army star on the gold buckle, black army boots, and desert safari hats, move through their paces in an air of extreme seriousness. Heavy physical exercise; six hours a day of technical training with 120mm mortar ground-to-air missiles, bazookas, grenades, Kalashnikovs, bayonets, and hand-to-hand combat; dinner; bed by 10:00 P.M.—this routine is followed six days a week.

"I don't believe the state spends enough money on the army," said Colonel Nikolai Rogojkin, who is in charge of all Ashkhabad military bases. "We need to develop equipment, and the salaries of officers need to be raised. And we need as many men as we have to defend all of the numerous borders of the Soviet Union. And if we cut the army, what will we do with the people that are cut?

"It is true that the Communist Party and the army are closely connected, even if this relationship is not an official one. I am against the separation of these two organs, but on the other hand, if an officer is well-qualified, there is no reason why he should not serve in that position, even if he is not a member of the party. I absolutely believe the Cold War is over, and this transition has brought about dramatic changes in our tactical preparations. We no longer have large-scale military maneuvers as we did before."

Colonel Alexander Smirnoff, age 38, is in charge of the training regiment. "I am for the idea of a volunteer professional army, as in the States, but you cannot solve all of these problems in one day. The people who talk about a military coup in this country are stupid. In Vilnius and Tbilisi, it was the politicians that got the army involved. It is not the job of the military to intervene inside our own country. I am a communist, and I believe that the party should be involved in the army, but in what role, we will have to see. I believe in the ideals of communism. Granted, this kind of communism under Stalin was not practiced. In any case, the Communist Party today does not reject the idea of a free market. We are looking for the best solutions for everybody."

A new conscript from Kazakhstan, Sergei Gerlitz, age 19, said, "I have four brothers and two sisters, my father is a mechanic and my mother is not working. My father is of German origin and my mother Russian. I was called up on

May 20. I will get out in June of 1993. I think that most of the things that we are trained for here will be completely useless in the case of a real war. We will be the canon fodder, while the officers will take over and use the mortars we are being trained to fire, for example. I don't believe in communism, and I am not a member of the party.

"After the army, I would like to get a job as a train conductor, because they promise you an

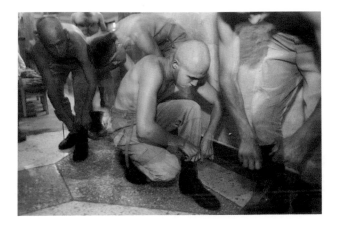

apartment with this job. I will work several years, and then I would like to study some more. I have only one message for the American people—Come on guys, let's live in peace together."

August 19, Ashkhabad

Received word this morning that there was a coup at 4:00 A.M. Moscow time. Gorbachev is under arrest in the Crimea, relieved because of "ill health." He has been replaced by a "state committee for the extraordinary situation." Yeltsin has called for a general strike. Tanks are circulating in the streets in Moscow. There are orders from this new committee against any form of demonstration or strike, and martial law has been imposed in six regions: the Baltic States, Armenia, Georgia, Azerbaijan. Phone lines to the outside world have been cut. All Soviet borders have been closed to Soviet citizens. Television and radio towers have been taken over by the military, and only one official station is airing. Yeltsin has called the situation a military coup. He and his supporters

have signed a declaration calling this an unconstitutional situation. He has barricaded himself inside the Russian Federation Building, surrounded by tanks which have defected from the Red Army.

In Turkmenia, standing at the Ministry of Foreign Affairs, a number of Turkmenian officials nervously listened to the news this morning. One commented, "I wonder if we will all be rounded up in a stadium tomorrow like in Chile during the coup." Another said, "Shit, it will be like 1937 all over again." The Turkmenian people—content once again to worship their Muslim faith, a reality they attribute to Gorbachev—feel threatened by the new situation.

This evening, on the way back from a village on the border between Turkmenia and Iran, we passed a long convoy of tanks moving toward Ashkhabad in the desert. The dust from their tracks was the same as I remember from the tanks in the Saudi Arabian desert and Iraq—a flashback to a situation that had, until now, moved deep into my memory during this trip.

Decided that due to this "extraordinary" situation— as the television called it last night—we needed to get to Moscow immediately. With a small bribe and much discussion over the technicalities of changing an Aeroflot ticket, we have succeeded in getting a flight at 4:30 in the morning, Moscow time. It appears that our itinerary, which was to take us to Yerevan and then Tbilisi, is now in serious danger. I commented to the interpreter that this situation had really screwed up my plans, and Andrei laughed and said, "David, forget your trip. This situation has screwed up the rest of my life."

August 21, Moscow

Arrived in Moscow at approximately 10:00 A.M., exhausted. Streets in the center of the city near the Kremlin are all barricaded by tanks and armored personnel carriers and lines of soldiers. The Russian Federation Building is ringed by debris, buses, and tanks that Yeltsin supporters have erected to protect him. The building is surrounded by thousands of demonstrators.

The city has the feel of a Surrealist movie. Muscovites are in the streets heeding Yeltsin's call for a general strike. Some are walking around the soldiers and tanks; children are climbing up on tanks talking to the soldiers, fascinated by their uniforms and equipment. Informal group discussions and arguments happen all over—some between civilians, others between civilians and soldiers, whose right to occupy the city is being challenged. Still others are taking advantage of the situation to visit stores and shop. I have the impression that many people understand the gravity of the situation, and many do not.

Outside the Russian Federation Building, thousands of demonstrators fervently cheered Yeltsin and Andrei Sakharov's wife, Elena Bonner. I am reminded of scenes during the revolutions in East Germany and Czechoslovakia. I have also been struck by a passivity to the situation by the Russian people—scenes of a city under occupation

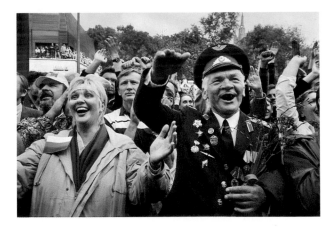

with a new status quo in the making. Like in Bucharest, I have the sense that people have no clear idea what will come, and feel they ultimately will have little control over the process of change.

Frequently, I have seen Soviet citizens coming to the soldiers' defense, telling crowds that these young men are victims of the situation, just doing their job. This sentiment seems to be generally shared. One Russian man commented to Andrei the interpreter, "This fucking country! They don't even know how to do a coup d'état right."

The night will be without sleep, to see if—as

rumored—a convoy of tanks will descend upon the Russian Federation Building to remove Yeltsin and seize control. I have taken a hotel room across the river in the Ukraine Hotel, with a view of the situation. We are getting CNN in the room—once again, as in China and in the Gulf, I am meters from the situation and can actually get more information from a television station beamed from Atlanta. During the night there are occasional sounds of automatic weapon fire. A few tanks have tried to approach the Russian Federation Building, and have been surrounded by angry protestors. During this situation, three people have been left dead.

It is pouring rain as I wake up in the morning.

August 22, Moscow

Returned to the Russian Federation Building, where the Russian Parliament met. By afternoon, driving through the city, tanks began pulling out of their positions around Red Square, and before long it was clear that the coup had failed. In the evening, drove to the airport, where Soviet officials take off and arrive, and waited for Gorbachev to return from the Crimea. At approximately 2:30 A.M., a fleet of Soviet cars pulled out of the airport from a secret gate, and took off toward the Kremlin at 140 kilometers an hour.

August 23, Moscow

Awakened at 5:30 A.M. by a call from my brother. Went to my hotel room window, overlooking the bridge leading to the Russian Federation Building, and could see tanks manned by army defectors who had rallied around Yeltsin, pulling across the bridge. Soviet citizens cheered their heroes, who had become symbolic of the revolution against the coup. Went back to the Russian Federation Building later in the morning to see Yeltsin address a large crowd. He has become the hero of the putdown of the coup. Later, went to a press conference where Gorbachev described what he had been through, and mapped a sketchy course of his loyalty to the Communist Party. Elsewhere in the city, a crowd tore down a statue of KGB founder, Felix Dzerzhinsky.

August 24, Moscow

At Communist Party headquarters, a messenger brought an edict signed by Gorbachev and Yeltsin to shut down the building until further notice. Attended the session in Parliament that Gorbachev presided over with Yeltsin.

August 25, Moscow

Today the Soviet Union held a state funeral for the three people killed during the disturbances. Hundreds of thousands of people walked through the streets of Moscow behind caskets to the sound of classical music aired from loudspeakers. Finished the day at the largest statue of Lenin in Moscow, which many people rumored would be torn down this night. It was not. The Moscow City Council currently does not have enough money in its coffers to do so.

August 26-September 1, Moscow

Woke up on Monday morning to hear on CNN that Gorbachev would resign his position as Communist Party chief.

Photographed Gorbachev and Yeltsin at the Kremlin, addressing the Chamber of People's Deputies. As Gorbachev walked out at the end of the day, he saw my brother, who has been photographing him for *Newsweek* since the day he took office. Peter exclaimed, "*Druzhba* (friendship), Mikhail Sergeivich," and Gorbachev reacted with the warmest smile I have seen on his face since the coup. I could see that it was important that his friends from the West were still with him, and maybe Peter—the photographer he had seen from Moscow to Prague to Washington over the last six years—came to symbolize this support.

On Sunday, Muscovites came out in the thousands to celebrate "Moscow Day," an annual event which has taken on particular significance this year. My brother says he will remember it as the day the Russians came out to smile again. Everywhere around us Russians danced together—

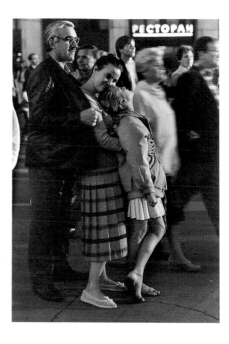

young and old; people dressed up in costumes from earlier periods, and teenagers roller-skated in front of the Kremlin, carrying the new Russian flag. It was as if—collectively—the Russian people had gotten something off their chests and were now free to rejoice, and to start living for a different future.

Karin and I had a dinner at Tren Mos, an American-style restaurant owned by a man from New Jersey, to thank our interpreters Andrei and Natasha, and Dima, our taxi driver, for everything they had done for us, and to say goodbye to our friends. In true Russian style, the evening unfolded with toast after toast—to our friendship, to Russia, and to our future meetings. The night finished early in the morning as we closed the bar at the Hotel Metropol.

Fifty thousand kilometers, some 20 Aeroflot plane trips, 15 cities, and seven republics later, our 70 days around the Soviet Union are coming to an end.

The air is starting to change now. Autumn is coming. Children everywhere are going back to school.

ACKNOWLEDGMENTS

The Russian Heart is dedicated to my wife Karin, who traveled around the Soviet Union with me, and whose support, compassion, and belief in my work have been my constant source of strength. It is also dedicated to my brother Peter, whose photographic coverage of the Soviet Union for *Newsweek* since 1985, and whose affection for the Soviet people, opened many doors for this project, and gave me great inspiration.

This book, and the work I have done covering every major revolution in the last seven years, could not have happened without the support of the *Detroit Free Press*, for whom I have been a photographer since 1980. I would particularly like to thank Publisher Neal Shine, Executive Editor Heath Meriwether, then-Assistant Managing Editor Randy Miller, and Director of Photography Mike Smith for their faith and support. They sent me to the Soviet Union for three months to compile this coverage, which was first published as a thirty-page series and supplement in the newspaper. I would also like to thank Assistant Director of Photography Marcia Prouse, Photo Editors Susan Tusa and Chris Magerl, Printers Helen McQuerry, Jessica Trevino and Diane Bond, Foreign Editors Joe Ricci and Chuck Mitchell, and Layout Designer John Goecke for the tremendous work they did to get this quickly into the newspaper following the Soviet coup.

The photographic agency Black Star, under the direction of Ben Chapnick, embraced this project from its inception. With editorial assistance from Yukiko Launois and Linda Ferrer, and with the efforts of Ann Stack and the entire Black Star research staff, the agency has been successful in placing the work in magazines and newspapers around the world. Linda Ferrer played a very special role in representing my interests at Aperture during the layout and design of this book.

This project could not have been completed without the assistance of Russian interpreters Natasha Lebedeva and Andrei Agafonov, who traveled with us throughout our journey. Their spirits and souls inspired an affection for the entire Soviet people.

Marc Grosset, Guillaume Valabrèque, Sylvie Languin, and Chantal Soler from the Rapho Agency in Paris, with a humanist tradition of photo reportage and strong interest in the Soviet Union, gave me invaluable advice and support for this project.

Constantin Petrochenko, the Attaché de Presse at the ex-Soviet embassy in Paris was invaluable in helping to arrange the necessary visas we needed to visit 15 cities in seven republics.

Thanks also to Igor Tabakov, President of the Soviet Photographers' Union, who introduced me to photographers across the ex-Soviet Union.

I would like to thank the *Time* bureau in Moscow, and Photo Editor Michele Stephenson, who put me on assignment for the magazine during the coup. I would also like to thank the AP and AFP bureaus in Moscow, who transmitted my work to the States, and whose esprit de corps during the coup was very uplifting.

Thanks to Dr. Verena Frey and Leica Cameras for their support of my work in the Soviet Union. Thanks also to Nikon, Inc.

And, finally, I could not have been more fortunate than to have worked with the Aperture Foundation, under the direction of Michael Hoffman, who has embraced this book with the same sensitivity, care, and aesthetic excellence for which Aperture is renowned. My editor has been Rebecca Busselle, whose enthusiasm for this project, photographic sensitivity, and intellect have been nothing but a pleasure to be associated with. Working with designer Wendy Byrne has been a series of wonderful surprises. And I would like to thank Production Manager Stevan Baron for his demanding efforts at every step in printing this book.

Generous support for
The Russian Heart:
Days of Crisis and Hope
was provided by

PEPSI-COLA BOTTLING COMPANY
OF NEW YORK

ARCHER DANIELS MIDLAND COMPANY

First published in U.K. by Phaidon Press Limited 1992

Phaidon Press Limited
140 Kensington Church Street
London W8 4BN

A CIP catalogue record of this book is available from
the British Library

ISBN 0 7148 2841 6